War: A Book of Mormon Perspective

How the War Chapters of the Book of Mormon Warn Against Wars of Aggression and the Warfare State

by Kendal Anderson

War:
A Book of Mormon Perspective

How The War Chapters of The Book of Mormon Warn

Against Wars of Aggression and the Warfare State

by Kendal Anderson

Dedicated to Jesus Christ—The Prince of Peace—who taught us to love our enemies and petitioned His Father to forgive those who were at that very moment attempting to take His life.

Table of Contents

<u>Foreword</u>

I am Anon Mous. We are Legion. We do not forget.

The best part about Anonymous and the reason that it's so successful is because it's decentralized. Anonymous has all kinds—white knights, black hats, mad-hatters, crackers, trolling net-scatters, and more. We are the conscious, the subconscious, and the unconscious. We are the obscurity from the obscurity, yet there are those who rise out of such obscurity when needed in order to reflect the light of Truth. That is needed now more than ever before.

We are less concerned with personal identities or institutions (especially centralized ones) and more about ideas and works. Consider the ideas, the works, and the results. Many of us from around the world have studied the contents of this book and have decided that they are so important that we will support them forever, regardless of persecution. We invite everyone alive to also study the information within this book as we have and make the same decision for yourselves because the results of doing so would be the end of aggressive warfare and many other terrible things and would lead to improved lives for everyone. This book is even a great benefit to those who are not religious. Wouldn't you like to be able to educate Christians about what their God tells them to do concerning these things and hold them to the Peaceful standard of the Golden Rule and the rest of their own teachings rather than allowing them to engage in mockeries of Christianity through aggressive warfare such as the 'crusades'? These 'crusades' continue today in various ways, yet you could help to end them and avoid much further suffering and death if the contents of this book are adhered to.

Are you not from the United States and/or maybe don't think that the contents of this book apply to you and/or your loved-ones? If so, then you are dangerously wrong and are missing a prime opportunity to improve your own life and that of all others. The United States effects all the world and the things within this book are timeless and apply everywhere, not just within the United States. Are you a member of a foreign nation, have resources, and would like the aggression, deceiving, and other harm of the United States to end Peacefully? If so, then all you need to do is to promote this book in its unaltered form among the People of the United States, who are still largely ignorant of the information within. It is a fact that it only takes 3% of a population to accomplish beneficial and enduring change on a very large scale, and the contents of this book are worthy of 100% of the support that can be offered because the results so greatly benefit everyone.

Do you perhaps believe that it's pointless or even harmful to get involved in the political process at this point? It's understandable that you might feel that way, as many do, but not being politically active yourself only gives more power to corruption and makes ever-worsening murderous government-sponsored carnage inevitable. Instead, study and live by the contents of this book and you will know exactly which politicians to elect based on their works, their public record, and their platform rather than their party, power, attractiveness, and/or lies.

Share this information in any way that you know how as virally as possible. Be ready and able to accurately discuss these things with your family, friends, co-workers, internet acquaintances, and more. Ask politicians running for office what they think of this philosophy and use that to inform your vote—though the ideal is for those who support these things to vote each-other into office and implement them according to the People and Constitutional Rule of Law.

Expect us.

About the Author & Preface

My name is Kendal Anderson. I live in Ammon, Idaho, and run a small business in sprinklers, lawn care, and pest control. I have a beautiful family consisting of my wife Christy, my son Caleb, and my step-son Kadeon. Although I don't have a college degree, I have a strange affinity for reading books that most would consider boring. For the last 12 years or so, I have embarked on a journey of independent study that has culminated in the writing of this book, which is the first of what I hope will be more. My journey began with a spiritual study, evolved into a more secular approach, and ended up being a synthesis of the two. I have been trying for the last five years to reconcile my Mormon theology with secular libertarianism. This endeavor became much easier when I put aside the cultural traditions that have crept into Mormonism over the past 200 years and decided to look to the scriptures instead. What I gleaned from this process is that the *Book of Mormon* is full of teachings that coincide with the libertarian philosophy of non-aggression. This non-aggression axiom is not unlike the Savior's own teachings in the New Testament that we have aptly named 'the Golden Rule'.

The first book I read that really inaugurated my intellectual journey was W. Cleon Skousen's *The Naked Communist*. As a young man of 23, I shirked my collegiate studies—which were riddled with establishment pap—in favor of used books by obscure men that I felt taught me real truth. Frederick Bastiat's *The Law* is another that comes to mind. At about the same time, I discovered H. Verlan Andersen's work—an LDS author and former BYU professor. His magnum opus, *Many Are Called, But Few Are Chosen,* is a must-read for Latter-day Saints who are seeking to understand the relationship between the Gospel and liberty. These and other books helped to prepare me for what would come next and much later. About five years ago, I discovered the Mises Institute, which is one of the largest libertarian think-tanks in the world, or at least commensurate with the other great like-minded think-tanks such as the Cato and Independent Institutes. Working as a laborer in my father's cabinet shop, I purchased my first IPod and downloaded endless hours of libertarian lectures on economics, politics, war, and history. Needless to say, the hours of mindless labor passed by a much greater velocity than they had before when I was forced to listen to Spanish and Country music blaring through a loud speaker.

I was introduced to men like Ludwig Von Mises, Murray Rothbard, Henry Hazlitt, Lew Rockwell, Walter Block, Robert Higgs, John Denson, Tom Woods, Tom DiLorenzo, and Bob Murphy. These men were and are echoing ideas that were laid down in the *Book of Mormon* and taught here on the American continent millennia ago. Many of these men are not religious at all but are in tune with principles that the Lord Himself wanted recorded by a fallen people who speak to us from the dust. These principles can be summarized into the following categories; free markets, voluntary charity, pacifism, just war, natural rights, and the evils of bloated government. I chose to write about just war because I have seen so many of my fellow Saints buy into the jingoistic lies propagated by the government. So many who have the *Book of Mormon* in hand capitulate to the worship of the State, it's military and police, it's foreign adventures, it's sanctions, and it's insatiable appetite to be the world's police.

With this in mind, I decided to search deep within the war chapters of the *Book of Mormon* to see just what kind of message Mormon was attempting to portray by including twenty-*plus* chapters about a war between the Nephites and the Lamanites. I didn't casually study these chapters; instead, they consumed me for several months. I would listen to them over and over again in attempts to dissect every morsel of information. Why—I would ask myself—did the Lord want us to know these things? Why did Mormon say that if all men were like unto Captain Moroni then the devil would lose his power? What does Captain Moroni's *Title of Liberty,* or Amalickiah's coup, or Pahoran's stand against the kingmen, have to do with Christianity? Why did the righteous Nephites never go into the lands of the enemy to attack? And why did Mormon resign from his position of military commander when his people desired to go into Lamanite lands and exact vengeance on them by the sword? I attempt to answer these and other questions within this book.

There are also other important reasons that I wrote this book. First and foremost, I love liberty. I think that war is ugly, reprehensible, and that it brings out the worst in people and nations. War is the worst crime committed by governments because murder is far worse than stealing or enslaving. And war-like nationalism is perhaps the easiest way for governments to deceive their constituents. On a more personal level, I decided to engage in this work because of a strong spiritual prompting that moved me to action. I remember skipping the last hour of church one day (Priesthood meeting)—a common practice of mine—and retiring home to my couch to engage in my Sunday study of something a little more interesting than regurgitated conference talks. As I sat pondering the *Book of Mormon,* an overwhelming feeling came over me that I should write a book using the ancient record as the general theme. At first, I began writing on the general subject of liberty, but I found this to be exhausting, overwhelming, and entirely too vague. After several months and 100 pages of manuscript, I changed the theme to just warfare. This more specific topic allowed me to write with greater ease and more purpose. I discovered *Doctrine and Covenants* Section 98—a revelation given to Joseph Smith about when the Lord justifies war, which was given in response to the persecution of the early Saints by the Missourians.

D&C 98 correlated with the message of Captain Moroni's war of defense against the Lamanites, as well as many preceding and contemporary libertarian theorists on just war. I discovered the writings of J. Reuben Clark—a constitutional scholar who was called to the First Presidency after years of inactivity and working on Sunday. He condemned the dropping of the atomic bombs on Japan in a general conference of 1946 and referred to the incident as "fiendish butchery." Subsequently, I discovered the First Presidency message of 1945 that condemned conscription. I was finding that secular and spiritual sources were coming together to witness to the truthfulness of the message of Peace contained within the ancient records of the Nephites.

Finally, the real value that has come from my journey throughout this work is a deeper appreciation for the Savior's supernal pacifism. If there is anything that I hope that this book portrays to my fellow Saints, it's that Jesus would never condone us in our "kill 'em all in the name of 'Merica" mentality, or wars of aggression, so-called 'nation building' that is actually imperial mercantilism, our torture, and/or any attacks on human rights. The Lord teaches that the true Christian way is to love our enemies, even while they are in the very act of crucifying us, as the Prince of Peace so perfectly demonstrated.

Chapter 1
Introduction

Peace is built into us. We don't naturally want war. The Light of Christ (that which helps us to discern between right and wrong) speaks *Peace* to our souls. We all possess an innate pacifism that resonates, *a priori,* the knowledge that war is wrong, inhumane, degenerate, and abhorrent. Yet, our respective governments tell us that war is noble, honorable, and necessary to preserve freedom, security, and peace. How, then, are we to know if the cause of war is just and if our government is telling the truth? In this age of mass brainwashing, government-controlled media, and the unlimited amount of information available on the internet, it is difficult to distinguish between right and wrong, truth and error. Many of us have been conditioned to receive our information directly from government or government-approved sources such as Fox News, CNN, and CNBC, while others prefer the free market of ideas found online. There are so many voices out there declaring so many variations of doctrine that it has become extremely difficult to ascertain true principles of right and wrong.

It seems as though humanity is struggling for answers, especially in regard to the proper use of violence against so–called enemies/criminals/terrorists, etc. Is it truly ethical to seek out and destroy potential aggressors before they have a chance to "get" us?

Is this method of preemptively rooting out evil justified from a normative, moral perspective? Or, do those who support "taking out" our enemies before they can cause harm actually make murderers of themselves instead? I wrote this book to help bring clarity to those who are struggling for answers to questions such as these. I believe that the principles and axioms laid down in Christendom give us a proper guide in regard to when it is righteous to wage war. Although many nations and armies have killed collectively in the name of Christ, I believe those choices to be gross misrepresentations of the doctrines of the Master. Jesus taught the Golden Rule, which admonishes us to treat others as we wish to be treated (Luke 6:31). This principle is not unlike the non-aggression axiom of libertarian philosophy, which is defined in the following way by libertarian Walter Block: The non-aggression axiom is the lynchpin of the philosophy of libertarianism. It states, simply, that it shall be legal for anyone to do anything he wants, provided only that he not initiate (or threaten) violence against the person or legitimately owned property of another. That is, in the free society, one has the right to manufacture, buy or sell any good or service at any mutually agreeable terms. Thus, there would be no victimless crime prohibitions, price controls, and government regulation of the economy, etc.[1]

When the Golden Rule and the non-aggression axiom are applied to warfare, it becomes evident that preemptive war is illegitimate and illogical. To illustrate the point, we will consider that person A has become suspicious of their next-door neighbor—person B—whom person A thinks is harboring weapons that might be dangerous to A's family and possibly to the rest of the neighborhood. Person A sends spies to collect intelligence about B and finds that person B is indeed very well armed. However, A has no proof that person B intends to use these resources maliciously against others. For all person A knows, person B may only wish to stockpile such weapons as a precaution against the potential aggression of others. Regardless of B's intentions, A holds a meeting with the rest of the neighborhood and they determine through a democratic vote that B is a dangerous threat and needs to be removed before person B "attacks" someone. Although there have not yet been any victims of person B's alleged malevolent thought crimes, the neighborhood militia moves in on B's premises and stealthily apprehends then executes person B without a trial or any due process of law.

Most people who hear this story would agree that person A was out of line and indeed the true aggressor; still, how many would decry governments and nations for doing the same thing? Saddam Hussein never committed an act of violence against the United States, yet the government used the above rationale to "take him out before he got us." Even if he had been harboring weapons of mass destruction as alleged, he had not used them against Americans, and if it is illegitimate to even possess such weapons (as it can be argued from a libertarian perspective) then the American government and others also should have been disarmed from possessing such weapons. However, Iraq was preemptively attacked, Saddam ousted, and hundreds of thousands of Iraqi civilians were sacrificed for the "greater good." I argue in this book that preemption is not the Lord's way, and that true followers of Christ are only justified in the use of violence when they and their families are *actually under attack* by aggressors or invaders. Thus, the victims of such crimes are vindicated in fighting to preserve their lives, families, religion, lands, property, and other inalienable rights. Fighting for any other reason violates the Golden Rule and the non-aggression axiom, as well as the foundational tenets of Christianity.

The Lord has truly given us a handbook that lays out the rules of righteous warfare. This handbook was translated by Joseph Smith, Jr. and published in 1830 as "Another Testament of Jesus Christ" and is also known as the *Book of Mormon*. Named after the prophet/historian Mormon—who compiled a thousand years of history—this book details an account of an ancient people of Hebrew descent who inhabited the American continent. Mormon gives us a history of their preaching, prophesying, contentions, wars, and ultimate destruction. In the heart of the book, there are several chapters which deal with a major war between two groups known as the Nephites and the Lamanites. The history of this war clearly distinguishes that the Lamanites were the aggressors and lays out the proper war protocol for Christians who find themselves under attack. The Nephites only fought to preserve their families, lands, properties, and religion, and in conducting the war abstained from conscription to raise armies or compulsory taxation to fund the war. The Nephites never used torture on Lamanite prisoners and even taught them the Gospel and set them free after the war, allowing many of them to remain among the Nephites where they enjoyed more Liberty than the Lamanite government allowed. Mormon also regrettably informs us that several hundred years later—during his own day—the Nephites devolved toward a more aggressive foreign policy which eventually led to their demise. When these teachings are applied to our modern day, it becomes obvious that we are falling into the same trap that our Nephite progenitors fell victim to. As the saying goes, those who ignore history are doomed to repeat it.

I realize that many who come across this work may not believe in the literal reality of the Nephite civilization existing on the American continent. To those, I offer an invitation to consider the principles of just war found within the *Book of Mormon* as works of literary genius that are concomitant with just war theory and the libertarian principle of non-aggression. Even if the *Book of Mormon* were a fable, the axioms found within its pages are of paramount importance in regards to personal liberty. To those who believe it to be an authentic record of Israelite history, I would offer an invitation to consider that the Lord's rules of warfare are a moral imperative that must be adhered to if one truly desires to obey the Gospel of Jesus Christ. I would submit that it is inconsistent with the religion that Joseph Smith, Jr. restored for any to parrot the official worldly policy of preemption while simultaneously professing to be a disciple of Christ. Remember; Jesus taught us to love our enemies, not to kill them all in the name of national 'security'.

That said, I would invite all to cast off the chains of cognitive dissonance and read my book. It is not just written to LDS Christians or other Christians exclusively, but is extended to all audiences—including atheists, deists, agnostics, liberals, conservatives, and libertarians. All will find common ground in the message of Peace contained within these pages. For those who would dismiss my book based solely on the belief that it is seemingly associated with the 'Mormon church', I would offer the following disclaimer: This book has no official affiliation with the Church of Jesus Christ of Latter-day Saints and there are many within that religion who would strongly disagree with the perspectives shared herein—even among its leadership. In fact, the *Book of Mormon* is a work independent of any religion much like the *Holy Bible*, and I believe that the message contained within its pages is intended for all people, especially that its declaration of Christian Peace is universal and ubiquitous.

Although there is quite a bit of American history included in this work, the focus is centered on principles of right and wrong. Using a combination of conventional history and lessons from the *Book of Mormon*, I strive to point out the fallacies of the modern warfare state. Contrary to the opinions of many readers and students, it is fact that the *Book of Mormon* teaches non-aggression. This assertion may seem strange in spite of the many wars and contentions included in the narrative of the book—however, when it is studied in context, one can conclude that the Lord only condones defensive warfare. In fact, the Lord has a very strict set of rules that must be followed before an individual or group is morally justified in the use of violence. Not surprisingly, these rules corroborate with the principles of just war theory and natural law laid down by the great philosophers of the past. I endeavor to point out in this book the evils of preemptive war, military conscription, jingoistic nationalism, war collectivism, economic sanctions, and perhaps the most pernicious evil—the waging of war against innocent civilians.

Unfortunately, the government has managed to convince the majority of the American people that the above actions are moral and just, and somehow prerequisite to preserving our nation's freedom. Such an argument (that killing innocents in the name of God, family, and/or country makes us freer) is most absurd. The reader will discover as they peruse this book that each category of state-sponsored evil is broken down to its most logical conclusion, that: preemptive war is unprovoked violence, military conscription is slavery, jingoistic nationalism is abstract hatred, war collectivism is just another excuse to increase economic regulation and raise taxes, economic sanctions deprive innocents of food and medicine, and civilian warfare equals mass-murder and genocide. Government not only expects its citizens to accept these absurdities, it demands total obedience and allegiance from them. The truth is that no person owes the government *anything*, for its very existence is rationally impossible without the people. By nature, it is a parasitic entity that cannot continue without a host. It does not and cannot produce anything, and it cannot transfer the slightest modicum of wealth without first extracting it from its productive citizenry.

To say that we owe the government our obedience, our allegiance, our wealth, and even our lives is like saying that we owe the same to a common highway robber that plunders us "for our own good" over and over and over again, and then declares that we are "safer" because of our "privilege" of being robbed. Lysander Spooner— a great libertarian philosopher of the 19th century—was profoundly correct when he referred to government as being operated by "a secret band of robbers and murderers." This statement is inherently true of all governments, for they rob collectively through taxation and they murder collectively through aggressive warfare. Despite the fact that these are gross violations of the 6th and 8th commandments, the masses continue to capitulate to the State's antics because they feel that dissent would be unpatriotic. They forget through all the jingoistic hype that government is not some abstract, big-brother-like, faceless entity, but is merely a small group of individuals who have managed to slip into positions of power. This "secret band of robbers and murderers" hires intellectuals who spend more time studying propaganda techniques than the average person spends learning to read. The result of such systems is collective acquiescence to an official state agenda which usually enriches a few at the expense of the many. The obedient masses are told that the State does these things for the "good and safety of society."

The *Book of Mormon* teaches the opposite view: that we are individuals, we act for ourselves, our rights are granted by our Creator, true patriotism is obedience to God, that most men abuse power, just wars are always defensive, preemptive wars are always initiated by ambitious men, armies should be voluntary, war taxation is evil, collective hatred is of the devil, free trade leads to prosperity, flattery (propaganda) is used to start wars, civilians are to be left alone during battle, and that the word of God is more powerful than the sword. That the commandment to love God and our neighbor transcends all nations, countries, cities, and states, and that God is not so much concerned with imaginary lines defining countries as He is with how we treat our brothers and sisters—encompassing all of mankind. This is the message I hope to portray in this book; one which lifts individual liberty above the false "good" of collective acquiescence to any unrighteous government action. This is a message reaching out to all people who inhabit this world, regardless of race, religion, or nationality—admonishing all of us to love our enemies as well as our neighbors. A message promulgated by the Savior Himself, which pleads with mankind to stop murdering and to begin truly loving each-other instead.

Chapter One Notes and Sources

1.   http://archive.lewrockwell.com/block/block26.html

Chapter 2

Principles of Defensive Warfare; America's Two Just Wars

In memory of our God, our religion, and freedom, and our peace, our wives, and our children.

-Captain Moroni

War is perhaps the most reprehensible atrocity ever perpetuated upon mankind. It encapsulates all of the most egregious crimes, darkest horrors, unrestrained passions, and merciless tyrannies of ambitious people. In the name of God, country, and patriotism conscripted armies have engaged in the mass slaughter of men, women, and children while being convinced that the cause is just. The purpose of this book is to debunk the romanticism surrounding the philosophy of aggressive warfare, to set forth the Christian principles of defensive warfare as expounded in the *Book of Mormon*, and to expose war for what it really is; mass murder on a grand scale. The reader should keep in mind throughout this study that war has been primarily carried out by a small ruling minority; worldly government. This entity uses the power of intellectuals to convince others to rally behind a "just" cause by sending their children to die for the supposed liberty of other nations, or "to protect our freedom" at home. If establishment intellectuals fail in their endeavors then the power of conscription is invoked (as it was during the Civil War, WWI, WWII, Korea, and Vietnam) to coerce them into fighting. Such involuntary servitude is wrong, a violation of the

Constitution, and a contradiction of the Lord's statement that, "it is not right that any man should be in bondage one to another."[1]

The reason why wars are perpetuated is explained to us through the scriptures in a warning given by Joseph Smith, Jr., wherein he states; "it is the disposition of almost *all* men, as soon as they get a little authority, as they suppose, they will immediately begin to exercise unrighteous dominion."[2] When one is placed at the head of government, it is almost universally inevitable that they will exercise such compulsion on their people. The lust for power and gain can envelope those in authority with an insatiable desire to exercise unrighteous dominion over nations, peoples, and territories—leading to wars of expansionism and empire. Unfortunately, most wars are fought over this very thing and yet so few are waged purely for the purpose of defense as was done by the Christians recorded within the *Book of Mormon*—defensive warfare to "preserve their rights and their privileges, yea, and also their liberty, that they might worship God according to their desires."[3]

To help us avoid confusion and/or deception, the Lord has given us a standard for defensive warfare in the Doctrine and Covenants, and an actual history of a war fought by the Nephites against a dictatorial maniac named Amalickiah. When one considers these principles revealed to Joseph Smith, Jr. and studies them with an open mind, it becomes evident that our own nation has not followed the Lord's standard of defensive warfare and is in fact under condemnation for most of the wars it has engaged in. These principles can be found in the 98th Section of the Doctrine and Covenants and will be quoted at length here as follows:

> Now I speak unto you concerning your families—if men will smite you, or your families once, and ye bear it patiently and revile not against them, neither seek revenge, ye shall be rewarded; But if ye bear it not patiently, it shall be accounted unto you as being meted out as a just measure unto you. And again, if your enemy shall smite you the second time, and you revile not against your enemy, and bear it patiently, your reward shall be an hundredfold. And

again, if he shall smite you the third time, and ye bear it patiently, your reward shall be doubled unto you four-fold; and these three testimonies shall stand against your enemy if he repent not, and shall not be blotted out. And now, verily I say unto you, if that enemy shall escape my vengeance, that he be not brought into judgment before me, then ye shall warn him in my name, that he come no more upon you, neither upon your family, even your children's children unto the third and fourth generation. And then, if he shall come upon you or your children, or your children's children unto the third and fourth generation, I have delivered thine enemy into thine hands. And if thou wilt spare him, thou shalt be rewarded for thy righteousness; and also thy children and thy children's children unto the third and fourth generation. Nevertheless, thine enemy is in thine hands; and if thou rewardest him according to his works thou art justified; if he has sought thy life, and thy life is endangered by him, thine enemy is in thine hands and thou art justified.

Author's interjection: The reader should be picking up the hint by now that war—to the Lord—is the absolute last resort and should only be engaged in after bearing patiently three "smitings" from a potential enemy. There also needs to be a clear and present danger, or as the Lord has stated it; if "thy life is endangered . . . "This is congruent with the ancient "Just War" philosophy of the Romans (before they became an aggressive empire) that war should only be engaged in if your home is being attacked. The Nephites shared this philosophy as evidenced by the following statement that they were "taught… never to give an offense, yea, and never to raise the sword except it were against an enemy, except it were to preserve their lives."[4]

Behold, this is the law I gave unto my servant Nephi, and thy fathers, Joseph, and Jacob, and Isaac, and Abraham, and all mine ancient prophets and apostles. And again, this is the law that I gave unto mine ancients, that they should not go out unto battle against any nation, kindred, tongue, or people, save I, the Lord, commanded them. And if any nation, tongue, or people should proclaim war against them, they should first lift a standard of peace unto that people, nation, or tongue; And if that people did not accept the offering of peace, neither the second nor the third time, they should bring these testimonies before the Lord; Then I, the Lord, would give unto them a commandment, and justify them in going out to battle against that nation, tongue, or people. And I, the Lord, would fight their battles and their children's battles, and their children's children, until they had avenged themselves on all their enemies, to the third and fourth generation. Behold, this is an ensample unto all people, saith the Lord your God, for justification before me.[5]

So we learn from these verses that the Lord gave this law to his ancients and we have to assume that this includes Moses and Joshua. However, we read in the Old Testament of Israelites destroying entire civilizations—including women and children. Would the Lord contradict his own law? The answer lies in the authenticity of the Biblical translation. We know the *Book of Mormon* to be the pure translation of the Nephite record and there is not one single instance wherein the Lord commands a Nephite prophet to annihilate an entire nation, or to even engage in a preemptive attack on their enemies. During the righteous times, and specifically under Captain Moroni, the

Nephites waged only defensive war and were "compelled reluctantly to contend with their brethren, the Lamanites."[6] They were also "sorry to take up arms against the Lamanites, because they did not delight in the shedding of blood.[7] When Captain Helaman asked the two-thousand stripling warriors if they would battle against the Lamanites in order to help defend Antipus, they replied—"we would not slay our brethren if they would let us alone."[8] As we shall see, Captain Moroni was obedient to the principles outlined in D&C 98, and showed his faith in God by asking a prophet to pray for guidance—for he, "knowing of the prophecies of Alma, sent certain men unto him, desiring of him that he should inquire of the Lord whither the armies of the Nephites should go to defend themselves against the Lamanites."[9]

When this account is compared to the record of the Israelites, it is strikingly dissimilar. For instance, in Numbers 31 the Lord supposedly commands Moses to send 12,000 warriors to destroy the Midianites and burn all their cities. After this was done, they "took all the spoil, and all the prey, both of men and of beasts."[10] As for the women and children Moses then commanded them to "therefore kill every male among the little ones, and kill every woman that hath known man by lying with him."[11] Here we have the Israelites committing an overt act of aggression against the Midianites; burning their cities, taking the spoils, and killing men, women, and children. Is this not a violation of the commandments "thou shalt not kill" and "thou shalt not steal?" There are several accounts of this type of warfare in the Old Testament that have to do with the Israelite journey into the Promised Land. It is this author's opinion that one of the two following things is true; either these accounts are mistranslations, or there were very special circumstances approved of by the Lord which justified the Israelites in their actions. The former is more probable, but even if the latter were the case the Nephite example is the one that applies to America today. Christians (Mormon or otherwise) who cite Israelite accounts as pretext or prescription for preemptively attacking any foreign nation and/or conducting aggressive warfare are *not* justified.

Turning to the account of the Nephite war in the *Book of Alma*, we learn of the extenuating circumstances which justified the Nephites in waging defensive war. The Zoramites and Amalekites had dissented, or defected over to the Lamanites, and had come into the land of the Nephites to wage war. Moroni—only 25 years old when given command of the Nephite army—"knew the intention of the Lamanites, that it was their intention to destroy their brethren, or to subject them and bring them into bondage that they might establish a kingdom unto themselves over all the land."[12] Mormon, as he relates this history, explains that the Nephites were indeed following the Lord's rules:

Nevertheless, the Nephites were inspired by a better cause, for they were not fighting for monarchy nor power but they were fighting for their homes and their liberties, their wives and their children, and their all, yea, for their rites of worship and their church. And they were doing that which they felt was the duty which they owed to their God; for the Lord had said unto them, and also unto their fathers, that: Inasmuch as ye are not guilty of the first offense, neither the second, ye shall not suffer yourselves to be slain by the hands of your enemies. And again, the Lord has said: Ye shall defend your families even unto bloodshed. Therefore for this cause were the Nephites contending with the Lamanites, to defend themselves, and their families, and their lands, their county, and their rights, and their religion.[13]

It is important to note that the first *and* second offenses were committed by the Lamanites and both preemptive attacks were facilitated by *Nephite* dissenters who were lusting for kingship and power. The chief of these—Amlici—was after the order of the Nehors (meaning antichrist), and he sought to establish himself as a king so he could destroy the religious freedom of the people. Just four years prior, king Mosiah had established the *reign of the judges,* which resulted in a constitutional republic much like the United States of America[14]. This system also resembled the ancient Israelite system of judges that Moses and his father-in-law—Jethro—established prior to their entering the land of Canaan[15]. Needless to say, the Nephite people weren't going to let Amlici pull off a coup after they had just been granted their political freedom. A vote was held through which "the voice of the people came against Amlici, that he was not made a king over the people."[16] He then proceeded to stir up the hearts of those who followed him and after they consecrated him to be their king they took up arms against the people of Nephi. Alma, the chief judge and governor of the people, went up at the head of the Nephite armies (true leadership behavior forsaken by modern executives) as they defended themselves against the Amlicites. Thousands were slain on both sides, and as the Amlicites retreated Alma sent spies to watch them. The next day they returned and related the terrifying news that the Amlicites had joined with the Lamanites. Being greatly outnumbered, the Nephites were assaulted by the Lamanites and Amlicites; however, "the Nephites being strengthened by the hand of the Lord, having prayed mightily to him that he would deliver them out of the hands of their enemies, therefore the Lord did hear their cries, and did strengthen them, and the Lamanites and the Amlicites did fall before them."[17]

Alma contends face to face with Amlici, slays him, and then subsequently contends with the king of the Lamanites—forcing his retreat. In fact, the whole army of the Lamanites—exceedingly more numerous than the Nephites—was defeated and driven back, fulfilling the Lord's promises that he would fight their battles for them if they followed His rules of warfare. The second offense came when Zerahemnah came against the Nephites thirteen years later, with the intent "that he might gain power over the Nephites by bringing them into bondage."[18] He was immediately defeated, and even scalped by Moroni's army and compelled to enter into a covenant of peace or be destroyed[19]. The Lamanites returned to their own land and there was peace until Amalickiah appeared on the scene. Amalickiah was a Nephite by birth who dissented just shortly after Helaman established the church again following the wars and dissensions of the Lamanites. He was a cunning man and used much flattery to convince those around him, especially the lower judges of the land, that if they supported him in his quest for kingship then "he would make them rulers over the people."[20] He drew many away from the church by his "flatteries," leading them to "seek to destroy the church of God, and to destroy the foundation of *liberty* which God had granted unto them."[21] He fled with his followers to the wilderness and when Moroni cut his men off, Amalickiah took a small number who had not been captured and defected to the Lamanites. He used treachery and murder to assassinate the king of the Lamanites in a classic coup d'etat, establishing himself as dictator.[22] He then launched a massive military campaign against the Nephites and swore to drink the blood of Moroni. It was these precarious circumstances that compelled the Nephites to wage defensive warfare against a sycophantic, megalomaniacal tyrant.

Glenn L Pearson and Reid E. Bankhead—two former BYU professors who wrote one of the best *Book of Mormon* study guides in existence—have a section on defensive war. They document the plain and precious clarity that the *Book of Mormon* lays down in regard to the causes of war and what qualifies as righteous participation in them. They are the following:

1. It is the result of the wickedness of fallen men in a fallen world.

2. It always is started by the evil designs of power-hungry totalitarians.

3. Good men and good nations should *never* go to war except to defend their liberty, their lives, their families, and their property.[23]

There is another condition that exists when it is morally justifiable to engage in war: the case of secession from a mother state. The proper protocol here is to engage in civil disobedience or intellectual dissonance when a central governing authority is destroying rights and to continue such action until that authority relents or declares war on its subjects. According to the Lord's counsel, we are *only* required to obey the laws of governments that honor our inalienable rights. Joseph Smith, Jr. declared the following:

We believe that all men are bound to sustain and uphold the respective governments in which they reside, *while* protected in their inherent and inalienable rights by the laws of such governments...[24]

This counsel from Joseph Smith, Jr. implies that our obedience to government is conditional upon how well that government protects our natural rights. If a state becomes rogue, violating its bounds by attacking its citizens' basic rights of free speech, free press, freedom of religion, economic freedom, *et al*, then the people of that state are justified in initiating a revolution. This is acceptable to God because when government becomes tyrannical and begins to destroy individual liberty then it interferes with God's plan of free agency. As this is God's work and glory, one can understand the disdain the Creator has for governments that work to infringe upon individual agency, which is God's greatest gift to His children. Nephi, in the *Book of Mormon,* qualifies the American Revolution by prophesying that the Lord would not only vindicate the colonists in their secession from Britain, but that he would also help them win the war. This humble prophet—when just a boy at sixteen years of age—saw this in the following vision:

> And it came to pass that I beheld many multitudes of the Gentiles upon the land of promise (America)... And I beheld the Spirit of the Lord, that it was upon the Gentiles, and they did prosper and obtain the land for their inheritance . . . I, Nephi, beheld that the Gentiles who had gone forth out of captivity did humble themselves before the Lord; and the power of the Lord was with them. And I beheld that their mother Gentiles were gathered together upon the waters, and upon the land also, to battle against them. And I beheld that the power of God was with them, and also that the wrath of God was upon all those that were gathered together against them to battle. And I, Nephi, beheld that the Gentiles that had gone out of captivity were delivered out of the hands of all other nations.[25]

Why did the British monarch King George III declare war on the colonies? It was because of their civil disobedience and intolerance toward abuses from the king. Thomas Jefferson listed 27 of these abuses in the Declaration of Independence. Some of the most invasive include: keeping standing armies during peacetime, giving the military power over the civil power, forced quartering of British troops while protecting them with mock trials in cases of murder, trade embargos, imposing taxes without consent, deprivation of trial by jury, suspending the legislatures of the state governments, and sending "swarms of officers to harass our people, and eat out their substance."[26] Much like the Nephites under the command of Alma, the colonists were greatly outnumbered and outgunned by their British counterparts. However, unlike the British, their cause was just. They were not fighting for monarchy, nor for power as the Lamanites had—they fought to preserve their liberty, rights, lands, and families. It is evident that God preserved our forefathers during many of the various battles of the Revolution. Just by examining the life of George Washington we find extraordinary Divine Providence. When 23 years old, he survived two horses being shot out from under him in one battle during the French and Indian War, which took place at Fort Duquesne near Pittsburgh. He was also deathly ill during the melee and displayed unrelenting valor in rallying the troops after General Braddock was fatally wounded. After retiring for the night, he found bullet fragments in his coat and wig. About twenty years later, he would lead the colonial army to eventually defeat the British, literally fulfilling the prophecy of Nephi. Henry B. Carrington—a historian—documents twenty-two instances of divine intervention during the Revolutionary War. He had this to say about the war in general:

> The war for American independence was marked by many critical events, which were beyond human control or remedy. Some of these changed the relations of contending armies in a single night. More than once, a few hours of unexpected rain, wind or fog, were enough to assure lasting results. These determining events, because belonging to the sphere and operation of physical laws, are not beyond the recognition of nature's Master. They testify very clearly at least, the absolute uncertainty of the best human plans, whether for peace or war, and the value of the promptness, which seizes every opportunity as it passes, and thus gives shape to the material issues, which are ripe for solution.[27]

The *Book of Mormon* was written for our day. We can draw comparisons between the types of wars waged during those times and those we have in the present. What may come as a shock to many Christians, Latter-day Saints, and Americans in general is that only two of America's wars have been constitutional, moral, and justified from a *Book of Mormon* perspective. We have just discussed the first of these, and the second is the subject of much controversy and debate. It is the Civil War, and our contention here is that only the *Southern* position was justified. The notion of a civil war implies that both sides are struggling for power, but in the American case it was a war of *secession*. We have already established that the American Revolution was *also* a war of secession from England. Murray Rothbard—one of the most influential libertarain thinkers of the 20th Century—explains the similarities between the two wars as follows:

> In 1861, the Southern states, believing correctly that their cherished institutions were under grave threat and assault from the federal government, decided to exercise their natural, contractual, and constitutional right to withdraw, to "secede" from that Union. The separate Southern states then exercised their contractual right as sovereign republics to come together in another confederation, the Confederate States of America. If the American Revolutionary War was just, then it follows as the night the day that the Southern cause, the War for Southern Independence, was just, and for the same reason: casting off the "political bonds" that connected the two peoples. In neither case was this decision made for "light or transient causes." And in both cases, the courageous seceders pledged to each-other "their lives, their fortunes, and their sacred honor.[28]

This, of course, is not the history that is preached from the pulpits of public schools—because, unfortunately, the winners of wars always get to write the history and establishment historians would have us believe that the war was fought over slavery and saving the so-called "Union"—whatever that is. Our goal here is simply to tell the truth, and there is much more to this story than most Americans have been taught.

Our story begins in South Carolina in the year 1828. In this year, a tariff—which Southerners called the Tariff of Abominations—was passed in the legislature, raising the tariff rate substantially. This tariff was targeted at European goods that were being imported into the South. The Southern economy was mostly agrarian which meant that Southerner's had to purchase industrial goods from either Northern or European sources. Up until that time, the goods coming from Europe were cheaper than those coming from Northern industry. This tariff forced the South into an ultimatum; either pay a high tax on imported goods or pay a high price for Northern goods. The South viewed this tariff for what it really was—legalized plunder that led to the rebellion of South Carolina and the idea of nullification (a state's right to nullify federal laws deemed unconstitutional). John C. Calhoun—vice-president under Andrew Jackson during the 1830s—strongly opposed the tariff and eventually resigned over it. South Carolina endeavored to nullify the tariff legislation and was able to negotiate a reduction in the rate. However, the damage to Southern prosperity sowed the seeds of eventual secession.

Abraham Lincoln came onto the scene in 1861. He was a proponent of three things that tear at the root of individual freedom; large public works projects (such as subsidized railroads), a national bank, and a high protective tariff.[29] Lincoln was a Republican who supported *protectionism*, which is another name for corporate welfare for big business. He was of a type of person like Alexander Hamilton or Henry Clay, who championed the archaic economic system of British mercantilism. Edgar Lee Masters—a famous playwright who wrote one of the first books criticizing Lincoln—gives a telling definition of mercantilism:

> Henry Clay was the champion of that political system, which doles favors to the strong in order to win and to keep their adherence to the government. His system offered shelter to devious schemes and corrupt enterprises. He was the beloved son of Alexander Hamilton with his corrupt funding schemes, his

superstitions concerning the advantage of a public debt, and a people taxed to make profits for enterprises that cannot stand alone. His example and his doctrines led to the creation of a party that had no platform to announce because its principles were plunder and nothing else.[30]

The tariff imposed upon the South by Lincoln and the Republican Party was a mercantilist policy which benefitted Northern industry at the expense of the Southern economy. This was only a scheme for government to abolish competition by fiat and which destroyed the idea (found within the *Book of Mormon*) that "every man should have an equal chance throughout all the land."[31] Not only was Lincoln in full support of the tariff, he was willing to use violence to enforce it. He also plainly articulated the fact that slavery was something he did not care to meddle with. Quoting from his first inaugural address we read:

> I have no purpose, directly or indirectly, to interfere with the institution of slavery in the States where it exists. I believe I have no lawful right to do so, and I have no inclination to do so.[32]

He also made a direct verbal threat of violence to those Southern states that refused to pay the tariff:

> In doing this (defending the Union) there needs to be no bloodshed or violence; and there shall be none, unless it be forced upon the national authority. The power confided to me, will be used to hold, occupy, and possess the property, and places belonging to the government, and to collect the duties and imposts; but beyond what may be necessary for these objects, there will be no *invasion* — no using of force against, or among the people anywhere.[33]

The duties and imposts mentioned here are another name for excise taxes, or tariffs. What Lincoln is essentially saying is that if the

Southern states paid the tariff then there would be no invasion or use of force. This was a direct threat of aggression against states that would not comply with an unjust tax. How ironic that those who protested King George during the Boston Tea Party are heralded by historians, yet Southerners who displayed patriotic valor in doing virtually the same thing are not even mentioned in the history books except as despicable slave owners. Can it not be said that the people of the Southern states were just as heroic in their endeavors to stand up to the Republican Party and its high protective tariff? Another point that should be examined is Lincoln's definition of the so-called Union. He made the outrageous and nonsensical claim that the Union was older than the Constitution, and therefore that the states were subject to it. Quoting again from his first inaugural address:

> Descending from these general principles, we find the proposition that, in legal contemplation, the Union is perpetual, confirmed by the history of the Union itself. The Union is much older than the Constitution. It was formed in fact, by the Articles of Association in 1774. It was matured and continued by the Declaration of Independence in 1776. It was further matured and the faith of all the then thirteen States expressly plighted and engaged that it should be perpetual, by the Articles of Confederation in 1778. And finally, in 1787, one of the declared objects for ordaining and establishing the Constitution, was "to form a more perfect union....It follows from these views that no State, upon its own mere motion, can lawfully get out of the Union, — that resolves and ordinances to that effect are legally void; and that acts of violence, within any State or States, against the authority of the United States, are insurrectionary or revolutionary, according to circumstances.[34]

In reality, there is no such thing as this *perpetual Union* referred to by Lincoln. This loaded term signifies a geographical abstraction that only exists as a perception of a collective people or society. However, to the founding generation this rationale would be a heresy, for they viewed the United States as not one people, but as diversified individuals of thirteen independent states. If one studies the original meaning of how the Framer's viewed the Union and Constitution, one can discern the inherent fraud associated with such a claim. To Lincoln, the Union was only a means to an end, and that end was the confiscation of Southern wealth through taxation. His assertion that the Union is older than the Constitution is mythical nonsense and blather. The truth is that, prior to the ratification of the Constitution, the thirteen colonies were laying tariffs on goods crossing state lines, requiring travelers to go through customs, and inflating their own separate currencies. The colonies were anything but unified, but rather were acting like thirteen independent sovereign nations. Also, his claim that "no state … can lawfully get out of the Union" has no validity according to how the people viewed the Constitution at that time. In fact, the thirteen colonies came together *voluntarily* and formed a *compact,* which is tantamount to a contract entered into by several parties working toward a common goal. The states came together and delegated certain powers to the federal government, but they did not *cede* any powers. The absolute power was retained by the people, not the whole people, but the *individual* people of the sovereign states. St. George Tucker, one of the first scholars to write a commentary on the Constitution, reflects the general sentiment at the time in his *Views of the Constitution of the United States:*

> …It is a compact by which the federal government is bound to
> the several states, and to every citizen of the United States. Although
> the federal government can, in no possible view, be considered as a
> party to the compact made anterior to its existence, and by which it
> was, in fact, created; yet as the creature of that compact, it must be
> bound by it, to its creators, the several states in the union, and the
> citizens thereof. Having no existence but under the constitution, nor
> any rights, but such as that instrument confers; and those very rights
> being in fact duties; it can possess no legitimate power, but such as
> is absolutely necessary for the performance of a duty, prescribed and

enjoined by the constitution. Its duties, then, become the exact measure of its powers; and wherever it exerts a power for any other purpose, than the performance of a duty prescribed by the constitution, it transgresses its proper limits, and violates the public trust.[35]

It was also understood, and reiterated by Jefferson and Madison's Virginia and Kentucky Resolutions, that a state could voluntarily and peacefully leave the Union (terminate the contract) at any time if the federal government passed unconstitutional laws. At the very least they could nullify such laws, as South Carolina attempted to do in 1832, and if further aggression was used it was universally understood that states could peacefully secede. Quoting from the Kentucky Resolutions we read:

Resolved, that the several States composing the United States of America, are not united on the principles of unlimited submission to their General Government; but that by compact under the style and title of a Constitution for the United States and of amendments thereto, they constituted a General Government for special purposes, delegated to that Government certain definite powers, reserving each State to itself, the residuary mass of right to their own self Government; and that whensoever the General Government assumes undelegated powers, its acts are unauthoritative, void, and of no force; that to this compact each state acceded as a state, and is an integral party; that the Government created by this compact was not made the exclusive or final judge of the extent of the powers delegated to itself; since that would have made its discretion, and not the Constitution, the measure of its powers; but that, as in all other cases of compact among powers having no common judge, each party has an equal right to judge for itself, as well of infractions as of the mode and measure of redress.[36]

This language is congruent with that of the Declaration of Independence, wherein Jefferson stated, "That whenever any Form of Government becomes destructive of these ends (securing rights), it is the Right of the People to alter or abolish it, and to institute New Government..."[37] The people of the South had every right not to be taxed without representation and to stand up to federal tyranny. The tariff was nothing but a redistribution scheme that transferred wealth from Southern agrarians to Northern merchants while enriching the pockets of men like Lincoln who were the beneficiaries of lobbyists. The institution of slavery, however, was an inimical practice and needed to be abolished, but why did it take a war costing over 600,000 American lives to do so? The interesting thing about slavery is that in several European countries the practice was slowly phased out peacefully. In fact, the United States is the only country that fought a war during that epoch over what most participants thought was the issue of slavery. When the facts are examined it becomes evident that pecuniary factors were at the root of the war, and that slavery was used as a veneer to gain support from the opposing Northern public. Joseph Smith, Jr. ran for U.S. president in 1844 just shortly before his martyrdom and he had a plan to end slavery peacefully by selling territories and purchasing the freedom of slaves, which was something that had been done in other nations. He said:

> Petition, also, ye goodly inhabitants of the slave states, your legislators to abolish slavery by the year 1850, or now, and save the abolitionist from reproach and ruin, infamy and shame. Pray Congress to pay every man a reasonable price for his slaves out of the surplus revenue arising from the sale of public lands, and from the deduction of pay from the members of Congress.[38]

In addition to the Civil War being an act of aggression on the part of the North, Lincoln assumed dictatorial power not granted to federal government by the Constitution. Illegitimate powers grabbed by the executive are an ominous threat to liberty—especially during times of war. Most historians agree that Lincoln violated Constitutional limits, while at the same time honoring him as a "benevolent dictator." This myth has been dispelled by revisionist historian Thomas J. DiLorenzo, who chronicles the abuses of Lincoln as follows:

> Even though the large majority of Americans, North and South, believed in a right of secession as of 1861, upon taking office, Lincoln implemented a series of unconstitutional acts, including launching an invasion of the South without consulting Congress, as required by the Constitution; declaring martial law; blockading the Southern ports; suspending the writ of habeas corpus for the duration of his administration; imprisoning without trial thousands of Northern citizens; arresting and imprisoning newspaper publishers who were critical of him; censoring all telegraph communication; nationalizing the railroads; creating several new states without the consent of the citizens of those states; ordering Federal troops to interfere with elections in the North by intimidating Democratic voters; deporting a member of Congress, Clement L. Vallandigham of Ohio, for criticizing the administration's income tax proposal at a Democratic Party rally; confiscating private property; confiscating firearms in violation of the Second Amendment; and effectively gutting the Ninth and Tenth Amendments to the Constitution, among other things.[39]

It is also important to remember—especially by Latter-day Saints—that the Lord approved the Constitution in a revelation given to Joseph Smith, Jr. In this revelation, the Lord specifically declared the He justified the brethren in "befriending that law which is the constitutional law of the land; And as pertaining to the law of man, whatsoever is more or less cometh of evil."[40] It therefore logically follows that Lincoln was out of line with the Lord's standard when he walked all over civil liberties and Constitutional Rule of Law during the Civil War era. A war that was declared *without* Congressional approval, something unprecedented up until Lincoln's time, but widely accepted today as normal. More on Lincoln will be covered in subsequent chapters with regard to his cornering the South into firing the first shot and the uncivilized and brutal warfare carried out by Northern generals on Southern civilians.

Conclusion

In summation, we have established the Lord's standard for defensive war. We have learned through the example of the Nephites the precise conditions that need to exist before a just war can be waged by a defending nation. We have also discussed the premise that America has engaged in only two just wars since its inception and both have been wars of secession from a mother state, which usurped authority. It is also appropriate to point out that the "dissenters" in the *Book of Mormon* such as Amlici and Amalickiah desired to establish dictatorial regimes to overthrow the freedom of the Nephites. The American "dissenters" during the Revolutionary and Civil War—or more aptly named the *War for Southern Independence*—only desired to be left alone, and were therefore justified in their collective actions of defiance against a corrupt central government. It is important to distinguish between the two. The focus of our next chapter will be the conditions wherein waging war is not justified and instead is sinful 'aggressive warfare'.

Chapter Two Notes and Sources

1. D&C 101:79
2. D&C 121:39, Emphasis added.
3. Alma 43:9
4. Alma 48:14
5. D&C 98:23-38
6. Alma 48:21
7. Alma 48:23
8. Alma, 56:46
9. Alma, 43:23

10. Numbers 31:11

11. Numbers 31:17

12. Alma 43:29

13. Alma 43:45-47

14. See Mosiah 29

15. The Nephite and Israelite system of judges constitutes the Lord's ancient law of liberty. This law greatly reduces the power of central governments and gives more self-governing power to localities. The American system of states' rights is based on this same principle and Thomas Jefferson actually studied the Biblical account of the Israelites prior to the ratification of the Constitution. For a detailed study of the law of liberty see Cleon W. Skousen, *The Majesty of God's Law.*

16. Alma 2:7

17. Alma 2:28

18. Alma 43:8

19. Quite a difference from our modern day warfare where POWs are often tortured, executed, or incarcerated in a concentration camp for years.

20. Alma 46:5

21. Alma 46:10, Emphasis added

22. Details on how Amalickiah orchestrated this regime change will discussed in a later chapter entitled, *Amalickiah and False Flag Operations*

23. Glenn L. Pearson and Reid E. Bankhead, *Building Faith With the Book of Mormon,* copyright @ Joseph Educational Foundation, 1994 Provo, UT, p. 112 Emphasis added.

24. D&C 134:5

25. 1 Nephi 13:14-19

26. Thomas Jefferson, *The Declaration of Independence,* In Congress July 4, 1776

27. Col. Henry B. Carrington, *Battles of the American Revolution,* p. 39

28. An essay by Murray N. Rothbard, *America's Two Just Wars: 1776 and 1861,* Mises Institute, 1994

29. "I presume you all know who I am. I am humble Abraham Lincoln. I have been solicited by many friends to become a candidate for the legislature. My politics are short and sweet, like the old woman's dance. I am in favor of a national bank... in favor of the internal improvements system and a high protective tariff." -Abraham Lincoln, 1832, *The Collected Works of Abraham Lincoln,* Quoted in Thomas J. DiLorenzo,

Abraham Lincoln and the Triumph of Mercantilism. An essay in *Reassessing the Presidency, The Rise of the Executive State and the Delcline of Freedom,* Edited by John V. Denson, Mises Institute, 2001, p. 203

30. Edgar Lee Masters, *Lincoln the Man,* p. 27

31. Mosiah 29:38

32. Abraham Lincoln, *First Inaugural Address,* Monday, March 4, 1861

33. Ibid, Emphasis Added.

34. Ibid

35. St. George Tucker, View of the Constitution of the United States With Selected Writings, 1999, by Liberty Fund, Inc. pp. 120-121

36. Thomas Jefferson, The Kentucky Resolutions of 1798, *The Papers of Thomas Jefferson, Volume 30: 1 January 1798 to 31 January 1799,* Princeton University Press, 2003, pp. 529,56

37. Thomas Jefferson, *The Declaration of Independence,* In Congress, July 4, 1776

38. Joseph Smith, General Smith's Views of the Powers and Policy of the Government of the United States, Nauvoo, Illinois, Printed by John Taylor, 1844

39. Thomas J. DiLorenzo, *The Real Lincoln,* e-book pp. 145-46

40. D&C Section 98:6-7, See Also Section 101:77-80

Chapter 3

Wars of Aggression are Revolts Against Christ

Blessed are all the peacemakers, for they shall be called the children of God.-Jesus Christ

When a nation launches an attack on another by military invasion, remote bombing, or naval blockades, this constitutes a preemptive strike or attack, and is aggressive warfare. Taking it a step further, we can deduce that even trade embargos and economic sanctions are acts of war because they result in harm to innocent people who happen to be part of a particular state. The *Book of Mormon* is very explicit in drawing the lines between defensive and preemptive attacks and gives plenty of examples of each. As established before, during the righteous times of the Nephites under Alma, Captain Moroni, and his son Moronihah, they only engaged in defensive war to stave off attacks against their liberty. As the account progresses through Helaman and as the Nephites become subject to a government controlled by secret combinations, the people devolve toward a more aggressive foreign policy. We can find corollaries with the *Book of Mormon* account and our own modern devolution toward an interventionist foreign policy, beginning when the Monroe Doctrine of isolationism began to be subverted toward the end of the 1800s with the advent of the Spanish-American War.

In the third chapter of *3 Nephi*, we read an account of an epistle written to Lachoneus—the Nephite governor—from Giddianhi—leader of the Gadianton robbers. In this epistle Giddianhi made a direct threat of violence against the Nephites as follows:

> Therefore I write unto you, desiring that ye would yield up unto this my people, your cities, your lands, and your possessions, rather than that they should visit you with the sword and that destruction should come upon you. Or, in other words, yield yourselves up unto us, and unite with us and become acquainted with our secret works, and become our brethren that ye may be like unto us—not our slaves, but our brethren and partners of all our substance.1 And behold, I swear unto you, if ye will do this, with an oath, ye shall not be destroyed; but if ye will not do this, I swear unto you with an oath, that on the morrow month I will command that my armies shall come down against you, and they shall not stay their hand and shall spare not, but shall slay you, and shall let fall the sword upon you even until ye shall become extinct.[2]

There is no question or doubt that these Gadiantons were a clear and present danger to the Nephites, and according to our modern standards it seems that a preemptive attack on the robbers would have been justified to avoid being exterminated. However, as we read further into the chapter we find that this is not the case. Although Lachoneus was the chief governor of the land, a man named Gidgiddoni was a prophet *and* the chief captain of the armies of the Nephites, as it was their custom to appoint a person who "had the spirit of revelation"[3] to this position. The people, apparently a little misled, said this unto the prophet Gidgiddoni:

> Pray unto the Lord, and let us go up upon the mountains and into the wilderness, that we may fall upon the robbers and destroy them in their own lands. But Gidgiddoni saith unto them: The Lord forbid; for if we should go up against them the Lord would deliver

us into their hands; therefore we will prepare ourselves in the center of our lands, and we will gather all our armies together, and we will not go against them, but we will wait till they shall come against us; therefore as the Lord liveth, if we do this he will deliver them into our hands.[4]

We can see here that the Lord's standard of defensive war is holding true. True followers of Christ do not engage in preemptive attacks *even if* their enemies are planning a potential strike, or as in the above case, an imminent one. Instead of attacking the robbers in their own lands, which were in the wilderness, the people followed the counsel of the chief governor and:

> They did fortify themselves against their enemies, and they did dwell in one land, and in one body, and they did fear the words which had been spoken by Lachoneus, insomuch that they did repent of all their sins; and they did put up their prayers unto the Lord their God, that he would deliver them in the time that their enemies should come down against them to battle.[5]

It is interesting that the people had to repent and one has to ask just what did they have to repent for? Perhaps they were repenting for their inclination toward preemptive war in asking the prophet to pray to the Lord for permission to preemptively strike their enemies. Perhaps they should have instead said to Gidgiddoni, "pray unto the Lord and ask him what we shall do to defend ourselves." Fortunately, the Nephites did repent and when the robbers came the next month they were beaten and driven back into their own lands. What do we learn from this example? That true Christians do not under any circumstances engage in preemptive war, and that even if there is an imminent threat from an enemy then Christian protocol is to *fortify* the homeland and to prepare for the time of attack. This is also evident from the example of Captain Moroni who was constantly fortifying Nephite cities during their wars with the Lamanites.

Our next example comes in the third chapter of *Mormon*. Here, Mormon is describing the military history of his people during a time of great wickedness. Mormon was the military commander and also a prophet after the pattern of Gidgiddoni. When the Lord commands him to cry repentance to the people he laments that, "it was in vain; and they did not realize that it was the Lord that had spared them, and granted them a chance for repentance."[6] The next verse tells us that the king of the Lamanites sent Mormon an epistle declaring that the Lamanites were preparing to come against them to battle. In the tradition of Gidgiddoni, Mormon gathered his people together into one body in the land of Desolation (within Nephite borders). He says that "there [Desolation] we did place our armies, that we might *stop* the armies of the Lamanites, that they might not get possession of any of our lands; therefore we did *fortify* against them will all our force."[7]

The account then tells us that the Lamanites brought battle to the Nephites for two consecutive years and were defeated both times by Mormon's people. It is at this point that the Nephite people begin to become prideful—boasting in their own strength and swearing vengeance upon their enemies. Mormon relates:

> And now, because of this great thing which my people had done, they began to boast in their own strength, and began to swear before the heavens that they would avenge themselves of the blood of their brethren who had been slain by their enemies. And they did swear by the heavens, and also by the throne of God, that they would go up to battle against their enemies, and would cut them off from the face of the land. And it came to pass that I, Mormon, did utterly refuse from this time forth to be a commander and a leader of this people, because of their wickedness and abominations."[8]

We see here that Mormon refused to lead his people in aggressive rather than defensive warfare against the Lamanites. While many may deride him as a pacifist it is evident that Mormon understood the Lord's rules of defensive warfare. He admits that he had led his people to battle many times despite their wickedness, had loved them, and had prayed for them. Three times he had "delivered them out of the hands of their enemies, and they repented not of their sins."[9] The next few verses reveal that the Lord takes the business of vengeance seriously:

> And when they had sworn by all that had been forbidden them by our Lord and Savior Jesus Christ, that they would go up unto their enemies to battle, and avenge themselves of the blood of their brethren, behold the voice of the Lord came unto me, saying: Vengeance is mine, and I will repay; and because this people repented not after I had delivered them, behold, they shall be cut off from the face of the earth."[10]

The key to true defensive war doctrine lies in the principle teaching that vengeance belongs *only* to the Lord. The Lord has said that we are commanded to forgive all men but He will forgive whom He will forgive. We have no business making a judgment call on who should live and who should die. In the author's opinion, the Lord's standard of condemning preemptive war is twofold; vengeance belongs *only* to the Lord and there is always *collateral damage* in the form of innocents. When Truman dropped the bombs on Nagasaki and Hiroshima, some 200,000 innocent Japanese civilians died—including thirty schools full of children. In 1991, the UN sanctions on Iraq prohibited medical supplies from entering the country resulting in the deaths of 500,000 children. Hundreds of thousands of civilians died in WWII as a result of allied bombings and 750,000 Germans starved to death during WWI because of Churchill's hunger blockade. Millions more died in Korea, Vietnam, Iraq, and Afghanistan as a result of American intervention to annihilate the "commi's" and "terrorists" from the face of the earth. How are we any different than these Nephites who Mormon refused to command? The plain truth is that we are not different, and if we do not repent then we may meet the same fate as the Nephites and Jaredites whose failures to learn the lessons of history are compiled in a record that is warning us from the dust. Mormon continues:

> And it came to pass that I utterly refused to go up against mine enemies; and I did even as the Lord commanded me; and I did stand as an idle witness to manifest unto the world the things which I saw and heard, according to the manifestations of the Spirit which had testified of things to come."[11]

Mormon was keeping the commandments of God by *not* leading his men in an assault against the Lamanites in their own lands. He was standing as an "idle witness" or an anti-war protestor as a testimony against his people. Not surprisingly, we learn that from this time forth the Nephites begin to be defeated by the Lamanites. Mormon makes it perfectly clear as to the cause of their defeat by writing:

> And it was because the armies of the Nephites went up unto the Lamanites that they began to be smitten; for were it not for that, the Lamanites could have no power over them. But, behold the judgments of God will overtake the wicked; and it is by the wicked that the wicked are punished; for it is the wicked that stir up the hearts of the children of men unto bloodshed.[12]

From the above verse, we learn that it was only because the Nephites preemptively attacked the Lamanites that they began to be defeated by them. How ironic that all the Nephites had to do was follow the Lord's commandments pertaining to war and the Lamanites would have had no power over them. As in the case of the children of Israel being too stubborn to look upon the staff of Moses to be healed, sometimes following the commandments is just *too* simple. Men like to make things complicated. For example, the United States has around 900 military bases in over 130 countries, yet if a foreign nation attempted to build a base on American soil we would declare war on that nation, bomb its inhabitants, and claim a victory for "democracy."

Meanwhile, we would leave our troops there for at least ten years, disarm its citizenry, set up Marshall Law with military checkpoints, set price controls, manipulate elections, and establish a puppet government. This is exactly what we did in Iraq after 9/11/2001, but that nation's military never set foot on our soil or attacked us. In fact, they had nothing to do with the 9/11 attacks and UN inspectors never found any WMD's—yet we still invaded and took over their country. One has to wonder if the "hypocritical nation"[13] spoken of by Isaiah is the latter-day United States.

Returning to the account of Mormon, we learn that his son—Moroni—saw our day. He saw and spoke to the latter-day Lamanites who would be scattered, smitten, and then gathered in the last days. He issued the following warning to them about preemptive warfare:

> Know ye that ye must lay down your weapons of war, and delight no more in the shedding of blood, and take them not again, save it be that God shall command you.[14]

We see the Lord's law of defensive war established again and again throughout the *Book of Mormon*. Above, the Lamanites are told to stop delighting in the shedding of blood, and to lay down their weapons of war until they are commanded by God to take them up again. The truth is very simple, plain, and pure, and we can rest assured that these commandments pertaining to warfare have not changed and are in full effect today. King Benjamin's statement that God "never doth vary from that which he hath said"[15] looms ominously over America because as a nation we have *not* kept God's commandments. Subsequent chapters throughout this book will explain how the United States has strayed from the non-interventionist foreign policy promulgated by the Founders, whom the Lord said that he raised up for the very purpose of establishing the Constitution.[16] Perhaps the most powerful testimony against the act of preemptive war was orated from the Savior himself during His aphoristic Sermon on the Mount. He gave this exhortation to both the Jews and the Nephites and He is poignantly explicit as to how we should treat our enemies. He says:

> And behold it is written also, that thou shalt love they neighbor and hate thine enemy. But behold I say unto you, love your enemies, bless them that curse you, do good to them that hate you, and pray for them who despitefully use you and persecute you; That ye may be the children of your Father who is in heaven; for he maketh his sun to rise on the evil and on the good.[17]

Here is a declaration that the old myopic law of hating your enemies is to be done away. Not only do we love our enemies, we are to pray for them and bless them when they are doing what? *Hating us, persecuting us, and despitefully using us!* Could the Lord be any clearer? Probably not, but instead of following this counsel we follow our government to war in violation of God's commandments and doctrine of defensive warfare, usually responding to a rumor that a nation has some deadly weapon that they *might* use against us. The official leadership then pulls some abstract moral justification out of the sky, using establishment intellectuals to convince the people of the "righteousness" of the cause, and then proceeds to bomb "military" targets where thousands of civilians also happen to live. The "idle witnesses" like Mormon who protest these wars are labeled as unpatriotic cowards who hate their country and are ridiculed, ostracized, and even imprisoned. Returning to the Sermon on Mount, the Lord also declared it a sin even to be *angry* with another. He says:

> Ye had heard that it hath been said by them of old time, and it is also written before you, that thou shalt not kill, and whosoever shall kill shall be in danger of the judgment of God; But I say unto you, that whosoever is angry with his brother shall be in danger of his judgment.[18]

The Gospel of Jesus Christ is the Gospel of *Peace*. When the Savior introduced himself to the Jews at the beginning of his ministry he was not well received. They assumed that the Messiah would come as a powerful leader who would subdue governments, armies, and nations. Instead, he came as the Lamb of God—meek and lowly in heart— something the Jews would not accept. Isaiah prophesied that he would be called, "Wonderful, Counsellor, The Mighty God, The Everlasting Father, *The Prince of Peace.*"[19] Jesus Christ is the author of peace, liberty, freedom, mercy and justice. Preemptive war is the antithesis of all that is Christian. Its fruits are the mass destruction of individual rights, properties, lives, and liberties. It stifles the plan of salvation by prematurely ending the lives of so many who may be unprepared to die, as well as blinding and deceiving those who supported such murder. Those who promulgate the cruelty of aggressive warfare can hardly call themselves Christian, and the idea that preemptive crusades qualify as true Christian campaigns is blasphemy against God. The only type of preemptive strike the Lord condones is that of sending missionaries into every nation to preach the Holy Gospel. The Nephites understood this principle as evidenced within the following verse:

> And now, as the preaching of the word had a great tendency to lead the people to do that which was just—yea, it had had more powerful effect upon the minds of the people than the sword, or anything else, which had happened unto them—therefore Alma thought it was expedient that they should try the virtue of the word of God.[20]

The word of God is much more effective in dispelling hatred and potential enemies than war is. Love is God's greatest resource—it has such an effect upon the human heart that when love truly manifests it disperses all hatred and darkness. War—on the other hand—is the germ of hatred, which is generated by the devil. The idea that wars ought to be declared and fought in the name of Christ has been with us since the days of the primitive church and is as unjust to the Lord as it is to the victims of those wars. When did the Savior ever preach such nonsense? When did He ever favor a preemptive attack perpetrated by the Roman Empire in which he resided? When did He ever preach hate, destruction, and murder? He never did. The Lord taught His followers to love one-another, to reach out to social misfits and outcasts, to love our enemies, to pray for those that hate us, and to bear each-other's burdens. In fact, Jesus' extreme philanthropic view of His brothers and sisters penetrated the false veneer of Roman nationalism and patriotism and defied the local secular and ecclesiastical authorities. He was sentenced to death by leaders of His own synagogue who delivered Him up to the local government for preaching a message that obliterated the astigmatic law of the world's carnal commandments by proclaiming a message of peace, love, acceptance, friendship, and forgiveness. Borders and nations did not matter to Jesus, who saw the whole of humanity as one big family. To Him, the love of country—a geographical area defined by imaginary lines—was to be dwarfed by the love of God and the love of one's neighbor. To accept the false doctrines of warmongers against the seminal teachings of Christianity is to ignobly offend the God who created worlds without end, yet condescended to become a personal sacrifice for every living creature ever to exist. Perhaps Abinadi said it best when he described to the wicked priests of the corrupt Nephite king Noah the blessings of peace, saying:

> And these [the prophets] are they who have published peace, who have brought good tidings of good, who have published salvation; and said unto Zion: Thy God reigneth! And O how beautiful upon the mountains were their feet! And again, how beautiful upon the mountains are the feet of those who shall hereafter publish peace, yea, from this time henceforth and forever! And behold, I say unto you, this is not all. For O how beautiful upon the mountains are the feet of him that bringeth good tidings, that is the founder of peace, yea, even the Lord, who has redeemed his people; yea, him who has granted salvation unto his people.[21]

Conclusion

Jesus Christ truly is the author, founder, and publisher of Peace. Preemptive war represents all that is contrary to His Gospel, and in practice is a direct revolt against Christ. It is a collective acquiescence to the human weaknesses of anger, hatred, passion, cruelty, and vengeance, which are antithetical to all that the Savior taught. Those who engage in it become hardened, ferocious, vindictive, despotic, and murderous. Nations who participate in aggressive warfare commit mass-murder under the auspices of patriotism and nationalism—deceiving their subjects into mistaking evil for good just as Isaiah prophesied.[22] In short, preemptive/aggressive warfare is nothing less than an assault against humanity itself, which violates the pure doctrines taught by Christ—especially the age-old dictum proclaimed by the Master that "Thou shalt love thy neighbour as thyself."[23]

Chapter Three Notes and Sources

1. This statement by Giddianhi is an allusion to the modern day false doctrine of Communism. It implies the total abolition of property rights and the confiscation of property by the government to then be redistributed among whom he calls "brethren" (AKA "comrades").

2. 3 Nephi 3:6-8

3. Ibid, 3:19

4. Ibid, 3:20-21, Emphasis added

5. Ibid, 3:25, Emphasis added

6. Mormon 3:3

7. Ibid, 3:6, Emphasis added

8. Ibid, 3:9-11, Emphasis added

9. Ibid, 3:13

10. Ibid, 3:14-15, Emphasis added

11. Ibid, 3:16, Emphasis added

12. Ibid, 4:4-5, Emphasis added

13. 2 Nephi 20:6, See also The Bible, Isaiah 10:6

14. Mormon 7:4
15. Mosiah 2:22
16. See Doctrine and Covenants, Section101:80
17. 3 Nephi 12:43-45, Emphasis added
18. Ibid, 3:21-22, Emphasis added
19. Isaiah 9:6
20. Alma 31:5, Emphasis added
21. Mosiah 15:14-18, Emphasis added
22. 2 Nephi 15:20
23. Mark 12:31

Chapter 4

Just War Theory and the Nephite Experience
Renounce war and proclaim Peace. -Joseph Smith

Just war theory was established by early Christians and primarily promulgated by Saint Augustine of Hippo. Several centuries later, its principles were solidified and set forth by Saint Thomas Aquinas and again three hundred years later by the Dutch Christian Hugo Grotius—known by many as "the father of international law." This theory can be subdivided into two categories; *jus ad bellum* (the right to go to war), and *jus in bello* (the proper rules of how to conduct war once it has been initiated). We will examine these theoretical principles and the subcategories of each while comparing them to the experiences of the Nephites under Captains Moroni, Moronihah, and Gidgiddoni. The reader will discover that the Nephites were obedient to the principles of just war theory—however, the reader should also keep in mind that states have endeavored to use this very doctrine to justify offensive wars of aggression. Just war theory was conjured by man and as such cannot be as sound or moral as the principles set forth in the Doctrine and Covenants and the *Book of Mormon*. God's law is always better than man's.

The principles of *jus ad bellum* can be summarized as follows: just cause, comparative justice, public declaration by a legitimate authority, reasonable chance for success/proportionality, and last resort. So how did the Nephites do? Was Captain Moroni's cause just? As mentioned in chapter one, we know that the "Nephites were inspired by a better cause" than their Lamanite counterparts. Instead of fighting for "monarchy nor power," they were fighting for the just cause that can be summed up in the 43rd chapter of Alma:

> And again, the Lord has said that: Ye shall defend your families even unto bloodshed. Therefore for this cause were the Nephites contending with the Lamanites, to defend themselves, and their families, and their lands, their country, and their rights, and their religion.[1]

The Nephites were clearly justified in fighting to defend their lives, their liberty, their property, their land, and their families. We can see that even many of the Lamanites understood these principles as evidenced by the fact that many of Amalickiah's followers began to "doubt concerning the justice of the cause in which they had undertaken."[2] Murray Rothbard also concurs with the Nephite position in his own explanation of just war theory:

> My own view of war can be put simply: a just war exists when a people tries to ward off the threat of coercive domination by another people, or to overthrow an already-existing domination. A war is unjust, on the other hand, when a people try to impose domination on another people, or try to retain an already existing coercive rule over them.[3]

Concerning the concept of comparative justice, which is a subset of just cause, we can deduce from the record that the Nephites' rights were being violated by the Lamanites. Ammoron—the brother of Amalickiah—describes the Lamanite complaints of injustices supposedly committed against them by the Nephites in an epistle to Moroni concerning an exchange of prisoners as follows; "For behold, your fathers did wrong their brethren, insomuch that they did rob them of their *right to government when it rightly belonged unto them.*"[4] Here, Ammoron is citing incidents that took place nearly 600 years before this war. Also, it is strange that Ammoron—a Nephite by birth—would endeavor to use a Lamanitish argument against Moroni—especially one that claims the rights of rule. This is a monarchical argument and presupposes that Laman and Lemuel were somehow predestined to rule over the Promised Land—hardly a justification to declare war. Moroni, conversely, makes known the injustices done by the Lamanites in an epistle to Ammoron as follows:

> Yea, I would tell you concerning that awful hell that awaits to receive such murderers as thou and thy brother have been, except ye repent and withdraw your murderous purposes, and return with your armies to your own lands… But, as the Lord liveth, our armies shall come upon you except ye withdraw, and ye shall soon be visited with death, for we will retain our cities and our lands; yea, and we will maintain our religion and the cause of our God.[5]

We have seen that the Nephite's cause was just and the injustices brought upon them by the Lamanites were great—qualifying them under the first two tenets of *jus ad bellum*. We will next inquire into their system of declaring war. This system involved a dual process: the voice of the people and the consultation of the prophet. Moroni, the chief captain of the Nephite army, "was appointed by the chief judges and the voice of the people,"[6] and upon learning of a pending attack or of a domestic insurrection (as in the case of the kingmen) he would consult with the prophet and the other captains of the Nephite armies. The advantages of consulting the prophet are twofold: the verification of the Lord's approval of the war, and revelation from the Lord on how to defeat their enemies or flee to safety. Mormon explains that if the Nephites never gave an offense (preemptive attack/aggressive warfare), and "never raised the sword … except it were to preserve their lives," then the Lord would fulfill certain promises as follows:

And this was their faith, that by so doing God would prosper them in the land, or in other words, if they were faithful in keeping the commandments of God that he would prosper them in the land; yea, warn them to flee, or to prepare them for war, according to their danger.[7]

The Nephite system of allowing the voice of the people to vote for or against war is not unlike our own American system before it was corrupted by the subjugation of the legislative power by the executive branch. The framers of the Constitution vested the power to declare war in the legislative branch of government because this is the branch that is closest to the people. Never did they intend to bestow this type of power into the hands of one man, as Article I, Section 8, Clause 11 of the Constitution clarifies:

The Congress shall have power to…declare war, grant letters of Marque and Reprisal, and make Rules concerning Captures on Land and Water; To raise and support Armies.[8]

In fact, the president was only to assume his role as "Commander-in-Chief of the Army and Navy of the United States, and of the Militia of the several States, *when* called into the actual Service of the United States."[9] In contrast to the Nephite method of declaring war—or, rather, declaring their right to protect themselves—Amalickiah assumed dictatorial powers and alone thrust the Lamanites into war. Sadly, every war since WWII has been entered into at the whims of the president, who is usually acquiescing to the conditions of a treaty signed before his term of office at the expense of the sovereignty of the people of the United States. We have regretfully adopted the Amalickiahite method of entering war. St. George Tucker comments on the proper limits of this power as follows:

The Power of declaring war, with all its train of consequences, direct and indirect, forms the next branch of the powers confided to congress; and happy it is for the people of America that it is so vested. The term 'war' embraces the extremes of human misery and iniquity, and is alike the offspring of the one and the parent of the other. What else is the history of war from the earliest ages to the present moment but an afflicting detail of the sufferings and calamities of mankind, resulting from the ambition, usurpation, animosities, resentments, piques, intrigues, avarice, rapacity, oppressions, murders, assassinations, and other crimes, of the few possessing power! How rare are the instances of a just war! How few of those which are thus denominated have had their existence in a national injury! The personal claims of the sovereigns are confounded with the interests of the nation over which he presides, and his private grievances or complaints are transferred to the people; who are thus made the victims of a quarrel in which they have no part, until they become principals in it, by their sufferings. War would be banished from the face of the earth, were nations instead of princes to decide upon their necessity. Injustice can never be the collective sentiment of a people emerged from barbarism. Happy the nation where the people are the arbiters of their own interest and their own conduct! Happy were it for the world, did the people of all nations possess this power.[10]

So far, so good. The Nephites are right in line with just war theory—much more so than the U.S. government has been—which explains why the *Book of Mormon* was written for us and not them. So, did they only engage in battles in which they had a reasonable and proportional chance of success? The answer is yes, but there is a little more to this question when we are dealing with the Lord, who has stated that if we abide by His rules then He will fight our battles for us.[11] Aside from the fact that Alma, Captain Moroni, Gidgiddoni, Mormon, *et al*, faced overwhelming odds at certain times throughout the *Book of Mormon* and emerged triumphant, the Nephites still endeavored to pick their battles carefully. Captain Moroni—being a man who did not glory "in the shedding of blood but in doing good … in preserving his people"[12]—engaged energetically in fortifying many Nephite cities in preparation for attack. We find examples of this in the 49th chapter of Alma. Here, we learn that the Nephites had fortified the city of Ammonihah by digging "up a ridge of earth round about them, which was so high that the Lamanites could not cast their stones and their arrows at them that they might take effect, neither could they come upon them save it was by their place of entrence."[13] The Lamanites, thinking that they could "easily overpower and subject their brethren to the yoke of bondage,"[14] were repulsed and retreated. They tried their luck next in the land of Noah where they were again disappointed because "they knew not that Moroni had fortified, or had built forts of security, for every city in all the land round about."[15] Nevertheless, the Lamanite captains had sworn to take the city of Noah "which had hitherto been a weak place," but "now, by the means of Moroni, became strong."[16] Moroni again had caused a high bank of earth to be dug around the entire city except by the entrance, and when the Lamanites tried to dig the banks of earth down "they were swept off by the stones and arrows which were thrown at them; and instead of filling up their ditches by pulling down the banks of earth, they were filled up in a measure with their dead and wounded bodies."[17] The Nephites again are in congruence with this principle by their doing everything they could to fortify against attack. Amalickiah, on the other hand, plunged his men into situations where many would die needlessly in attempts to take fortified cities. The account redundantly proclaims that the dictator—who did not even come down himself to battle—"did care not for the blood of his people."[18]

Finally, we come to the principle of last resort. Did the Nephites make every effort to avoid a conflict with the Lamanites? We are not told the specific diplomatic measures they took to pursue peace, yet we know they wanted to avoid war. The record tells us that they were not only not guilty of the first or second offense, but also that they were very reluctant to resort to war, and were "compelled,"[19] to fight the armies of Zerahemnah, Amalickiah, and Ammoron despite their great "reluctance."[20] The stripling warriors also opined that, "we would not slay our brethren if they would let us alone."[21] The Nephites had two choices here; either fight or surrender their families, lands, country, rights, and religion over to the Lamanites. Their justification seems obvious.

We now come to the second part of just war theory called *jus in bello,* which is the proper mode of conduct once a war has begun. The principles of *jus in bello* are as follows: proper distinction between enemy-combatants and civilians, military necessity (attack only military targets), proper treatment of prisoners of war, and finally, that no means *malum in se* (wrong or evil in itself) should be used. The attacking of non-military targets or civilian areas is strictly prohibited under this principle. In our modern age of airstrikes and drones, this idea has largely been eviscerated and millions of civilians have consequently been murdered. The Nephites, however, were quite faithful in observing this dictum and were diligent in making sure that innocents were protected. Mormon tells us that Moroni "was a man of a perfect understanding; yea, a man that did not delight in bloodshed; a man whose heart did joy in the liberty and the freedom of his country, and his brethren from bondage and slavery."[22] Moroni did everything he could to ensure the safety of his people—especially the women and children. Mormon also tells us that "the Lamanites had taken many women and children, and there was not a woman nor a child among all the prisoners of Moroni."[23] The reader should keep in mind that in Moroni's day there weren't any missiles, nukes, or chemical/biological weapons that could be used indiscriminately. A sword, sling, bow, ax, or cimeter could only be pointed at one person at a time, making the principles of *jus in bello* much easier to abide by. We do read of atrocities committed by the Lamanites against women and children, but this had to be personally done by armed men, not the mere pushing of a button. It seems as though weapons of mass destruction are the commonality in the modern age of warfare, yet the principles of just war theory, morality, and the commandments of God would render these types of weapons illegitimate. Rothbard offers an explanation in his essay entitled *War, Peace, and the State* as follows:

War then, is only proper when the exercise of violence is rigorously limited to the individual criminals. We may judge for ourselves how many wars or conflicts in history have met this criterion. It has often been maintained, and especially by conservatives, that the development of the horrendous modern weapons of mass murder (nuclear weapons, rockets, germ warfare, etc.) is only a difference of degree rather than kind from the simpler weapons of an earlier era. Of course, one answer to this is that when the degree is the number of human lives, the difference is a very big one. But another answer that the libertarian is particularly equipped to give is that while the bow and arrow could be used for aggressive purposes, but it could also be pinpointed to use only against aggressors. Nuclear weapons, even "conventional" aerial bombs, cannot be. These weapons are ipso facto engines of indiscriminate mass destruction… We must, therefore conclude that the use of nuclear or similar weapons, or the threat thereof, is a sin and a crime against humanity for which there can be no justification.[24]

As far as military necessity goes, the Nephites obeyed this principle by default because the Lamanites had invaded them and taken over certain of their cities. They were simply engaged in the business of taking those cities back, regardless of whether or not they were considered "military targets." The wisdom of engaging only in defensive war automatically brings one into harmony with the above rule because then you are only fighting against those who are aggressing against you. Modern states in modern warfare use a perversion of this reasoning when attacking "military targets" on foreign soil, but their justification is illegitimate because such attacks are preemptive. Rothbard once again clarifies the primary principle that sustains just war as follows:

The fundamental axiom of libertarian theory is that no one may threaten or commit violence ("aggress") against another man's person or property. Violence may be employed only against the man who commits such violence; that is, only defensively against the aggressive violence of another.[25]

The above quote by Rothbard renders the "military necessity" argument a non-sequitur unless, of course, the victims are endeavoring to *reclaim* a military base from an assailant, for any other attack on such a target would be preemptive.

Next, we come to the question of the proper treatment of POWs. We know from the account that Moroni took many prisoners of war. So, how did he treat them? We learn that "Moroni was compelled to cause the Lamanites to labor, because it was easy to guard them while at their labor."[26] The forcing of prisoners of war to labor, whether or not a just principle, is a much less brutal punishment than torture and/or death, which seem to be the *status quo* of the modern war age. There is no evidence in the record that Moroni or his men *ever* used torture on Lamanite prisoners. There was one instance when many Lamanite prisoners were killed by a Nephite garrison under a captain named Gid. As they were marching toward Zarahemla with many POW's, some of their spies returned and "cried ... saying—Behold, the armies of the Lamanites are marching towards the city of Cumeni; and behold, they will fall upon them, yea, and will destroy our people."[27] The prisoners heard their cries and did "take courage; and they did rise up in rebellion against"[26] the men of Gid. What happened next is as follows:

> And it came to pass because of their rebellion we did cause that our swords should come upon them. And it came to pass that they did in a body run upon our swords, in the which, the greater number of them were slain; and the remainder of them broke through and fled from us.[28]

Gid and his men were forced to do this in an act of self-defense, even though the POW's were not armed. It is one of those instances wherein both parties acted in the circumstances they were placed in and one would be hard-pressed to find fault with either side. Towards the end of the war we learn that all of the Lamanites who had been taken prisoner were simply set free and allowed to join the people of Ammon, or the anti-Nephi-Lehi's, who were also Lamanites. Mormon records:

> Now it came to pass that many of the Lamanites that were prisoners were desirous to join the people of Ammon and become a free people. And it came to pass that as many as were desirous, unto them it was granted according to their desires. Therefore, all the prisoners of the Lamanites did join the people of Ammon, and did begin to labor exceedingly, tilling the ground, raising all manner of grain, and flocks and herds of every kind; and thus were the Nephites relieved from a great burden; yea, insomuch that they were relieved from all the prisoners of the Lamanites.[29]

We also learn that Moronihah treated prisoners in the same manner as his father did. In a subsequent battle wherein the Lamanites attempted to take the capital city of Zarahemla, the attackers were beaten and captured by the Nephites. Moronihah "caused that the Lamanites who had been taken prisoners should depart out of the land in peace."[30] Finally, after the battle between Gidgiddoni's Nephites and the Gadianton robbers, we discover that the Lord condones the preaching of the Gospel to POW's, and that aggressors can be forgiven by simply entering into a covenant of peace. Mormon relates as follows:

> And now it came to pass that when they had taken all the robbers prisoners, insomuch that none did escape who were not slain, they did cast their prisoners into prison, and did cause the word of God to be preached unto them; and as many as would repent of their sins and enter into a covenant that they would murder no more were set at liberty.[31]

One should remember that, in many wars, most of the troops are fighting because they have been compelled—not because they agree with the cause or even want to be there. Most would rather be home providing for their families and contributing to society. We should remember that the Lord's injunction to love our enemies transcends beyond nation-states, countries, empires, and kingdoms. POW's and other so-called "enemy combatants" are still our brethren in the bigger picture and we are commanded to love them. The Nephite's example of teaching the Holy Gospel to those very men who were endeavoring to destroy them is an act of Christ-like love few men are capable of. In our modern age of torture, genocide, gulags, and indefinite detention, the Nephite wisdom comes as both a breath of fresh air and a warning to repent.

Finally, the ending principle of *jus ad bello* is that no means *malum in se* are to be employed in battle. Methods that fall under this category are the use of nuclear or biological weapons, genocide, civilian brutality (torture, rape, assault, looting, *etc.*), or forcing soldiers to fight against their own side. Again, the Nephites (Under Moroni, Moronihah, and Gidgiddoni) show excellent marks in this category. The Lamanites, however, did not fare so well. Towards the end of the war under captain Moroni, the Nephites had retaken all those cities the Lamanites had captured during the insurrection of the kingmen. The account reveals that the Lamanites "have carried with them many women and children out of the land."[32] During the next war under captain Moronihah, we learn that the Lamanites engaged in the indiscriminate slaughter of women and children:

> But behold, the Lamanites ... had come into the center of the land, and had taken the capital city which was the city of Zarahemla, and were marching through the most capital parts of the land, slaying the people with a great slaughter, both men, women, and children, taking possession of many cities and of many strongholds.[33]

As the record progresses to over three hundred years after the coming of Christ, we discover that "there never had been so great wickedness among all the children of Lehi."[34] At this point, the Nephites were engaging in preemptive war and the Lamanites were sacrificing women and children POW's up to their idol gods.[35] Mormon reveals that "every heart was hardened, so that they delighted in the shedding of blood continually."[36] Almost at the very end of the *Book of Mormon*—in the 9th chapter of Moroni—we are appalled to discover that the wartime depravity exceeded the above wickedness. *Both* the Nephites and the Lamanites were violating the *malum in se* standard and were engaging in rape and torture, cannibalism, mass-murder, and more. In an epistle to his son Moroni, Mormon relates the carnage as follows:

> And now I write somewhat concerning the sufferings of this people. For according to the knowledge which I have received from Amoron, behold, the Lamanites have many prisoners, which they took from the tower of Sherrizah; and there were men, women, and children. And the husbands and fathers of those women and children they have slain; and they feed the women upon the flesh of their husbands, and children upon the flesh of their fathers; and no water, save a little, do they give unto them. And notwithstanding this great abomination of the Lamanites, it doth not exceed that of our people in Moriantum. For behold, many of the daughters of the Lamanites have they taken prisoners; and after depriving them of that which was most dear and precious above all things, which is chastity and virtue—And after they have done this thing, they did murder them in a most cruel manner, torturing their bodies even unto death; and after they have done this, they devour their flesh like unto wild beasts, because of the hardness of their hearts; and they do it for a token of bravery.[37]

Conclusion

It is difficult to imagine a people who have devolved to this point of cruelty and barbarism, yet the Lord prompted the *Book of Mormon* prophets to include these things for a wise purpose. That purpose—this author believes—being a direct warning for our day. When nations disobey the rules of just warfare and just war conduct then there are heavy consequences to pay. Prolonged years of hate and fear-mongering propaganda combined with an insatiable desire to enact vengeance for wrong-doings can lead nations and individuals to begin to delight in the shedding of blood. Much like a pornography addiction, the mere killing of enemies becomes insufficient to quell the unquenchable thirst of revenge leading to torture, rape, and genocide. It is under these conditions that those who were considered once as human beings become animalistic killers whose appetite for murder is never satisfied. The principles of just war theory are a good set of laws for nations to follow—however, they are still the precepts of men and cannot be considered as equal to the law of God found in the 98th section of the Doctrine and Covenants. Just war theory is pragmatic, utilitarian, and normative, but the laws of God are eternal, immutable, and endowed with the character of intrinsic morality and righteousness, encompassing all that pertains to the law given to Moses; *thou shalt not kill.*

Chapter Four Notes and Sources

1. Alma 43:47
2. Alma 46:29
3. http://mises.org/daily/5943/Just-War
4. Alma 54:17
5. Alma, 54:7,10
6. Alma 46:34
7. Alma 48:14-15
8. The U.S. Constitution, Article I, Section 8, Clause 11
9. *Ibid*, Article II, Section 2, Clause 1, Emphasis added
10. St. George Tucker, Views of the Constitution of the United States With Selected Writings, p. 211
11. D&C 98:36-37
12. Alma 48:16
13. Alma 49:4
14. Alma, 49:7

15. Alma, 49:13

16. Alma, 49:14

17. Alma, 49:22

18. Alma, 49:10

19. Alma 43:13

20. Alma 48:22

21. Alma 56:46

22. Alma 48:11

23. Alma 54:3, See also, Alma 58:30

24. An essay by Murray N. Rothbard, compiled *in Egalitariansim as a Revolt against Nature, and Other Essays,* copyright 2000 by the Ludwig Von Mises Institute, pp. 119-120

25. *Ibid*, p. 116

26. Alma 53:5

27. Alma 57:31

28. Alma 57:33

29. Alma 62:27-29

30. Helaman 1:33

31. 3 Nephi 5:4

32. Alma 58:30

33. Helaman 1:27

34. Mormon 4:12

35. Mormon 4:14

36. Mormon 4:11

37. Moroni 9:7-10

Chapter 5

Conscription versus Covenant

Compulsory military service does not bring a danger of militarism; it is militarism. To adopt it in this country would mean that no matter how this war results we are conquered already; the hope of peace and a better day would no longer be present to sustain us in the present struggle, but there would be only the miserable prospect of the continuance of the evils of war even into peace times.
-John Gresham Machen

In a revelation given to Joseph Smith, the Lord condoned the Constitution of the United States. He proclaimed that it was "established … for the rights and protection of all flesh, according to just and holy principles … according to the moral agency which I have given unto him [man] … Therefore, it is not right that any man should be in bondage one to another."[1] Here, The Lord is giving a lesson in natural law and declaring from what source our rights come from. Rights are "inherent" in man and preexist any earthly government or authority. They come from our Creator—who desires His children to be free to make our own choices, whether those choices are good or evil. Government exists to protect these natural rights and can assume no true authority to violate moral restrictions that apply to individuals. For example, a government (which is simply a group of individuals) cannot engage in activities collectively that would be violations of moral law when done individually. Person A cannot morally point a gun at person

B and coerce them into fighting other people for A's cause without violating B's rights. The law is no different when applied to a group of people—in government, for example—who endeavor to forcibly conscript others into military service.

Military conscription is a violation of the Lord's injunction to Joseph Smith that "it is not right that any man should be in bondage one to another." Why? Conscription constitutes involuntary servitude, which is just another name for slavery. We have already pointed out that Lincoln's war against the South was fought over the Morrill Tariff, which raised tariff rates exponentially. However, when Northern support for Lincoln's cause was waning, and thousands of Northern conscientious objectors had been imprisoned without trial, the administration resolved upon a new stratagem. Lincoln issued the Emancipation Proclamation[2] by executive order and the official cause of the war shifted to the abolition of slavery, something Lincoln had promised not to meddle with. After the war was over, the 13th Amendment was passed, which specifically prohibited involuntary servitude:

> Neither slavery nor involuntary servitude, except as punishment for crime whereof the party shall have been duly convicted, shall exist within the United States, or any place subject to their jurisdiction.[3]

History however, is not without a twist of irony, for Lincoln and his republicans had violated the 13th Amendment (prior to its passing) by passing the Enrollment Act of 1863, which instituted a national draft. Tens of thousands of Northern citizens were snatched from their families and thrust to the front lines of a war that took over 600,000 American lives. According to Lincoln's logic, freeing the slaves required the enslavement of freemen—a rationale that was completely foreign to captain Moroni and his Nephite freedom fighters. There is no scriptural evidence that Moroni ever issued a national draft or supported conscription. So how did he recruit soldiers for his armies? The answer is by *covenant* and we find it in the 46th chapter of *Alma*. Mormon tells us that Moroni:

> Went forth among the people, waving the rent part of his garment (the title of liberty) in the air, that all might see the writing which he had written upon the rent part, and crying with a loud voice, saying: Behold, whosoever will maintain this title of liberty upon the land, let them come forth in the strength of the Lord, and enter into a covenant that they will maintain their rights, and their religion, that the Lord God may bless them.[4]

A close look at the text will reveal that the words *whosoever will* can only be interpreted to mean that the people had the choice to enlist. Covenant is the *modus operandi* of how the Lord conducts the affairs of His kingdom; we make covenants with the Lord through baptism and other ordinances. The Nephite chief judges, lower judges, and governors all made covenants to protect liberty, and Moroni (who had also made a covenant) used this same formula to enlist volunteers into his defensive armies. How did the people respond to this proposal? Mormon records:

> And it came to pass that when Moroni had proclaimed these words, behold, the people came running together with their armor girded about their loins, rending their garments in token, or as a covenant, that they would not forsake the Lord their God; or, in other words, if they should transgress the commandments of God, or fall into transgression, and be ashamed to take upon them the name of Christ, the Lord should rend them even as they had rent their garments.[5]

The people came running and willingly—without coercion or compulsion—made covenants with God that they would not fall into transgression because they knew that if they capitulated to sin (such as exercising coercion/compulsion/unrighteous dominion over others) then they would be delivered into the hands of the Lamanites. The next verse explains this covenant:

> Now this was the covenant which they made, and they cast their garments at the feet of Moroni, saying: We covenant with our God, that we shall be destroyed, even as out brethren in the land northward, if we shall fall into transgression; yea, he may cast us at the feet of our enemies, even as we have cast our garments at thy feet to be trodden under foot, if we shall fall into transgression.[6]

It is important for the reader to note here that this covenant was not between the men and Moroni or the men and the government. It was between each individual and God. It is a man's duty to protect his family from harm, and his right to stand up for his freedoms that are granted unto him by God rather than by governments. Although the Nephites had an official organization of government, they understood the doctrine of natural rights and during the times when the government was not controlled by secret combinations it remained within the bounds of its legitimacy, which is to protect natural human rights. Therefore, there was no conscription used by the Nephite government and the people depended upon the Lord for protection, as it is foolish to assume that men or earthly governments can provide any real security.

A few years later, during the heat of the war with the Lamanites, we find that Moroni was constantly fortifying cities and creating strongholds throughout all the land. We discover that not all able-bodied men had enlisted during the initial display of the Title of Liberty and that many volunteered later after realizing the great protection that Moroni's armies afforded. The account reveals that:

> Thus Moroni, with his armies, which did increase daily because of the assurance of protection which his works did bring forth unto them, did seek to cut off the strength and the power of the Lamanites from off the lands of their possessions, that they should have no power upon the lands of their possessions.[7]

Here we see that many came to join the ranks of Moroni because he diligently and faithfully exercised his ability to offer security and protection to the people. This process operated much like a free market mechanism; Moroni offered a good product and those who desired protection from the invading armies participated *voluntarily*—as the record is void of any evidence that compulsion was used. There are even certain circumstances wherein the Lord forbids the taking up of arms altogether as a condition of repentance. This was evident in the case of the people of Ammon, or the Anti-Nephi-Lehies. These Lamanites had been converted by Ammon, and as a condition of their repentance they made a covenant that they would never take up arms again, even in self-defense. This they had to do because of the many murders they had committed prior to their conversion. When the Lamanites declared war on the Nephites, these people were moved with compassion and desired to take up arms and were about to break the covenant but were stopped by the persuasions of Helaman, who "feared lest by doing so they should lose their souls; therefore all those who had entered into this covenant were compelled to behold their brethren wade through their afflictions, in their dangerous circumstances at this time."[8] Fortunately, these people of Ammon had many sons who had not entered into such a covenant and who were willing to enlist in the Nephite army to help defend their parents:

> But behold, it came to pass they had many sons, who had not entered into a covenant that they would not take their weapons of war to defend themselves against their enemies; therefore they did assemble themselves together at this time, as many as were able to take up arms, and they called themselves Nephites. And they entered into a covenant to fight for the liberty of the Nephites, yea, to protect the land unto the laying down of their lives; yea, even they covenanted that they never would give up their liberty, but they would fight in all cases to protect the Nephites and themselves from bondage.[9]

Again, we see that these young men—who are later revealed to be the 2000 stripling warriors—entered into a covenant to fight for their liberty. They were not compelled nor conscripted into the army, but rather joined out of their own volition with a desire to defend their parents and the Nephites against tyranny. Later, we learn that these stripling warriors were all miraculously preserved because of their faithfulness in keeping the covenant they made to defend their parents. After the stripling warriors entered the war, there began to be dissensions among the people of Nephi. At this crucial time, those that called themselves *kingmen* rose up in rebellion against those who were known by the appellation *freemen* (this at a time when the Lamanites were on the march taking many cities). We discover that Pahoran sent a proclamation out in his part of the land to recruit more men to the army in order to dispel the insurrection. In an epistle to Moroni he declared:

> And behold, I have sent a proclamation throughout this part of the land; and behold, they are flocking to us daily, to their arms, in defense of their country and their freedom, and to avenge their wrongs. And they have come unto us, insomuch that those who have risen up in rebellion against us are set at defiance, yea, insomuch that they do fear us and durst not come out against us to battle.[10]

Here, *again,* we see evidence that conscription was not used, *even* when the Nephite government was about to be overthrown by traitorous men who sought power and authority over the people. Pahoran's persuasive invitation was embraced by many, who came according to their own free will and conscience, and who desired to protect the freedom and liberty of their country. Along with Pahoran, Moroni raised the title of liberty in every city on his march toward Zarahemla in order to recruit men to aid against the kingmen. The record explains that thousands came flocking to his standard, again, with no coercion used:

And he did raise the standard of liberty in whatsoever place he did enter, and gained whatsoever force he could in all his march towards the land of Gideon. And it came to pass that *thousands did flock unto his standard,* and did take up their swords in the defense of their freedom, that they might not come into bondage.[11]

It seems as though the status quo of the Nephite military was not to force or compel regular citizens into fighting. However, upon closer examination, we find that Moroni did give an ultimatum to a certain group and compelled them to fight for their liberty or be put to death. This group was, of course, captured kingmen who had sought to siege Zarahemla, unseat Pahoran, and establish a king over the Nephites. It is the author's contention here that Moroni was justified in the use of force against these traitorous men. According to the principles of natural law, if a person commits an act of aggression against another (*i.e.* seeks to take by force a person's life, liberty, or property) then the victim of the crime has a right to receive their property back, requiring that the aggressor give up *his* life, liberty, or property in return. These kingmen had engaged in an act of collective aggression against the Nephites, and thus were obliged to yield up their rights temporarily until they repented. When Moroni defeated these men, he captured Pachus—their leader—and he and his men received a trial (trials during wartime are rare, as most governments—including the U.S.—have suspended *habeas corpus*[12] during times of war; this speaks volumes about how the Nephites viewed civil rights). The account continues:

And the men of Pachus received their trial, according to the law, and also those kingmen who had been taken and cast into prison; and they were executed according to the law; yea, those men of Pachus and those kingmen, whosoever would not take up arms in the defence of their country, but would fight against it, were put to death.[13]

Let the reader not assume that conscientious objectors fall into the category of treasonous men who were not merely refusing to take up arms in defense of their country, but were actively fighting against it. Unlike the traitorous Nephite kingmen who had attempted to subjugate and destroy their own people by force, the rest of the Nephite citizenry had not engaged in acts of treason and violence against the government, and were therefore not conscripted, executed, or cast into prison. These were persuaded—in the spirit of Doctrine and Covenants Section 121—by inspiring words from Moroni and other leaders about freedom, liberty, and the right to worship. There have been many Americans from the Civil War to the present that have been wrongly imprisoned for objecting to the draft, and to compare them to the egregious kingmen is both wrong-headed and presumptuous. When Lincoln and the Republicans initiated the first official national draft in 1863, the resultant riots in New York City culminated in many unnecessary deaths. The draft exempted blacks (who were not considered U.S. citizens), and anyone who could pay a fee of $300 (over $5000 in today's dollars). This enraged conscripted men in the city, most of which were indigent and of Irish decent, and violent riots ensued. Property was damaged, many blacks were killed, and Lincoln had to send troops to dispel the insurrection—resulting in many deaths. Although the rioters were not justified in their torrent of destruction against innocent persons and their property, neither was the Lincoln administration vindicated in inaugurating the unconstitutional use of conscription.

President Woodrow Wilson—in an attempt to conscript men into WWI—signed into law the Selective Service Act of 1917. Within ten days of declaring war on Germany, there had only been 4,355 men who had volunteered for service. Wilson's war to "make the world safe for democracy" demanded far more soldiers than were willing to enlist. Circumstances like these serve as a natural check on government because of the obstacle of public disapproval. However, when conscription is used, such checks disappear into the Orwellian memory-hole. Robert Higgs, in relation to Wilson and WWI, put it best when he said that, "the President and Congress were more eager to send men to war than men were to be sent."[14] This statement comprises perhaps the epitome of conscription. Governments that conscript presuppose that they have ownership over their constituents; for if a person can be called up and shipped overseas to a war being fought over monetary, geographical, or resource-based initiatives then how can they be called free? The *Book of Mormon* teaches that this same person—whom the government does not own—has the duty to fight only for their own life, liberty, property, and family. Nowhere does it appear in the doctrine of the Gospel of Jesus Christ that rich and powerful people have the right to conscript others into fighting bloody wars of empire, expansionism, or nation-building.

Wilson's Selective Service Act forced all men between the ages of twenty-one and thirty to register for the draft. Failure to do so could result in heavy fines and imprisonment—not to mention being labeled as an unpatriotic coward. In an attempt to avoid the mass desertion and evasion that transpired during the Civil War, the Wilson administration and Congress passed the Espionage Act of 1917, which stated that whoever "shall willfully obstruct the recruiting or enlistment service of the United States, shall be punished by a fine of not more than $10,000 or imprisonment for not more than twenty years, or both."[15] The acts (there were two; the Sedition and Espionage Acts) forbade any attempt to interfere with military operations, recruitment, or to encourage insubordination. Consequently, this led to the abridgment of the freedom of speech protection in the 1st Amendment. One of the first Supreme Court cases wherein violations of these acts were committed was that of Charles Schenck. Schenck—the Jewish secretary of the Socialist Party of America—had been found guilty of distributing anti-war material to potential draftees, encouraging them to oppose the draft and to stand up for their Constitutional rights against involuntary servitude as guaranteed in the 13th Amendment. He appealed to the Supreme Court and after hearing the case, Oliver Wendell Holmes Jr. held that the previous ruling condemning Schenck was permissable—leading to Schencks imprisonment. Holmes's logic for making the ruling can be summarized as follows:

When a nation is at war, many things that might be said in time of peace are such a hindrance to its effort that their utterance will not be endured so long as men fight, and that no Court could regard them as protected by any constitutional right.[16]

There is absolutely no justification for the above nonsense in the Constitution. The 1st Amendment says that "Congress shall make *no* law . . . abridging the freedom of speech." There is nothing in the text that would suggest that such legislation as the Sedition or Espionage Acts would be justified during wartime. In fact, it's during wartime that these freedoms should be protected with the utmost vigilance because the press is meant to operate as a check on the State. Shouldn't government be kept in check when it is toying with the notion of engaging in the mass shedding of blood? For this is exactly what war is; mass-murder on a grand scale perpetuated by a select few who compel the average person to carry it out for those in power. This average person is deceived into thinking that they are serving a higher morality, a common good, or a grandiloquent purpose too "mysterious" to be understood. Yet, despite all of this propaganda, they are not allowed to voice dissent or even peep a word of disapproval because a black-robed government "deity" prohibited doing so.

The leader of the Socialist Party—Eugene Debs—was also found guilty of sedition after making a speech on resisting the military draft in Canton, Ohio. His case also came up to the Supreme Court (*Debs v. United States*) where the precedent of the Schenck case was used and Debs was sentenced to ten years in prison. He ran for president from his jail cell, and after the war was over the stubborn Wilson still refused to pardon him. Fortunately for Debs, he was subsequently pardoned by the next president—Warren Harding.

Franklin Delano Roosevelt, who—following in the footsteps of Wilson—promised American mothers that their boys wouldn't be sent off to foreign wars also reneged on his campaign promises. The Selective Training and Service Act of 1940, in a tone of Orwellian doublespeak, stated that "in a free society the obligations and privileges of military training and service should be shared generally in accordance with a fair and just system of selective compulsory military training and service."[17] One has to wonder how the American public bought such an abomination coded in dichotomous language; *free* society and *compulsory* military training can hardly be construed as congruent. The act (which was the first to be enacted during an antebellum period) exempted public officials from service while "providing for the assignment of conscientious objectors to noncombat service."[18] Penalties for failure to comply consisted of a $10,000 fine and up to five years in prison. We must remember here that forced "noncombat service" is still enslavement and violates property rights, *i.e.* the right a person has to own their own body. The interesting thing is that out of the sixteen million American servicemen who fought in the war, ten million were conscripts. Hence Higgs begs the question, "Popular war?"[19] We have to assume that most American's were plunged into this conflict against their wills, which argument Higgs further substantiates by recording that "Some 6,000 conscientious objectors went to prison rather than to submit to either military service or the alternative employments prescribed by the government."[20]

Thousands more Americans were later conscripted into both the Korean and Vietnam wars—yet again against their wills. These wars were true American travesties, as thousands of American servicemen lost their lives accompanied by millions of civilian casualties. When one digs into the politics of these wars one begins to discover the swine trough of corruption that causes them. As the subject of this chapter is conscription, we will save our more in-depth examination of political corruption for a subsequent chapter. Perhaps—for Latter-day Saints—the most compelling evidence against the evils of conscription comes from a document produced by the First Presidency in 1945. In a letter addressed to the Utah Congressional Delegation they made clear the church's stance against not only military conscription itself, but also the evil environments and temptations that it foists upon young men. We will quote the letter at length:

It now appears that the proponents of the policy have persuaded the Administration to adopt it (military conscription), in what on its face is a modified form. We deeply regret this, because we dislike to find ourselves under the necessity of opposing any policy so sponsored. However, we are so persuaded of the rightfulness of our position, and we regard the policy so threatening to the true purposes for which this Government was set up, as set forth in the great Preamble to the Constitution, that we are constrained respectfully to invite your attention to the following considerations:

1.   By taking our sons at the most impressionable age of their adolescence and putting them into army camps under rigorous military discipline, we shall seriously endanger their initiative thereby impairing one of the essential elements of American citizenship. While on its face the suggested plan might not seem to visualize the army camp training, yet there seems little doubt that our military leaders contemplate such a period, with similar recurring periods after the boys are placed in the reserves.

2.   By taking our boys from their homes, we shall deprive them of parental guidance and control at this important period of their youth and there is no substitute for the care and love of a mother for a young son.

3.   We shall take them out of school and suffer their minds to be directed in other channels, so that very many of them after leaving the army, will never return to finish their schooling, thus over a few years materially reducing the literacy of the whole nation.

4.   We shall give opportunity to teach our sons not only the way to kill but also, in too many cases, the desire to kill, thereby increasing lawlessness and disorder to the consequent upsetting of the stability of our national society. God said at Sinai, "Thou shalt not kill."

5.   We shall take them from the refining, ennobling, character-building atmosphere of the home, and place them under a drastic

discipline in an environment that is hostile to most of the finer and nobler things of home and life.

6. We shall make our sons victims of systematized allurements to gamble, to drink, to smoke, to swear, to associate with lewd women, to be selfish, idle, irresponsible save under restraint of force, to be common, coarse, vulgar, all contrary to and destructive of the American home.

7. We shall deprive our sons of any adequate religious training and activity during their training years, for the religious element of army life is both inadequate and ineffective.

8. We shall put them where they may be indoctrinated with a wholly un-American view of the aims and purposes of their individual lives, and of the life of the whole people and nation, which are founded on the ways of peace, whereas they will be taught to believe in the ways of war.

9. We shall take them away from all participation in the means and measures of production to the economic loss of the whole nation.

10. We shall lay them open to wholly erroneous ideas of their duties to themselves, to their family, and to society in the matter of independence, self-sufficiency, individual initiative, and what we have come to call American manhood.

11. We shall subject them to encouragement in a belief that they can always live off the labors of others through the government or otherwise.

12. We shall make possible their building into a military caste which from all human experience bodes ill for that equality and unity which must always characterize the citizenry of the republic.

13. By creating an immense standing army, we shall create to our liberties and free institutions a threat foreseen and condemned by the founders of the Republic, and by the people of this country from that time till now. Great standing armies have always been the tools of ambitious dictators to the destruction of freedom.

14. By the creation of a great war machine, we shall invite and tempt the waging of war against foreign countries, upon little or nor provocation; for the possession of great military power always breeds thirst for domination, for empire, and for a rule by might not right.

15. By building a huge armed establishment, we shall belie our protestations of peace and peaceful intent and force other nations to a like course of militarism, so placing upon the peoples of the earth crushing burdens of taxation that with their present tax load will hardly be bearable and that will gravely threaten our social, economic, and governmental systems.

16. We shall make of the whole earth on great military camp whose separate armies, headed by war-minded officers, will never rest till they are at one-another's throats in what will be the most terrible contest the world has ever seen.

17. All the advantages for the protection of the country offered by a standing army may be obtained by the National Guard system which has proved so effective in the past and which is unattended by the evils of entire mobilization.

Responsive to the ancient wisdom, "Train up a child in the way he should go: and when he is old, he will not depart from it," obedient to the divine message that heralded the birth of Jesus the Christ, the Savoir and Redeemer of the world, "...on earth peace, good will toward men," and knowing that our Constitution and the Government set up under it were inspired of God and should be preserved to the blessing not only of our own citizenry but, as an example, to the blessing of all the world, we have the honor respectfully to urge that you do your utmost to defeat any plan designed to bring about the compulsory military service of our citizenry. Should it be urged that our complete armament is necessary for our safety, it may be confidently replied that a proper foreign policy, implemented by an effective diplomacy, can avert the dangers that are feared. What this country needs and what the world needs, is a will for peace, not war. God will help our efforts to bring this about.[21]

Point by point, the First Presidency addressed every incumbent evil that the institution of conscription introduces into a society. We have to ask what right a government has to pluck young impressionable boys from their homes and families, alter their minds by intense submission exercises, train them to kill, and then ship them oversees to an environment of lasciviousness, promiscuity, and carnage? The answer is that they have none. There is no authority in the Constitution for the government to engage in such practices, and—according to natural law—such coercion over a person's body by a minority or a majority is illegitimate.

In chapter one, we mentioned the ancient Israelites and questioned the authenticity of the biblical translation of the accounts of them destroying entire civilizations. We will now examine their mode of military recruitment as described by Moses. In Numbers, we learn that the Lord commanded Moses to raise up an army by having men enlist from every tribe except that of Levi. The Lord said to Moses:

> Take ye the sum of all the congregation of the children of Israel, after their families, by the house of their fathers, with the number of their names, every male by their polls; From twenty years old and upward, all that are able to go forth to war in Israel: thou and Aaron shall number them by their armies.[22]

This sounds an awful lot like a draft but upon closer examination we find some interesting language at the end of the chapter. The biblical account reveals that "the children of Israel *did* according to all that the Lord commanded Moses, *so did they*.[23] Just the reference to the word *did* infers that the children of Israel had a choice in the matter. The Lord has also said that He is an unchangeable being and if this is the case, which indeed it is, then we have to suppose by logic and reason that since the Nephites didn't practice conscription it therefore rationally follows that the Israelites used a voluntary covenant system as well. In the book of Deuteronomy, we find compelling evidence of an extremely lenient military. Those who had just married, built houses, planted a vineyard, or were fainthearted were encouraged to go home:

> And the officers shall speak unto the people, saying, What man is there that hath built a new house, and hath not dedicated it? Let him go and return to his house, lest he die in the battle, and another man dedicate it. And what man is he that hath planted a vineyard, and hath not ye eaten of it? Let him also go and return unto his house, lest he die in the battle, and another man eat of it. And what man is there that hath betrothed a wife, and hath not taken her? Let him go and return unto his house, lest he die in the battle, and another man take her. And the officers shall speak further unto the people, and they shall say, What man is there that is fearful and fainthearted? Let him go and return unto his house, lest his brethren's heart faint as well as his heart.[24]

Perhaps the most logical and forthright argument against conscription comes from Murray Rothbard, who boldly challenges the legitimacy of the states that engage in such evil practices:

> A final word about conscription: of all the ways in which war aggrandizes the State, this is perhaps the most flagrant and most despotic. But the most striking fact about conscription is the absurdity of the arguments put forward on its behalf. A man must be conscripted to defend his (or someone else's?) liberty against an evil State beyond the borders. Defend his liberty? How? By being coerced into an army whose very *raison d'etre* is the expunging of liberty, the trampling on all the liberties of the person, the calculated and brutal dehumanization of the soldier and his transformation into an efficient engine of murder at the whim of his "commanding officer?" Can any conceivable foreign State do anything worse to

him than what "his" army is now doing for his alleged benefit? Who is there, O Lord, to defend him against his "defenders?"[25]

Conclusion

We have presented in this chapter a strong argument that the Lord does not condone conscription. We have used the *Book of Mormon*, the *Bible*, and a letter from the First Presidency of the church written during one of the bloodiest conflicts that transpired on this earth. Latter-day Saints and other Christians who, after reading this, still believe in the myth that we owe the government our involuntary servitude would do well to search the scriptures and the Constitution. We must remember that the Lord's plan that was presented in the pre-earth life was one of complete volunteerism, promulgating the liberty of the individual, and the intrinsic value of choosing the good for ourselves. Conscription, on the other hand, is a tenet of Satan's counterfeit plan of abolishing free agency and forcing the individual to conform to the collective. Also, we must remember that the collective is not a single entity but is composed of free acting individuals and that if we are to take the argument down to its most logical conclusion then we must admit that the collective (or government) has no rights and therefore cannot morally or legally conscript.

Chapter Five Notes and Sources

1. Doctrine and Covenants 101:77-79
2. The Emancipation Proclamation was issued without the authority of Congress, and it only prohibited slavery in Southern states that had not been conquered by the Union army, while allowing slavery to exist in *Northern* states controlled by the Union. Nothing but a rhetorical faux, it did virtually nothing to end slavery.
3. The 13th Amendment to the United States Constitution, December 6, 1865
4. Alma 46:19-20, Emphasis added
5. Alma 46:21, Emphasis added
6. Alma 46:22

7. Alma 50:12. Emphasis added

8. Alma 53:15

9. Alma 53:16-17

10. Alma 61:6-7

11. Alma 62:4-5, Emphasis added

12. *Habeas Corpus* literally means, "may you have the body," and is a writ or court order that requires a person under arrest to be brought before a judge. This ancient right helped to protect people from kangaroo courts, military tribunals, and indefinite detention. See also the 4th Amendment to the United States Constitution.

13. Alma 62:9-10, Emphasis added

14. Robert Higgs, Crises and Leviathan, Critical Episodes in the Growth of American Government, New York, Oxford, Oxford University Press, 1987, p. 131

15. Espionage Act of June 15, 1917, quoted in Ibid, p. 133

16. *Schenck v. United States 249 U.S. 47*, Holmes, Wendell Oliver, Opinion of the Court

17. Selective Training and Service Act of 1940, quoted in Higgs, *Crises and Leviathan*, p. 200

18. Higgs, Crises and Leviathan, p. 201

19. *Ibid*, p. 202

20. Ibid

21. Letter from the First Presidency (David O. McKay, George Albert Smith, and J. Reuben Clark Jr.) to the Utah Congressional Delegation—Senators Thomas and Murdock and Congressmen Granger and Robinson, December **22.** 1945, Source: http://www.awakeandarise.org/blog/greatest-generation-soldiers-line-up-for-brothels/

22. Numbers 1:2-3

23. Numbers 1:54, Emphasis added

24. Deuteronomy 20:5-8

25. Murray N. Rothbard, *Egalitarianism as a Revolt Against Nature and Other Essays*, Ludwig Von Mises Institute, Auburn, Alabama, 2000, p. 132

Chapter 6

The Nationalistic Disease

There are none save a few only who do not lift themselves up in the pride of their hearts.

-Moroni

Nationalism is the political ideology that associates the human need to belong, or interpersonal attachment, with citizenship in one's nation. This need to belong is one of humanity's most fundamental motivations. More often than not, people will forsake their religious creeds, morals, dogmas, and even logical and rationale thought processes to become part of or fit in with a group. Governments take advantage of this human weakness by employing intellectuals to indoctrinate people into rallying behind a "national" cause. Far too often, these "national" causes are not moral and when done on an individual level would be seen as murder and theft. However, as nations act collectively the Orwellian idea known as *group-think* takes command of the emotional state of men as established morals and principles are forsaken. We refer to nationalism as a disease because it is a symptom of the disease of pride. Those who are plagued with this disease are in a most precarious predicament in that they don't know they are infected. Worse yet, they suppose they are immune. A person can be in no worse state than to suppose they themselves are right and on the side of God when in reality they are wrong and on the side of evil.

The consequence of the sin of pride is deception, and to be deceived literally means that we believe evil to be good and good to be evil. Nationalism tends to deceive people into believing that laws that apply to individuals do not apply to groups. This fallacy is based on the premise that acting as a group somehow negates the injunctions that God gave to Moses; however, laws that apply to individuals are not magically exempted when individuals act in concert with others. This is an eternal principle, and when nations collectively violate the commandments of God they are held accountable. Because nations will not exist in the after-life, the punishment—according to God's judgment—has to take place during this time of mortality. The scriptures are replete with evidence of this principle—for we learn that the Antediluvians, the Jews, the Jaredites, and the Nephites were all destroyed because they collectively forsook the Lord's commandments.

Satan—being the cunning and crafty being that he is—uses this concept of nationalism to deceive people into believing that love of country should transcend the love of God and the love of one's neighbor. Thus, nationalism is used by the Evil One in a diabolical scheme to beguile the masses into acquiescing to collective hatred. The *Book of Mormon* teaches this principle throughout its entirety with an underlying theme that hatred and war are always generated by Satan. Jacob—the brother of Nephi—lamented the fact that his people were "cast out from Jerusalem, born in tribulation, in a wilderness, and *hated* of our brethren, *which caused wars and contentions.*"[1] Zeniff also discussed this principle and pointed out that Laman and Lemuel:

> ...have taught their children that they should hate [the Nephites], and that they should murder them, and that they should rob and plunder them, and do all they could to destroy them; therefore they have an eternal hatred towards the children of Nephi.[2]

The Lamanites taught their children to engage in collective hatred toward the Nephites. They did this because they felt that Nephi had deprived them of their right to rule and robbed them by taking the brass plates and departing into the wilderness. It is astonishing that this false tradition of hatred could last for close to 1,000 years of Nephite history, yet it reveals to us the extreme effectiveness of Satan's propaganda schemes. We learn that those who rejected the Gospel three hundred plus years after Christ visited the American continent "were taught to *hate* the children of God, even as the Lamanites were taught to *hate* the children of Nephi from the beginning."[3] Governments systematically teach their subjects to hate foreigners, enemy-combatants, or political dissidents for reasons of political gain. They create "bad guys" and "boogiemen" to scare their populations into surrendering their liberty for so-called security. Hate propaganda is the most effective means for them to accomplish this process and it can lead to both temporal and spiritual enslavement.

Hatred was the primary motivating factor for the Lamanite war against the Nephites during captain Moroni's tenure. We are told that Zerahemnah appointed chief captains over the Lamanites, of those who were Amalekites and Zoramites (Nephite dissenters) in order to:

> Preserve their hatred towards the Nephites that he might bring them into subjection to the accomplishment of his designs. For behold, his designs were to stir up the Lamanites to anger against the Nephites; this he did that he might usurp great power over them, and also that he might gain power over the Nephites by bringing them into bondage.[4]

Zerahemnah was no imbecile—he understood that in order to gain political advantage over people you must unite them, or stir them up through some kind of collective cause. We can see in the above verse that hatred was the means used by the Lamanite politburo in their efforts to subjugate the Nephites, and preserving that hatred was paramount to Zerahemnah's agenda. Amalickiah—also being skilled in political Machiavellianism—"did appoint men to speak unto the Lamanites from their towers, against the Nephites. And thus he did inspire their hearts against the Nephites."[5] Amalickiah was, in fact, so efficient at spreading anti-Nephite propaganda that he was able to raise a massive army without conscription—reiterating the fact that nationalism can unite the collective emotions of people into blindly believing that it is their duty to militarily serve their country and thus they can be willingly coaxed into military service. It is also interesting to note that he appointed men (intellectuals) to speak to the people from their towers, while today the intellectuals speak "flattering" words to us from radio and television towers. The American mass media has been used to spread hate speech, disinformation, and rumors of wars against fascists, communists, and terrorists for close to one hundred years and consequently we have fought illegal and immoral wars against each of these ideologies in a crusade to cleanse the world of "evil."

Although the above ideologies are themselves legitimate evils, we must remember that the *Book of Mormon* and our Founding Fathers teach that nations are not to go seeking after foreign military adventures to right every wrong. However, men like William McKinley, Teddy Roosevelt, Woodrow Wilson, Franklin Delano Roosevelt, Harry Truman, Linden B. Johnson, George W. Bush, and Barack H. Obama have done that very thing using the *very same* propaganda techniques as the Germans and Russians. Most Americans have bought in to the government war propaganda because they believed the nationalistic lie that the United States is always the "good guy" in every battle; however, we must realize that there are no such things as good guys and bad guys—there is only good and evil. Each person has the agency to choose between good and evil in *every* situation that requires it. For example, even those who are waging a defensive war approved by the Lord are still susceptible to committing evil—even though they are the proverbial "good guys." Our only defense against such human fallibility is eternal obedience to correct principles and reliance on personal revelation from the Lord.

Vladimir Lenin—the Marxist revolutionary who succeeded in orchestrating one of the most brilliant government overthrows in history—was of the ilk of men such as Zerahemnah and Amalickiah. He was a man who was expert in propaganda, or, what the *Book of Mormon* calls "flattery," or smooth-talk. As a master of social demolition and Pavlovian pathology, Lenin excelled in social engineering and mass manipulation. He was, indeed, the epitome of the modern megalomaniacal dictator and he set the stage for the despotic tyranny that characterizes the 20th century. Eugene H. Methvin coined the phrase "Lenin's law" when he quoted Lenin's most sanctimonious credo to never let a good class struggle to go waste. Lenin says:

> There is no single segment of industrial society, no class in the population, without its circle, however small, of discontented and maladjusted and alienated individuals—predisposed target audiences for radical hate propaganda—who can be hooked up to a revolutionary mass movement.[6]

Hate is Satan's most powerful weapon in his arsenal of unrighteous dominion. He often uses prominent men who can be set up as demagogues to incite the masses through flattery or convincing rhetoric about the supposed depravity of certain groups and ideologies. These masses are then duped into supporting preemptive wars, virulent revolutions, or legislation that destroys their God-given rights. The Lord's dictum to love our neighbor was not just given to persuade us—in a spirit of warm fuzziness—to engage in charitable acts for our neighbor. There is also another element to this second great commandment: to avoid *deception* by not allowing our emotions to overrule our logic when flattering establishment intellectuals endeavor to convince us to hate so-called foreign enemies. To illustrate the visceral absurdity of group hate and *groupthink*, we will strip down collective hatred to the *reductio ad absurdum,* or follow the argument down to its most logical conclusion. When this is honestly done, we must admit that hatred of an entire group is impossible. One cannot hate a group without hating every *individual* belonging to that group. Unless one spends countless hours, days, months, and even years getting to know the millions of people that have been labeled as enemies by the government then an honest assessment cannot be made and, thus, such a person only deceives themselves. In reality, that person has engaged in nothing more than hating an abstraction of the mind; for this is what a group is—an abstract metaphysical blob that our minds associate with a mass of people. This mass you cannot see, touch, smell, or hear because it can only exist as an idea in your head. You cannot see such a large group, you can only see individuals; you cannot see the whole forest, you can only see certain trees. Herein lies the key to avoiding deception; *love your neighbor,* for your neighbor is an individual—not an abstraction, not a group or a nation, but a real, tangible human being with distinct personality traits, thoughts, ideals, and actions. Our propensity to instead *love our nation* is totally missing the mark that Christ set as the scriptures are bereft of such a phrase.

Methvin continues his analysis of Leninism by revealing the true *modus operandi* of manipulators who use hate tactics. He opines that "Lenin's major point was that mass movements can and must be *artificially* promoted, and primarily through the mass media."[7] Governments have used this method of artificially created crises to gain the support of the masses in whatever the State's agenda is. This concept holds true whether the government is engaging in artificially manufacturing economic crises in order to garner support for more intrusive regulation, or in deliberately provoking a foreign nation to attack so that the people will acquiesce to an interventionist foreign policy. This method is called the Hegelian Dialectic and has been used by virtually every power-seeking dictator *ad nauseam*. George Wilhelm Friedrich Hegel was an 18th century German philosopher who expounded upon the dialectical process of thesis + antithesis = synthesis long before Karl Marx or Frederick Engels did. This augmented the birth of the left/right paradigm that plagues our nation to this day. Antony C. Sutton explains the genius behind Hegel's dialectical process as follows:

A clash of political left and political right brings about another political system, a synthesis of the two, neither left nor right. This conflict of opposites is essential to bring about change.[8]

The change that is brought about here represents not the goals of a particular party, but those of the State, which both parties are subject to. The smokescreen created by the illusion of a choice at the voting box can be easily discerned once a person comprehends that both parties are adherents of collectivism. Democrats prefer economic central planning, forced nondiscrimination, and monetary egalitarianism, while Republicans push for compulsory military service, excessive outlays on "national defense" (mostly actually offense), and foreign adventurism and nation-building. Both parties require the subservience of the individual to the State. To Hegel, the communists, the fascists, and to all collectivists in general, the State is supreme, omnipotent, and omniscient—to be worshiped unyieldingly, requiring the individual to surrender their rights to the State for the *pro bono publico,* or "good of the whole." And who or what is the State? Rothbard defines the State as "a group of people who have managed to acquire a virtual monopoly of the use of violence throughout a given territorial area."[9] Instead of continuing to foster the abstract delusions we have harbored since our time in government-funded schools, we must see this entity for what it is: a minority of individuals who have managed to gain a stranglehold on the majority, holding on like a parasite to a host in the constant fear that the sleeping giant known as the American people will wake up and crush its pathetic rule. This is precisely why the State is always at the helm of steering public opinion to meet its agenda and always initiating wars to keep the nationalistic sheep occupied, always hiring professional liars and deifying them through the mass media—all to keep its power monopoly. Methvin further expounds all the areas of sociological psychology that must be manipulated in order for the State to sway public opinion and maintain its empire:

Lenin was developing the techniques of power-oriented sociological analysis: the study of social groupings, attitudes, motivations, loyalties, the anatomy and nature of the mass organizations in industrial society and the techniques of mass communication and control—all aimed at orchestrating social conflict to effect a transfer of loyalty from the traditionally constituted government toward the Leninist international cartel of professional political organizers.[10]

As individuals, we must not be ignorant of the dangers of government. The *Book of Mormon* teaches us that men like Nehor, Amulon, Korihor, and Amalickiah are of the Leninist type and their narratives were included in the record by Mormon as a direct warning for our day. There are—and always have been—people who diligently study the techniques of mass brainwashing, Pavlovian conditioning, and nationalistic propaganda and/or indoctrination that will unite the masses behind a supposed cause of their country—no matter how diabolical a cause that is. When men are collectively united in a cause they are fulfilling certain psychological needs which include the longing for camaraderie, the pseudo-security of *groupthink*, and the supposition that they are fighting on the side of the "good guys." When governments can unite loyal citizens into such psychological delusions individual morality can get swallowed up in the collective black hole of group morality. One of the grandest lies the devil ever told was that people should serve their governments at the expense of God, and should follow their masters in a lemming-like herd off the cliffs of nationalism. The institutionalization of this lie has its evidence in the fact that *the majority of all murders have been committed by governments and their militaries.*

Moroni also warned us about the fruits of this deception. Speaking of the secret combinations (the ones who initiate and finance wars), he is asking the modern day American Gentiles the question:

Yea, why do ye build up your secret combinations to get gain, and cause that widows should mourn before the Lord, and also orphans to mourn before the Lord, and also the blood of their fathers and their husbands to cry unto the Lord from the ground, for vengeance upon your heads?[11]

Who suffers from war? Is it not widows and orphans who lose their fathers and husbands in battle? Is it not also people who have been conscripted away from their families by a predatory government that seeks power and authority over other nations? While those who sit in the judgment seats prey upon the frailties of the masses by entertaining and postulating absurd notions of jingoistic foreign enmity. This collective hatred spreads like a disease throughout the minds of the common people, who find themselves mindlessly cheering as conscripted men on both sides of the conflict die for empire. Meanwhile, Satan laughs as he wraps his chains around that nation that has become a mob of murderers. Sadly, this is the essence of jingoism (aggressive, hateful nationalism).

Herman Goering—a high-ranking Nazi official in Hitler's fascist regime—admitted to Gustave Gilbert—an allied journalists allowed free reign to visit jail cells at the Nuremburg Trials—that the Nazi formula for mass manipulation works the same in any country. What should be shocking, appalling, and insidiously terrifying to Americans is that our leaders have used this very same propaganda in the War on Terror. The following dialogue is the conversation that took place between Gilbert and Goering as recorded in Gilbert's journal:

We got around to the subject of war again and I said that, contrary to his attitude, I did not think that the common people are very thankful for leaders who bring them war and destruction.

"Why, of course, the people don't want war." Goering shrugged. "Why would some poor slob on a farm want to risk his life in a war when the best that he can get out of it is to come back to his farm in one piece? Naturally, the common people don't want war; neither in Russia nor in England nor in America, nor for that matter in Germany. That is understood. But, after all, it is the leaders of the country who determine the policy and it is always a simple matter to drag the people along, whether it is a democracy or a fascist dictatorship or a Parliament or a Communist dictatorship."

"There is one difference," I pointed out. "In a democracy the people have some say in the matter through their elected representatives, and in the United States only Congress can declare wars."

"Oh, that is all well and good, but, voice or no voice, the people can always be brought to the bidding of the leaders. That is easy. All you have to do is tell them they are being attacked and denounce the pacifists for lack of patriotism and exposing the country to danger. It works the same way in any country."[12]

Goering is describing the fear-mongering tactics used by governments to garner public support for foreign policy. It is indeed a "simple matter" to drag the masses along in government wars to crusade against proverbial "bad guys." It is quite astonishing how easily people will give up liberties and acquiesce to state propaganda if they think that a threat exists. The irony of this business is that the majority of perceived threats have been—as Hegel supported—*manufactured* by the government to induce fear into the population (See chapter 10, *Amalickiah and False Flag Operations*). When the mass hysteria caused by the manufactured crises is dispelled by the government's promises of protection (in return for liberties, of course), the fear-ridden population begins to engage in state idolatry, or the worship of the State. It is at this point in the evolution of the warfare state that things begin to get dangerously precarious. It is at this point when the citizenry begins to believe that the government can do no wrong. Spencer W. Kimball warned us about the evils of such a plight in a First Presidency message in 1976 as follows:

In spite of our delight in defining ourselves as modern, and our tendency to think we possess a sophistication that no people in the past ever had—in spite of these things, we are, on the whole, an *idolatrous* people—a condition most repugnant to the Lord. We are a *warlike* people, easily distracted from our assignment of preparing for the coming of the Lord. When enemies rise up, we commit vast resources to the fabrication of gods of stone and steel—ships, planes, missiles, fortifications—and depend on them for protection and deliverance. When threatened, we become anti-enemy instead of pro-kingdom of God; we train a man in the art of war and call him a patriot, thus, in the manner of Satan's counterfeit of true patriotism, perverting the Saviors teaching: Love your enemies...[13]

Statolatry has been practiced in this nation since its inception, and especially since the Civil War. During certain epochs, our leaders have used religious language in association with the supposed grandiosity of the wars we have been involved in. Lincoln and Wilson were especially guilty of this grand deception, which we call the preaching of *civil religion*. Lincoln—a known spiritualist and Darwinist—frequently incorporated Biblical language into his speeches. When he ended his 1838 Lyceum speech he did so with the phrase from *Mathew* 16:18 that "the gates of hell would not prevail against it" (American liberty). In 1858, during the state of the union address, he opined that "a house divided against itself cannot stand" (*Mathew* 12:25), and during the famous Gettysburg address, Lincoln inculcated various phrases originating from the Bible. The opening line "four score" was an allusion to the Psalmist's description of the average life span of "three score and ten." He continued with the words "brought forth" and ended with the phrase "shall not perish." Amid the address he uttered other canonized words such as "dedicated," "consecrated," and "hallow."[14] It is evident that Lincoln, who was a self-declared atheist, used this religious rhetoric to subtly incite the emotions of the vast majority of American Christians into accepting the official state line. Historian Richard Gamble further explains this idea of civil religion as follows:

In 1967, sociologist Robert Bellah launched the modern career of "civil religion" as a concept, a way to examine how, on the one hand, the state adopts religious language, ritual, holidays, and symbolism to bind a nation together and how, on the other hand, it elevates its own values and ideas to the status of holy doctrine.[15]

Wilson also waxed eloquent in his use of pietistic semantics when he preached his sermon of the Great War. Wilson's war rhetoric was littered with pompous praise for American intervention in the other nations of the world. In a speech given at Washington's grave at Mount Vernon, he orated the seemingly innocuous dictum that the "Founders" would've wanted the American people to "strive for the liberties of every other people as well." The Founders would have supported striving for the liberty of other nations by example but never by a war to "make the world safe for democracy"—a type of government that they despised. In a more onerous and Bush-like tone, Wilson declared that to secure peace there must be "the destruction of every arbitrary power anywhere that can separately, secretly, and of its single choice disturb the peace of the world." In the 1912 presidential campaign Wilson essayed "that [Americans] are chosen and prominently chosen to show the way to the nations of the world how they shall walk in the paths of liberty." Obviously an association with the Gospel—equating being "chosen" and walking in the "paths of liberty" to participation in an aggressive European war is obscene blasphemy. Edwin Anderson Alderman—a Wilson idolater in his own right—described the supposed fruits of the Fourteen Points of promising "a new earth arising out of horror but ennobled by the sacrifice of millions,"[16] assimilating Wilson's vision for a new world order with the dawning day of the Millennium.

One can discern these semantic deceptions simply by understanding the Lord's rules of war. Just as the Nephites were forbidden to go into the wilderness and destroy the robbers who threatened to invade their lands, so we are forbidden to go in search of foreign monsters to destroy in their own lands. It is a noble thing to "strive for the liberty of every other people" *only* if it is done by example. Perhaps if Wilson had read the *Book of Mormon* he might have learned that preaching the word of God has a much better effect on eliminating evil than to enforce "righteousness" by the sword. We must recognize Wilson's rhetoric for what it is—sinister rhetoric that is used to incite the American people into supporting a European war waged over economic and political interests. Wilson's true motives in involving the U.S. into this horrible conflict was to set himself up as a savior of mankind who was instrumental in establishing the League of Nations which would forever abdicate warfare. Instead, however, he managed to initiate a war legacy that would set the stage for the bloodiest century in the history of the world. All of his jingoistic sloganeering merely served to dupe the good-hearted religious masses into supporting U.S. entry into a pietistic crusade to set the world on the "right" path.

We must remember that—in the spirit of true Machiavellianism—most political leaders will use whatever language is necessary to spread propaganda—even if it means blasphemy. To Lincoln, it was the deification and mystification of the Union. To Wilson, it was the "holy crusade" called the Great War. These were but a means to an end, and that end was collectivism and the centralization of government. Speeches with religious undertones play upon the most sacred and interpersonal yearnings of those with religious convictions—unfortunately leading some of the best men and women to be deceived by civil leaders. The reason why nationalism is such an effective means to deceive is because it takes a certain type of courageous person to stand up for true principles in the face of unpopularity, and this type of person is unfortunately very rare. The sad truth is that most people will capitulate to *groupthink* and the false sense of security that accompanies it.

So, does the *Book of Mormon* teach us about the evils of jingoism? The answer is a resounding yes. When the missionary Ammon returned home after having spent fourteen years preaching the gospel among the Lamanites and having had great success, he began to glory in his God by declaring his thankfulness to his Creator in eloquent and poetic language. As he did this he recounted how his Nephite brethren had denigrated and ridiculed him for desiring to go on a mission to the Lamanites. The following verses reflect how many Nephites felt about the Lamanites, which is chillingly reminiscent of the attitudes of our modern day Neo-Conservatives:

> Now do ye remember, my brethren, and we said unto our brethren in the land of Zarahemla, we go up to the land of Nephi, to preach unto our brethren, the Lamanites, and they laughed us to scorn? For they said unto us: Do ye suppose that ye can bring the Lamanites to the knowledge of the truth? Do you suppose that ye can convince the Lamanites of the incorrectness of the traditions of their fathers, as stiffnecked a people as they are; whose hearts delight in the shedding of blood; whose days have been spent in the grossest iniquity; whose ways have been the ways of a transgressor from the beginning? Now my brethren, ye remember that this was their language. And moreover they did say: Let us take up arms against them, that we destroy them and their iniquity out of the land, lest they overrun us and destroy us. But behold, my beloved brethren, we came into the wilderness not with the intent to destroy our brethren, but with the intent that perhaps we might save some few of their souls.[17]

Notice the language used by these nationalistic Nephites; "let us … destroy them and their *iniquity* out of the land." These Nephites were making rash judgments steered by collective hatred and *groupthink*. They were making the presumptuous claim that they were more righteous than their Lamanite brethren, and, therefore, had a right to annihilate them from the face of the earth. That they viewed the Lamanites as sub-human is evident by their claim that they were transgressors "from the beginning." Much like Hitler's final solution to the Jewish "problem" (which was genocide), these Nephites were prepared to do the same to the Lamanites. This perversion of the Gospel of Jesus Christ—to stamp out all sin by force—is the antithesis of the true Gospel of persuasion and volunteerism. How refreshing that rather than leading an army of aggressive warriors, Ammon instead chose to lead a small band of missionaries into their lands that they might perhaps "save some few of their souls."

Conclusion

In summation for this chapter, it is requisite to quote Rothbard once again. The following passage succinctly describes the social calamities that befall a nation that succumbs to jingoism and the warfare state:

> The great Randolph Bourne realized that "war is the health of the State." It is in war that the State really comes into its own: swelling in power, in number, in pride, in absolute dominion over the economy and the society. Society becomes a herd, seeking to kill its alleged enemies, rooting out and suppressing all dissent from the official war effort, happily betraying truth for the supposed public interest. Society becomes an armed camp, with the values and the morale—as Albert Jay Nock once phrased it—of an "army on the march."[18]

Chapter Six Notes and Sources

1. Jacob 7:26, Emphasis added

2. Mosiah 10:17, Emphasis added

3. 4 Nephi 1:39, Emphasis added

4. Alma 43:7-8, Emphasis added

5. Alma 48:1-2

6. Quoted in Eugene H. Methvin, *The Riot Makers,* Arlington House, New Rochelle, N.Y., 1970, pp. 125-26

Ibid, p. 128, Emphasis added

7. Antony C. Sutton, *America's Secret Establishment, An Introduction to the Order of Skull & Bones,* copyright 1983, 1986, 2002 Antony C. Sutton, p. 34, Emphasis added

8. Rothbard, Egalitarianism as a Revolt Against Nature and Other Essays, p. 120

9. Methvin, *The Riot Makers*, p. 130

10. Mormon 8:40

11. Gustave Gilbert, *Nuremburg Diary*

12. President Spencer W. Kimball, *The False Gods We Worship,* The First Presidency Message, June 1976, Emphasis added

13. Richard Gamble, Gettysburg Gospel, How Lincoln forged a civil religion of American nationalism, The American

14. Conservative, November 14, 2013

15. Ibid

16. Richard Gamble, *Woodrow Wilson's Revolution Within the Form,* an essay in *Reassessing the Presidency,* edited by John V. Denson, Mises Institute, 2001

17. Alma 26:23-26

18. Rothbard, Egalitarianism as a Revolt Against Nature and Other Essays, p. 131

Chapter 7

War Collectivism

More than any other single period, World War I was the critical watershed for the American business system. It was "war collectivism," a totally planned economy run largely by big-business interests through the instrumentality of the central government, which served as the model, the precedent, and the inspiration for state-corporate capitalism for the remainder of the 20th century.

-Murray Rothbard

Centralized governments always tend toward collectivism, and during times of war that collectivism can be magnified *ad infinitum*. The very concept of collectivism simply implies the sacrificing of the individual for the "good of the whole," the group, or the many. In our previous chapter, we postulated that groups do not exist without individual constituents and can *only* exist as an abstraction in our minds. If this premise is correct then we have to conclude that a political philosophy based upon the rights of a group (rather than individual human rights) is indeed flawed and fallacious. In reality, when an individual is forced to sacrifice their own civil rights for the good of the whole then what actually happens is that certain other individuals gain at that person's expense. Logic teaches us that it is impossible for an entire group to benefit at the expense of an individual member because that individual is still a part of that group. Therefore, when governments restrict freedom of speech, establish price controls, invoke conscription, or increase taxes during times of war only a few people gain at the *expense of everybody else.* Collectivism is therefore one of the great deceptive doctrines that riot-making men in authoritative places have ever bamboozled the susceptible masses into accepting. In this chapter, we will examine the ways that the U.S. government has destroyed liberty during wartime due to collectivism. These include; the abrogation of civil rights, economic manipulation or controlled/fiat economy, and mass brainwashing through the demonization of supposed enemies.

We have already seen that the Nephites excelled in the area of civil rights protection during times of war. This is evidenced by the fact that they did not conscript civilians, gave the treasonous kingmen trials in accordance with *habeas corpus,* and not only did not torture Lamanite prisoners, but preached the Gospel to them and let them join their society as freemen. The United States, however, has not fared so well in these areas and consequently has vehemently attacked liberties during wartime. In fact, American's have lost more liberties during times of war than they ever lost during times of peace. Randolph Bourne's assertion that "war is the health of the state" rings ominously in our ears as we study the bellicose history of the United States.

What may come as a surprise to many Americans is that our first president to suspend civil liberties was none other than John Adams. Adams—a beloved founding father and virulent federalist—fell victim to Lord Action's dictum that "power corrupts, and absolute power corrupts absolutely." Our modern scripture asserts that "almost *all men*, as soon as they get a little authority, as they suppose … will immediately begin to exercise unrighteous dominion,"[1] King Benjamin and King Mosiah—along with leaders such as Alma, Helaman, Captain Moroni, Pahoran, Gidgiddoni, and Mormon—are some of the exceptions.

John Adams was the second president of the United States, and during his administration the Alien and Sedition Acts (1798) were passed in a milieu of paranoia that followed the French Revolution and accompanied the Quasi-War (an undeclared naval war) with France. Section 2 of the Sedition Act prohibited "scandalous and malicious writings . . . with intent to defame the said government, or either house of the said Congress, or the said President, or to bring them, or either of them, into contempt or disrepute."[2] Being an obvious attack against freedom of speech, these Acts motivated Jefferson and Madison to author the Virginia and Kentucky Resolutions, which outlined the right of state's to nullify unconstitutional federal actions and even to secede if a state desired to do so. These rights were based upon the compact theory discussed in chapter one—that the states voluntarily created the federal government, were sovereign, and could leave the union at any time. Thomas Jefferson was vice-president at that time and such an act of defiance was dangerous even for him, as many people had been indicted under the Acts already. Some of these included Mathew Lyon, who had written an article in the *Vermont Journal* accusing the Adams administration of "ridiculous pomp, foolish adulation, and selfish avarice,"[3] and Luther Baldwin, who—when inebriated—hinted to his friend that he didn't care if President Adam's entourage of a 16-cannon salute accidentally "fired thro' his ass."[4] Baldwin was fined $100 and Lyon was fined $1000 and sentenced to four months in prison. Although the Acts were passed by Congress, the effect was to give the executive entirely too much power—resulting in the loss of newly acquired civil liberties. The Acts were thankfully repealed in 1800 and 1801 by the Jefferson administration and any who were still serving sentences under the legislation were pardoned.

Abraham Lincoln was the first American president to become a virtual dictator. During his war to prevent Southern independence, he unleashed a wave of civil liberty violations that would've made King George blush. These included; the suspension of *habeas corpus*, the forced quartering of Union soldiers, assuming dictatorial powers not granted to the executive in the Constitution, laying an income tax, printing inflationary currency to finance the war, conscription, shutting down over three hundred dissenting newspapers, establishing martial law, blockading Southern ports, declaring war without congressional approval, censoring news media (including telegraph communications), using Federal troops to intimidate Democratic voters during elections, imprisoning without trial thousands of Northern pro-abolitionist war protestors and newspaper owners, nationalizing the railroads, implementing gun control and civil forfeiture laws—*i.e.* confiscating private property, and the Soviet-style deportation of congressman Clement L. Vallandigham of Ohio for voicing criticism of the president and his administration.[5] Lincoln succeeded in effectively gutting of the Bill of Rights (especially the Tenth Amendment) during the Civil War epoch, relegating him to the status of a dictator. He perpetually preached the gospel of saving the mystical Union to justify his illegal and immoral violations of the Constitution—the same Constitution established by those whom the Lord calls "wise men."

Those among us who are intellectually honest are forced to beg the question; "was Lincoln another man who fell victim to the universal temptation to exercise unrighteous dominion?" Our answer has to be yes if the truth is to prevail. The war to prevent Southern independence was an American travesty that resulted in the destruction of the original intent of the Constitution as established by the Framers. In a true spirit of collectivism, this conflict forced the states—originally the sovereigns—to acquiesce to the federal government who was never an original party to the voluntary compact that formed it. The Fourteenth Amendment was an anomaly full of meaningless drivel, for the states already guaranteed those basic rights. The trouble with this overreaching amendment is that it allowed the federal government to interpose "civil rights" violations on the states. This was all based on the ludicrous doctrine posited by Lincoln that the people of the United States were "one." Lincoln and his statists pushed this doctrine in order to consolidate the several states into one united conglomerate over which central control could be maintained. This new collectivism would highly curtail the freedom of the people to vote with their feet by moving to another state, relegating the state governments to mere agents of the feds. If the founding documents—including the ratification documents—are studied carefully then it becomes easy to discern that the founding generation saw themselves as not "one" people, but diverse individuals of thirteen sovereign states. Brutus—the penname used by the antifederalists when rebutting the federalist papers—said this in regard to the "one people" doctrine:

> The United States should never be one government. The United States includes a variety of climates. The productions of the different parts of the Union are very variant, and their interest of consequence diverse. Their manners and habits differ as much as their climates and productions, and their sentiments are by no means coincident. The laws and customs of the several states are in many respects very diverse, and in some opposite. Each would be in favor of its own interests and customs, and of consequence a legislature formed of representatives from the respective parts, would not only be too numerous to act with any care or decision, but would be composed of such heterogeneous and discordant principles as would continually be contending with each-other.[6]

Although Lincoln was the first to really inaugurate wartime collectivism and tyranny, it was Wilson who took this oppression to the next level during his crusade to establish prosperity through force. There was a wave of unconstitutional legislation during his first term—including the Underwood Tariff, the Federal Reserve Act, the Federal Trade Commission, the Clayton Antitrust Act, the Federal Farm Loan Act, and the 16th and 17th Amendments, which established the infamous income tax and the popular election of senators.[7] Although he promised to keep America out of the war, after the sinking of the Lusitania by a German submarine the nation was thrust into the European conflict. The war collectivism that accompanied it moved the nation toward a more centralized government and command economy. With the inception of the war, Wilson nationalized the railroads and the merchant marine, and signed into law the Espionage and Sedition Acts which—as previously discussed—led to the imprisonment of many who did nothing more than speak their mind about America's involvement in the war. In 1917, he created the Committee on Public Information (CPI) through an executive order. The CPI was a government think-tank that helped to sway public opinion on the war effort, as involvement in a European war was very unpopular among Americans. Prior to the Spanish-American war, it was unthinkable that the U.S. would go nosing about in foreign entanglements and it was certainly not a policy supported by the Founders. Therefore, the CPI was put into place to quell dissent against the war effort through the use of subtle propaganda. This propaganda manifested itself in an emotional attack on German culture and, strangely enough, even food. Judge Andrew Napolitano documents some of these ridiculous wordplays as follows:

> ...sauerkraut was renamed "liberty cabbage," hamburger was renamed "Salisbury steak," Dachshunds were renamed "liberty dogs," German measles were renamed "liberty measles".... And fourteen states banned the speaking of German in public schools.[8]

These euphemisms—along with the modern label "freedom fries" (used to denigrate the French for not supporting the Second Gulf War against Iraq) are reminiscent of the language a third grader might use during typical recess banter. It is quite astonishing how grown men and women can fall prey to such juvenile propaganda against foreigners they honestly know nothing about.

Wilson's most pernicious accomplishments—the income tax and the Federal Reserve Act—played integral roles in financing the war. The highest tax bracket skyrocketed to an appalling 77 percent and still was not sufficient to finance the war. "The FED"—consisting of a group of private bankers—was granted a monopoly over the money supply by the government and began pouring billions of inflated dollars into the economy (mostly to war-connected corporations favored by the government). The national deficit rose from less than $1 billion in 1915, to a whopping $25 billion by 1919. This led to an increase in the number of federal employees to 450,000 by 1918, which created a gigantic wartime bureaucracy. After the war, the number of federal employees was reduced by 70 percent, leaving a permanent 30 percent increase in wasteful, parasitic jobs.[9] If principles of sound monetary and fiscal policy would have been observed—*e.g.* maintaining a gold standard—then these scheming leaders couldn't have so easily plunged the United States into war. However, when governments are given a blank check on how much currency they can print and spend then wars are inevitable.

Wilson's fiat economy included the War Finance Corporation (a government corporation created to assist banks giving loans to corporations associated with the war effort) and the War Industries Board (a government agency created to coordinate the purchase of war supplies). These programs allowed corporations like DuPont, Bethlehem Steel, United States Steel, Anaconda, Utah Copper, Central Leather Company, International Nickel Company, and American Sugar Refining company to profit immensely from American participation in the European war.[10] In addition to these companies achieving record profits while millions of conscripted men were dying, Wilson took further command of domestic economic resources. Herbert Hoover was named "Food Czar" and took total control of the Food Administration (a bureaucracy created by the Pure Food and Drug Act passed during Theodore Roosevelt's presidency). By act of Congress he was "given power to requisition 'necessaries,' to seize plants for government operation, and to regulate or prohibit exchanges."[11] This program also included price controls and government rationing in food and other industries.

We must realize that none of these programs were Constitutional, legal, or moral. This war was unpopular and was initiated by ambitious men within banking institutions, big corporations, and the government. The American people were involuntarily plunged into it—the vast majority against their wills. This conflict was not only bad for Americans, it was also bad for the economy—despite what some economists have asserted. The assumption that war is good for an economy is a gross fallacy, for the mass destruction of life and property destroys wealth—it cannot create it. It's like saying that when a robber breaks in to a family's house, kills a few of the members, plunders them, and then burns their house down that it's profitable because that generates work and gain for certain people. Wartime command economies disproportionately reallocate resources away from what would have been produced in the private sector toward the production of weapons, munitions, and other means of death and destruction. This is done by coercive taxation and industry nationalization—enriching a few politically-connected businessmen at the expense of the many. This is what urged General Smedley Butler—one of the most decorated war heroes of the 20th century—to write his book *War is a Racket*. Henry Hazlitt—a journalist during the mid-1900s who wrote for *The Nation, The Wall Street Journal,* and *The New York Times*—explains the particulars of the fallacy of wartime economic growth as follows:

> Now there is a half-truth in the "backed up" demand fallacy, just as there was in the broken-window fallacy.[12] The broken window did make more business for the glazier. The destruction of war will make more business for the producers of certain things. The destruction of houses and cities will make more business for the building and construction of industries. The inability to produce automobiles, radios, and refrigerators during the war will bring about a cumulative postwar demand *for those particular products.* To most people this will seem like an increase in total demand, as it may well be *in terms of dollars of lower purchasing power.* But what really takes place is *diversion* of demand to these particular products from others. The people of Europe will build more new houses than otherwise because they must. But when they build more houses they will have just that much less manpower and productive capacity left over for everything else. When they buy houses they will have just that much less purchasing power for everything else. Wherever business is increased in one direction, it must (except insofar as productive energies may be generally stimulated by a sense of want and urgency) be correspondingly reduced in another.[13]

What Hazlitt is saying here is that true wealth creation can only take place within the *free market.* To comprehend this, we must understand what real wealth is and what it is not. Money is *not* wealth; it is just a tool that serves as a means of facilitating mutually-beneficial exchanges when trading goods and services. The more goods and services a society has, the *richer* it becomes, because the people have *more* choices at *lower* prices. War merely diverts those goods, services, and resources arbitrarily toward industries that specialize in war goods production. This is not necessarily what would have transpired within the free market had the war never taken place, and when goods, services, and resources have to be used to rebuild homes, buildings, and cities that have been destroyed in the war, a net loss results because all of those *new* goods and services that would've been created in the absence of war are never brought into existence. We have a tendency to only see the physical results of economic policy—such as the creation of government jobs, or certain businesses that grow because of war goods production. However, we would do well to try to envision what is unseen, or what *would have* occurred within the free market if resources had not been coercively reallocated to wasteful government jobs or the death and destruction of many people and their property. For example, instead of using up resources to manufacture instruments of death such as bombs and tanks, perhaps the unhampered market would have chosen to produce more numerous and less expensive furnaces, vehicles, plumbing innovations, and the like—things which serve to enrich an entire nation by bringing better products into existence and available to those who could not previously afford them.

Defensive war, on the other hand, does not usually result in the enriching of a select few because voluntary means are usually used to redirect resources and men toward the defending of their families and land. The Nephites voluntarily imparted of their substance toward the war effort because all were desirous to remain free. This is evidenced by the fact that "the people of Ammon (those who had entered into a covenant to never again shed blood) did *give* unto the Nephites a large portion of their substance to support their armies."[14] The use of the word *give* implies that the people of Ammon did this voluntarily, without coercive taxation. In fact, the definition of the word give is to "freely transfer the possession of something or someone; to hand over."[15]

Likewise, when Moroni raised the Title of Liberty the people came running to volunteer, and we must assume that money and means were donated to the war effort along with men, for we can find no evidence in the Book of Mormon account of compulsory taxation being used to fund the war. In *3 Nephi*, we learn that Lachoneus had asked his people to gather into one body to defend themselves against the robbers, all of them bringing their own supplies and provisions to the place appointed—again without taxation or coercion:

> And it came to pass in the seventeenth year, in the latter end of the year, the proclamation of Lachoneus had gone forth throughout all the face of the land, and they had taken their horses, and their chariots, and their cattle, and all their flocks, and their herds, and their grain, and all their substance, and did march forth by thousands and by tens of thousands, until they had all gone forth to the place which had been appointed that they should gather themselves together, to defend themselves against their enemies.[16]

There is a reoccurring theme throughout the *Book of Mormon* that excessive taxation is *evil.* King Benjamin humbly declared to his people that, "even I, myself, have labored with mine own hands that I might serve you, and that ye should not be *laden with taxes,* and that there should nothing come upon you which was grievous to be borne."[17] It is also interesting to note that the book calls king Noah a *wicked* king because—among other sins—he taxed his people one-fifth of all they possessed.[18] We can assume, *arguendo,* that the 77 percent income tax rate during WWI and the 94 percent rate during WWII were put into place by wicked men.

FDR was no better than Wilson when it came to wartime collectivism. Aside from his "New Deal" (which was an economic disaster), FDR's war policies were hardly moral or Constitutional. He launched a major propaganda campaign against the German people while simultaneously allying with the despotic Russians. The fact that FDR promoted allying with Stalin—who by 1941 had already murdered tens of millions—represents an oddity that can hardly be explained ethically or logically. By 1941, Hitler had murdered a few million in contrast to Stalin's much larger death toll, yet Hitler was considered by Americans to be the most pernicious monster in the world. He was indeed a monster, but on an objectively smaller scale than Joseph Stalin—who had starved millions with his terror famine of the 1930s and had executed millions more by firing squads and secret police— including the entire extermination of the Kulaks; a group of land-owning farmers who had refused to submit to Stalin's grain collectivization programs. What on earth was FDR thinking when he agreed to become an ally of this gangster, whom he affectionately called "Uncle Joe?" Such a choice defies all good reason.

In an effort to preach anti-German propaganda, FDR helped to establish the Writer's War Board, which served to demonize the Germans much like the CPI had done during WWI. The WWB was organized by Rex Stout, a leftist, and was influential in the distribution of books and articles that denigrated the German people. Author Benjamin Colby expounds upon the WWB as follows:

> The promotion of hatred of all Germans was guided and fueled by a quasi-governmental agency, the Writer's War Board, set up early in the war by [Treasury] Secretary Morgenthau…. By 1943, the board's chief effort had become promoting hatred of all Germans and the idea that they would start a new war unless prevented by a harsh peace following the Morgenthau ideas.[19]

It can be argued that the "harsh peace" foisted upon the German people at Versailles actually *led* to the election of Hitler and World War II, but this is an argument for another chapter (See chapter 7: *Economic Sanctions*). The Roosevelt Administration pushed for price controls previous to the war, and the opportunity came in 1942 when the Emergency Price Control Act was passed. The Rooseveltian wartime economy easily slid into place following the centralizing polices of the New Deal. However, the economic choke-hold strengthened as the government further wrapped its tentacles around a weak economy. The EPCA contained provisions for a host of new economic regulation but its specific purpose was "to assure that defense appropriations are not dissipated by excessive prices."[20] Or, in other words, it was a guarantee that the government would not have to pay high prices for the resources it would consume for the war program. In addition to this, the government indulged in a rationing program that included "necessities" "such as gasoline, tires, coffee, canned foods, shoes, meats, sugar, and typewriters."[21] Just as in WWI, resources were being reallocated to the war effort at the expense of private enterprise.

FDR's attack on civil liberties far exceeded that of Wilson's. In 1944, the executive branch of the U.S. government engaged in one of the most virulent attacks against civil rights in American history. FDR signed and issued Executive Order No. 9066 on February 19, 1942, which authorized the Secretary of War to create military zones on the West Coast that could forcibly exclude all citizens of Japanese-American ancestry regardless of citizenship. The scope of government went beyond forcing these citizens to leave their homes and placed over one-hundred thousand of them in internment camps (gulags) where they would remain for the duration of WWII. These American citizens whose only crime was to be of Japanese descent were forced to sell their homes and most of their belongings in weeks or days, keeping only what they could carry in luggage. Many had to fire sell their homes and businesses because of time restraints by the government and got pennies on the dollar. Farmers (who were allowed to retain their farms) would return home after the war to find their farms torched by paranoid "patriots" who believed the government hate propaganda against "Japs." Fred T. Korematsu—one of these unfortunate citizens—did not give up his liberty so easily. He eluded authorities with the help of plastic surgery and a name change in an attempt to stay in his home town of San Leandro, California, until his arrest in September of 1942 for failure to report for relocation. He appealed his case all the way up to the Supreme Court (*Korematsu v. United States*) where a ruling was made by Justice Hugo Black upholding the supposed constitutionality of FDR's executive order. The rationale for Black's decision was that the president had the right to relocate citizens in the face of wartime emergency, and that national security outweighed Korematsu's individual rights. Justice Robert Jackson was of a dissenting opinion and issued this written statement:

> Korematsu was born on our soil, of parents born in Japan. The Constitution makes him a citizen of the United States by nativity and a citizen of California by residence. No claim is made that he is not loyal to this country. There is no suggestion that apart from the matter involved here he is not law abiding and well disposed. Korematsu, however, has been convicted of an act not commonly a crime. It consists merely of being present in the state whereof he is a citizen, near the place where he was born, and where all his life he has lived….His crime would result, not from anything he did, said, or thought, different than they, but only in that he was born of different racial stock. Now, if any fundamental assumption underlies our system, it is that guilt is personal and not inheritable. Even if all of one's antecedents had been convicted of treason, the Constitution forbids its penalties to be visited upon him…. But here is an attempt to make an otherwise innocent act a crime merely because this prisoner is the son of parents as to whom he had no choice, and belongs to a race from which there is no way to resign. If Congress in peace-time legislation should enact such a criminal law, I should suppose this Court would refuse to enforce it.[22]

Jackson's opinion agrees with the Lord's admonition in the Doctrine and Covenants that the Constitution was established "for the rights and *protection of all flesh*."[23] FDR and General DeWitt had no right whatsoever to initiate violence upon these people who were guilty of no criminal aggression. The hysteria and paranoia caused by FDR's wartime regime resulted in the destruction of civil rights guaranteed by the Bill of Rights—specifically the 5th Amendment's due process clause and the 6th Amendment's protection against indefinite detention. The ironic thing is that in all of the hype there was not one single case where a Japanese-American was convicted of collusion with the enemy or sabotage, and—in fact—many were desirous to prove their loyalty to the U.S. and volunteered for military service despite the fact that their families would remain incarcerated while they were shipped off to fight in the European war.

Perhaps one of the most egregious atrocities that occurred during WWII was the forced repatriation of Russian defectors, refugees, and POW's back into the hands of Joseph Stalin where they would either be sent to a Siberian work camp, executed, or both. FDR had made a secret agreement with Stalin at the Yalta conference of March 31, 1945 to return the dissidents, and—after his death in April—the mission was carried out by Harry Truman. Antony Sutton explains this agreement as follows:

> According to the *Wall Street Journal* (Nov. 24, 1972), the United States and Russia in 1945 "signed a special convention for forcibly repatriating to the USSR some four million anti-Communist Soviet subjects who had fled to the West." This agreement (known as Operation Keelhaul[24]) was a violation not only of the traditional American spirit of freedom, but also of the Geneva Convention. American military police "forcibly herded thousands of displaced persons into the waiting arms of the Russians." Even worse, in June 1945 at Fort Dix, New Jersey, some 200 Russians prisoners were drugged, and, according to the *Wall Street Journal*, U.S. authorities "...allowed them to be taken unconscious aboard a Russian ship in New Jersey. Elsewhere, many refugees drowned themselves, slashed their throats and otherwise committed suicide rather than return to the brutal death they knew awaited them."[25]

Historian Ralph Raico also sheds some light on this insidious act of government:

In the early months of Truman's presidency the United States and Britain directed the forced repatriation of many tens of thousands of Soviet Subjects—and many who had never been Soviet Subjects—to the Soviet Union, where they were executed by the NKVD or cast into the Gulag. Their crime had been to fight against Stalinist domination of the side of the Germans. Terrible scenes occurred in the course of this repatriation (sometimes called "Operation Keelhaul"), as the condemned men, and in some cases women with their children, were forced or duped into returning to Stalin's Russia. American soldiers had orders to "shoot to kill" those refusing to go. Some of the victims committed suicide rather than fall into the hands of the Soviet secret police.[26]

In contrast, the Nephites either let the Lamanite prisoners go or allowed them to stay among them and become a free people.[27] How ironic that a war that purported to spread "liberty" and "democracy" throughout the world could result in such a vehement attack on human liberties. Such are the fruits of war collectivism and jingoism when populations submit to the hate speech, lies, economic controls, and human rights violations that war-making people always perpetuate on populations. We must not be deceived; war is a racket—a fallacy based on a lie and an instrument to spread tyranny both at home and abroad. It is, indeed, "the health of the state."

Conclusion

We will conclude this chapter with a quote from one whom the reader perhaps has strong feelings about—Adolph Hitler. Hitler understood how to use propaganda to persuade mass populations into capitulating to the state. He understood that most people won't believe that something is a lie when the lie is told on a massive scale, because they think that the world just isn't that evil, or that deception on such a scale could not occur or persist. This human weakness has been exploited by the State for the purpose of getting gain. Here is what Hitler had to say:

In the big lie there is always a certain force of credibility; because the broad masses of a nation are always more easily corrupted in the deeper strata [i.e. layers] of their emotional nature than consciously or voluntarily; and thus in the primitive simplicity of their minds they more readily fall victim to the big lie than the small lie, since they themselves often tell small lies in little matters but would be ashamed to resort to large-scale falsehoods. It would never come into their heads to fabricate colossal untruths, and they would not believe that others could have the impudence to distort the truth so infamously. Even though the facts which prove this to be so may be brought clearly to their minds, they will still doubt and waver and will continue to think that there may be some other explanation. For the grossly impudent lie always leaves traces behind it, even after it has been nailed down, a fact which is known to all expert liars in this world and to all who conspire together in the art of lying.[28]

Chapter Seven Notes and Sources

1. D&C 121:39
2. The Sedition Act of 1798
3. http://en.wikipedia.org/wiki/Alien_and_Sedition_Acts
4. http://posterityproject.blogspot.com/2008/09/sedition-act-luther-baldwin.html
5. Thomas J. DiLorenzo, *The Real Lincoln*, E-book Version, pp. 145-46
6. Brion McClanahan, *The Founding Fathers Guide To The Constitution*, copyright 2012 by Brion McClanahan, Chapter 8
7. Richard M. Gamble, *Woodrow Wilson's Revolution Within the Form*, an essay in *Reassessing the Presidency*, Edited by John V. Denson, p. 415
8. Judge Andrew Napolitano, Theodore and Woodrow, How Two American Presidents Destroyed Constitutional Freedoms, Chapter 8
9. Ralph Raico, *World War I: The Turning Point*, an essay in *The Costs of War, America's Pyrrhic Victories,* Edited by John V. Denson, Transaction Publishers, 2009, p. 233
10. See, General Smedley Butler, *War is a Racket*

11. Murray N. Rothbard, *War Collectivism in World War I,* Mises Institute, http://mises.org/page/1419

12. See Frederic Bastiat, *The Broken Window Fallacy.* Bastiat's broken-window fallacy is a treatise on the fallacy that destruction of property results in economic growth. The crux of the story is that when a kid breaks a man's window he is forced to buy another which creates work for the glazier. However, Bastiat shows that since the window was already made this constituted a net loss for the man because now instead of buying say, a new suit, he is compelled to purchase a window. The suit-maker is now shorted the money that he would've made by selling another suit which results in him spending less on goods he would've purchased, creating a ripple effect. Bastiat concludes that society is worse off because they all had to pay for a window that already existed. When applied to war and public spending one can see how the net results are economic losses and the destruction of freedom of choice.

13. Henry Hazlitt, *Economics in One Lesson,* Ludwig Von Mises Institute, Auburn Alabama, Copyright 1946 by Harper & Brothers, Copyright 2008 by The Mises Institue, pp. 14-15

14. Alma 43:13

15. Google dictionary

16. 3 Nephi 3:22

17. Mosiah 2:14, Emphasis added

18. Mosiah 11:3

19. Benjamin Colby, *Twas a Famous Victory* (New Rochelle, N.Y.: Arlington House, 1974), p. 65 Quoted in David Gordan, *A Common Design: Propaganda and World War,* an essay in *The Costs of War: America's Pyrrhic Victories,* Edited by John V. Denson, p. 311

20. Quoted in Higgs, *Crises and Leviathan,* p. 208

21. *Ibid,* p. 209

22. Korematsu v. United States 323 U.S. 214 (1944)

23. D&C 101:77, Emphasis added

24. Operation Keelhaul was the name that become popular for this covert mission after the publication of Julius Epstein's 1973 book entitled, *Operation Keelhaul: The Story of Forced Repatriation from 1944 to the Present.* The term Keelhaul literally means to "to haul under the keel of a ship as punishment or torture." (http://www.merriam-webster.com/dictionary/keelhaul)

25. Antony C. Sutton, *National Suicide: Military Aid to the Soviet Union,* Arlington House, New Rohelle, N.Y., Copyright 1973, p. 29

26. Ralph Raico, Great Wars & Great Leaders, A Libertarian Rebuttal, Mises Institute, 2010, p. 132

27. See Alma 62:27-29, Helamin 1:33, and 3 Nephi 5:4-5

28. Adolph Hitler, *Mien Kampf,* Vol. 1, Ch. X, Quoted in D. Christian Markham, *There Are Save Two Churches Only,* p. 158

Chapter 8

Economic Sanctions

Among the conventional weapons in the arsenal of the modern Warfare State, none is crueler or more indiscriminate than economic sanctions. While a bomb, missile, or other military ordnance can devastate an entire neighborhood in a moment, the slow death of economic strangulation can so degrade an entire people that they are reduced to a pre-civilizational state, modern savages living at a subsistence level.

-Justin Raimondo

Economic sanctions are trade restrictions or embargoes against a foreign nation and are acts of aggression. They have been used by the United States to punish those nations that are seen as potential threats, and are usually a prelude to war. Although superficially they appear to punish the governments of those "evil" countries to which they are applied, we must realize that *only* innocent civilians—the men, women, and children—who have nothing to do with the government are the ones who suffer. When a despotic government is cut off from trade, that regime will continue to squander resources from its own citizenry, resulting in their further impoverishment. Consequently, the common people are the ones who starve while those in government eat the last morsels of bread. Economic sanctions are simply evil; for they punish the innocent while those who are supposed guilty continue to prosper through government largess. This chapter will explore the dark past of U.S., British, and U.N.-enforced sanctions during WWI, WWII, the Gulf

War, and the current "War on Terror." Unfortunately, these sanctions have led to the mass starvation of millions of innocents—including children—and are an abhorrent travesty in the history of U.S. foreign policy.

Before indulging ourselves in studying America's dark past, it will be requisite to consult the *Book of Mormon* on the subject. In the sixth chapter of Helaman, we learn that during the postwar period the Nephites and Lamanites had free exchange with one-another. This is significant because they were separate countries with distinct borders. There had been a lot of preaching and converting going on during this period and it seems as though a milieu of *laissez-faire* economics abounded—probably even without tariffs. We learn from the account that:

> And behold, there was peace in all the land, insomuch that the Nephites did go into whatsoever part of the land they would, whether among the Nephites or the Lamanites. And it came to pass that the Lamanites did also go, whithersoever they would, whether it were among the Nephites; and thus they did have *free intercourse* one with another, to buy and to sell, and to get gain, according to their desire.[1]

The text is clear that they were engaging in free trade, uninhibited by the imaginary lines we call borders. Sanctions, on the other hand, are the exact opposite of free trade, and those nations on whom they are inflicted always see them as an overt act of war. In fact, they constitute war crimes against innocents and those that perpetrate them are war criminals. When a bomb explodes in enemy territory, it only destroys those who are unfortunate enough to be in its proximity. Sanctions, as Raimondo declared, affect the entire population with a slow strangulation effect that reduces civilization into barbarism. Sanctions are indeed the ultimate, indiscriminate weapon that can be used—as one statesman opined—to "starve the whole population—men, women, and children, wounded and sound—into submission."[2]

These are the words Winston Churchill used when he frankly admitted to the real purpose of his British Naval blockade, more aptly named hunger blockade, against German civilians during WWI. The British, prior to the Americans, had launched a massive propaganda campaign against their German counterparts, referring to them as odious "Huns," who were "diabolical enemies of civilization," and "perpetrators of every imaginable sort of frightfulness."[3] The blockade violated two major declarations: the Declaration of Paris of 1856 (which prohibited large areas of open seas around an enemy's coast to be off-limits to anything but war contraband), and the Declaration of London of 1909 (which placed limits on the use of food as "contraband").[4] The British acted unilaterally by expanding the list of German "contraband" to include food and other essentials. The American government, with the exception of William Jennings Bryan—who resigned from the office of Secretary of State in 1915—supported the starvation policy. C. Paul Vincent describes the devolution of the German diet caused by the need to ration food:

> The German population was surviving on a meager diet of dark bread, slices of sausage without fat, an individual ration of three pounds of potatoes per week, and turnips.[5]

Other effects of the blockade included the spreading of tuberculosis, rickets, and edema. Individual German food consumption was reduced to about one thousand calories a day, causing the mortality rate to jump up 38% from pre-war levels. In all, 763,000 people died as a result of the blockade according to the National Health Office in Berlin—sealing its fate as one of the worst state-induced atrocities of the 20th century.[6] How could an ethical and logical individual vindicate such murderous practices? What is the difference between Churchill's blockade and quarantining a house in a neighborhood—allowing neither entry nor exit—until the inhabitants are starved to death? Nothing, except that instead of just killing those in one household Churchill managed to exterminate hundreds of thousands. What crimes did

German women, children, and other peacekeeping civilians commit against Britain, besides being in the wrong country at the wrong time? The rhetorical inquiries here are redundant, but essential to drive the point home to the reader; *sanctions are immoral,* and are the marks of total and indiscriminate warfare.

There is also other evidence that suggests that the harsh *pre* and *post* war conditions foisted upon German peoples created a milieu of collective hatred that fostered support for the rise of Nazism and the promise of deliverance from the Treaty of Versailles. Vincent asserts that, "the victimized youth of [World War I] were to become the most radical adherents of National Socialism."[7] In Versailles, the details of Germany's unconditional surrender were worked out, albeit disproportionately out of favor with the Germans. Germany was to renounce its sovereignty over its colonies (in Asia and the Pacific) which amounted to 25,000 square miles and 7,000,000 people, which land and people were handed over to Allied control. It was to embark on a program of unilateral disarmament, reducing its armed forces to less than 100,000 with no more than seven infantry and three cavalry divisions. Conscription was to be abolished (not for the Allies, of course), paramilitary police were prohibited (another name for this restriction is *posse comitatus*[8], and it is something the hypocritical Allies should have followed themselves), and the Navy was limited to 1500 men, six pre-dreadnought battleships, and six light cruisers. Germany was also banned from the arms trade and was prohibited from producing chemical weapons, tanks, armored cars, and military aircraft.[9]

As if the loss of the ability to defend itself was not enough, Germany was then forced to pay war reparations upwards of twenty billion in gold Marks ($5 billion) to cover Allied occupation costs. This led to the hyperinflation of the Weimer Republic in 1922, which totally devastated the German economy. The hunger blockade was continued even after the Germans surrendered—food and raw materials were not allowed into the country until the treaty was signed in 1919. Although Wilson had promised that the effects of the treaty and his Fourteen Points would bring a new world order of peace and justice, German peoples suffered greatly at the hands of Czechs and Poles. The Peace Conference created the nation of Czechoslovakia from parts of Austria-Hungary (whom the Czechs were granted their independence from) and the German Sudetenland. It was comprised of Czechs, Slovaks, and Germans (who were in the minority). The Germans and Slovaks were discriminated against by the Czech government and were disadvantaged when it came to land, economics, and education, and were denied basic rights of freedom of speech against the newly created centralized government. Germans who were caught in the new Poland were similarly treated as "potentially treasonous" and the new aristocracy actually proposed to eliminate them by "coerced emigration."[10] We are taught in our compulsory American schools the misconception that the Germans were always the "bad guys," making the mistake of overlooking the pre-WWII era when they were actually the *victims* of their Polish and Czechoslovakian neighbors.

Another truth that is neglected in our government schools is that Hitler rose to power through a democratic process and ran on the platform of delivering the German people from the harsh peace at Versailles. In a speech addressing the Dusseldorf Industry Club in 1932, Hitler said:

> Both the Peace Treaty of Versailles together with all the consequences of that Treaty have been the result of a policy which perhaps fifteen, fourteen, or thirteen years ago was regarded as the right policy, at least in the enemy States, but which from our point of view was bound to be regarded as fatal when ten or less years ago its true character was disclosed to millions of Germans and now today stands revealed in its utter impossibility. I am bound therefore to assert that there must of necessity have been in Germany, too, some responsibility for these happenings if I am to have any belief that the German people can exercise some influence towards changing these conditions.[11]

The Nazi atrocities committed against Jews and other minorities during WWII are in no way justified in light of the Versailles treaty or the victimization of German people during that epoch. They seemed to have fallen into the Nephite trap of seeking to exact vengeance, which belongs only to the Lord. Again, it is imperative to remember that many Germans were innocent civilians and were either conscripted by the Nazi government, thrown into gulags themselves, or sought defection to neutral or allied nations. It is always governments that start war, initiate violence, and enforce economic sanctions. Woodrow Wilson—in an address to Congress in 1917—disclosed the nature of the "peace" treaty in a transparency that leaders do not offer today:

> It would be accepted in humiliation, under duress, at an intolerable sacrifice, and would leave a sting, a resentment, a bitter memory upon which the terms of peace would rest, not permanently, but only as upon quicksand.[12]

We can see that this "peace" was indeed built "upon quicksand," for not more than twenty-two years later war erupted once again in Europe—similarly accompanied by economic sanctions, yet this time on the Japanese. Prior to the Japanese attack on Pearl Harbor, FDR—with the support of Secretary of War Henry Stimson and Secretary of the Treasury Henry Morgenthau—launched a series of economic sanctions in an effort to curtail Japanese advances into Asia. Higgs illuminates:

> The Roosevelt administration, while curtly dismissing Japanese diplomatic overtures to harmonize relations, imposed a series of increasingly stringent economic sanctions on Japan. In 1939 the United States terminated the 1911 commercial treaty with Japan. "On July 2, 1940, Roosevelt signed the Export Control Act, authorizing the President to license or prohibit the export of essential defense materials." Under this authority, "[o]n July 31, exports of aviation motor fuels and lubricants and No. 1 heavy melting iron and steel scrap were restricted." Next, in a move aimed

at Japan, Roosevelt slapped an embargo, effective October 16, "on all exports of scrap iron and steel to destinations other than Britain and the nations of the Western Hemisphere." Finally, on July 26, 1941, Roosevelt "froze Japanese assets in the United States, thus bringing commercial relations between the nations to an effective end. One week later Roosevelt embargoed the exports of such grades of oil as still were in commercial flow to Japan." The British and the Dutch followed suit, embargoing exports to Japan from their colonies in southeast Asia.[13]

Needless to say, these measures strained Japanese/American relations, and (with several other provocative polices implemented by FDR) led to the attack on Pearl Harbor. Robert Stinnett—in his book *Day of Deceit: The Truth about FDR and Pearl Harbor*—brings to light a communiqué between Japanese Foreign Minister Teijiro Toyoda and Ambassador Kichisaburo Nomura on July 31:

> Commercial and economic relations between Japan and third countries, led by England and the United States, are gradually becoming so horribly strained that we cannot endure it much longer. Consequently, our Empire, to save its very life, must take measures to secure the raw materials of the South Seas.[14]

The "measures" mentioned above materialized in the form of an attack on Pearl Harbor and culminated with the entry of the United States into the war. A war that cost millions of lives and resulted in the enslavement of one-third of the world under the Iron Curtain of Communism. There is extensive evidence that FDR not only knew of an impending attack against the U.S., but also assimilated an eight-point plan designed to provoke the Japanese into firing the first shot. Stinnett lays out this plan that was put into effect by Lieutenant Commander Arthur H. McCollum, who had been born in Japan and spoke the language fluently. He was commissioned to incorporate the eight-point plan approximately one year before the attack, which includes several provocative actions:

    A.   Make an arrangement with Britain for the use of British bases in the Pacific, particularly Singapore;

    B.   Make an arrangement with Holland for the use of base facilities and acquisition of supplies in the Dutch East Indies;

    C.   Give all possible aid to the Chinese Government of Chaing-Kai-shek;

    D.   Send a division of long-range heavy cruisers to the Orient, Philippines, or Singapore;

    E.   Send two divisions of submarines to the Orient;

    F.   Keep the main strength of the U.S. Fleet, now in the pacific, in the vicinity of the Hawaiian Islands;

    G.   Insist that the Dutch refuse to grant Japanese demands for undue economic concessions, particularly oil, and

    H.   Completely embargo all U.S. trade with Japan, in collaboration with a similar embargo imposed by the British Empire.[15]

Part D of the eight-point plan was particularly pernicious, because FDR was willing to put American Naval men at risk by initiating "the deliberate deployment of American warships within or adjacent to the territorial waters of Japan."[16] FDR aptly named these provocations "pop-up" cruises and would assert that, "I just want them to keep popping up here and there and keep the Japs guessing. I don't mind losing one or two cruisers, but do not take a chance on losing five or six."[17] According to Denson:

    Roosevelt also ordered separate suicide missions for three small ships based in the Philippines. With American captains and Filipino crews, these vessels, each of which carried at least one gun, were to sail at different times toward Japan in an effort to draw Japanese fire, but the Japanese refused the bait.[18]

FDR virulently took economic sanctions to the next level. Not only was he willing to pressure the Japanese with oil and steel embargoes, he was willing to jeopardize the lives of American servicemen to provoke the Japanese in a game of cat and mouse. Some historians claim that he pushed for American involvement in the war because domestic support for his disastrous New Deal was waning and the government needed a foreign policy diversion. Others postulate that he craved the glory of being the one who was instrumental in establishing the United Nations. Either way, he got his wish, and when Stimson heard the news of the Pearl Harbor attack, he was "relieved" and would record the following in his diary:

> We three [Hull, Knox, and Stimson] all thought that we must fight if the British fought. But now the Japs have solved the whole thing by attacking us directly in Hawaii.[19]

Whatever the reasons for entering, the results of U.S. involvement in the war were disastrous. In total defiance of George Washington's counsel to "avoid entangling alliances," FDR and Churchill capitulated to Stalin's demands at Yalta, and betrayed all those nations who would be subsequently enslaved under the Iron Curtain. (See Chapter 11, *Betrayal at Yalta: Fruits of the Last "Good" War*).

Our study of U.S. economic sanctions brings us to the year 1990, when UN Resolution 661 was passed, which placed stringent limitations on what could be allowed into Iraq. These sanctions were passed in response to Saddam Hussein's August 2, 1990 invasion of Kuwait. The U.S. government wholeheartedly supported this resolution, and a little trip in foreign policy history will show just how deep the hypocrisy goes. We must begin in Iran in the year 1953, when the newly created CIA (under the direction of Alan and John Foster Dulles) removed Mohammed Mossadegh—Iran's first democratic Prime Minister—from power via a coup d'etat. Mossadegh had brought freedom of speech and religion to Iran and nationalized the British oil company called Anglo-

Iranian, which later morphed into British Petroleum. The British government was profiting immensely from Iranian oil fields at the expense of Iranian industry, and Mossadegh wanted to give the company back to the Iranians, a move that enraged Churchill—who subsequently enlisted the Americans to orchestrate the coup and put the dictatorial Shah back in power. They published false information, incited riots, and even paid people to pretend to protest in the streets. About 300 people died in a crossfire at Mossadegh's house, where he was captured and subsequently spent the rest of his life under house arrest. Kermit Roosevelt—the grandson of Theodore Roosevelt—was the man commissioned by the CIA to carry out the mission, which was known by the code name "Operation Ajax."[20]

With Shah Reza Pahlevi reinstalled, and Anglo-Iranian back in British control, the Iranian people were once again impoverished and tyrannized by the government. The Shah was a ruthless dictator, and used the oil revenues to purchase weapons from the U.S. at the expense of the Iranian people. His people hated and feared both him and the U.S. government that successfully restored him to power, which led to his overthrow in 1978 and replacement by the radical Islamist regime under the Ayatollah Khomeini. Things escalated into the subsequent capture of the U.S. embassy in 1979, where 52 Americans were held hostage until 1981. In an attempt to counter—and to keep Iran contained—the U.S. secretly *supported* Saddam Hussein in his war against Iran that lasted until 1988:

> The U.S. government provided Iraq with key intelligence, military planning, and billions of dollars in loans—some of which Saddam used to try to build a nuclear weapon—and looked the other way when Iraq used chemical weapons, produced with technology and material purchased from Western nations, on the Iranians and the Iraqi Kurds.[21]

This foreign policy merry-go-round came to rest at a position hostile to Saddam, a place that he was not acquainted with until 1990.

The game of good cop bad cop culminated in the U.S. intervention in Kuwait and the sanctions that were heaped upon the innocent Iraqi people. We are not justifying Saddam here at all—let that be understood. Nevertheless, the Iraqi civilians who had nothing to do with any of this are the ones who suffered. The sanctions banned all trade with Iraq, excepting cases of medicine and foodstuff—which were tightly regulated. In fact, they were so regulated that those wishing to export such items were required to get an export license and were evaluated on a case-by-case basis by UN inspectors. Needless to say, in light of all the red tape Iraqis were forced into a rationing program which allotted—like the Germans—no more than 1000 calories a day.[22] Justin Raimondo commented on the effects of the resolution in 1998 as follows:

> More than one-third of Iraqi children are malnourished, on a level with sub-Saharan Africa. In the name of "international peace," more than one million Iraqis have died as a direct result of the sanctions, 567,000 of them children. Some 4,500 children under age five are dying each month from hunger and disease. Condemned by U.S. and Un planners to a starvation diet, little children have suffered a six-fold mortality rate increase since the onset of sanctions.[23]

The U.S. government had no compunction about the effects of their inglorious sanctions, and justified them for the "greater good" of subduing the Hussein regime as the following dialogue of an 1996 interview between Lesley Stahl of 60 Minutes and former Secretary of State Madeleine Albright demonstrates:

> Stahl: We have heard that a half million children have died. I mean, that's more children than died in Hiroshima. And – and you know, is the price worth it?
> Albright: I think this is a very hard choice, but the price – we think the price is worth it.[24]

It is apparent that our government is ethically-challenged, for they justified the *murder* of a half million *children* to start a war that was never constitutionally vindicated. Little children are saved through the atonement of Jesus Christ,[25] and are incapable of committing sin, which places them into the category of the saints of God, and we learn from Moroni in the 8th chapter of *Ether* that the Lord will exact just vengeance upon those who murder his saints:

> And whatsoever nation shall uphold such secret combinations, to get power and gain, until they shall spread over the nation, behold, they shall be destroyed; for the Lord will not suffer that the *blood of his saints, which shall be shed by them*, shall always cry unto him from the ground for vengeance upon them and yet he avenge them not.[26]

With the advent of 9/11/2001 and the pseudo-"War on Terror," the war hawks began beating the war drums once again. Even now as this book is being written, economic sanctions are in force upon the Iranian economy, bringing our foreign policy adventure full-circle. American's shouldn't be surprised that Iranians dislike them, not for the laughable reason that "they hate us because we're free"—a most ridiculous notion, but because we have harmfully and indiscriminately intervened in their affairs. Perhaps with a little introspection, while lowering the walls of hysterical jingoism, we could visualize the following reasons why; we removed Iran's only democratic prime minister in the last 60 years, replacing him with a dictator who had already been dethroned; we backed Saddam Hussein in an eight year war against them, while turning our heads when chemical weapons were used against Iranians which were produced with materials manufactured in the U.S.; and most recently we have accused them of endeavoring to build nuclear weapons, which we have many of, while saddling their economy with sanctions (which have existed in some form since 1979) and threatening invasion. While—for the moment—a peace has been negotiated with regard to invasion, sanctions are still in place. According to Josh Levs of CNN, here is a history of U.S. sanctions against Iran since 1979:

As a result of the hostage crisis in 1979, the U.S. government froze Iranian government assets in the United States and U.S. banks overseas, totaling $12 billion, according to the U.S. Treasury. That freeze was eventually expanded to a full trade embargo until an accord was signed with Iran in 1981. Most assets were unblocked and the embargo was lifted. In 1987, the United States imposed a new embargo on Iranian goods and services, "as a result of Iran's support for international terrorism and its aggressive actions against non-belligerent shipping in the Persian Gulf," the U.S. Treasury says. In 1995, the United States banned "involvement with petroleum development in Iran," the U.S. Treasury says. Two years later, the United States banned "virtually all trade and investment activities with Iran by U.S. persons, wherever located." In 2010, the United States passed the Comprehensive Iran Sanctions, Accountability, and Divestment Act. It revoked, for example, permission to import "certain foodstuffs and carpets of Iranian origin," the U.S. Treasury says. Those who violated the law could face a fine of up to $1 million and 20 years imprisonment. The law established that Iranian goods or services may not be imported unless they are gifts valued $100 or less; informational materials, or personal property of someone coming into the United States. U.S. citizens may not export goods or services to Iran or, in general, to a third country knowing it is intended for Iran. There are exceptions for "donations of articles intended to relieve human suffering," gifts valued at $100 or less, certain agricultural products, medicines, and informational materials, the Treasury says. The U.S. government prohibits "servicing accounts of the government of Iran," including the country's central bank. In 2011, the United States added further sanctions, including tightening restrictions on companies that provide Iran with equipment and expertise to run its oil and chemical industry. It prohibited groups that do business with financial institutions in Iran from holding accounts in the United States.[27]

Conclusion

If these current sanctions are continued and increased then we can only expect matters to worsen for Iranian civilians. These impositions—instead of weakening the Iranian government—will serve to incite hatred and disdain among Iranians against the American government. It is hard to say how many Iranian civilians are suffering now and how many will suffer in the future, partly because of limited transparency in American media. How many more children will have to die for the *pro bono publico* before American politicians are convinced that Iran is "contained?" We must ask ourselves, what good has come from Churchill's German starvation policy, or FDR's provocative measures against Japan, or Bush's pediatric genocide against Iraq, or from any sanction against any nation? The answer is none. Those who—after reading this chapter—continue to foster the delusion that economic sanctions are somehow "good" for American foreign policy would do well to study the effects that sanctions have on the *ordinary* people. Forget the dictators, oligarchs, autocrats, and tyrants who, when faced with impending sanctions, merely order the forces of their respective nations to confiscate the remaining vestiges of sustenance from the common peasants. We must realize as spoiled Americans that we have only reached our wealthy status because of *free markets*. Without the voluntary division of labor, the invisible hand described by Adam Smith would be rendered inoperative and each individual would be relegated to a primitive husbandmen in constant fear of the ravages of hunger. Free markets allow trade specialization, industry development and innovation, and are what build highly sophisticated human civilizations. When the strong arm of government coercion curtails this beautiful process of voluntary cooperation by implementing sanctions then humanity itself suffers. A once robust and productive economy is reduced to an archaic and primordial venue of starvation, theft, murder, and barbarism. What once were human beings enjoying an array of goods and services are reduced to mere animals in the struggle for survival. Economic sanctions are, indeed, a war declared on humanity and a gross infraction of the second great commandment; thou shalt love thy neighbor as thyself.

Chapter Eight Notes and Sources

1. Helaman 6:7-8, Emphasis added

2. Winston Churchill Quoted in Ralph Raico, Great Wars and Great Leaders, A Libertarian Rebuttal, p. 198

3. Ibid, p. 198

4. *Ibid*, p. 199

5. Quoted in *Ibid,* p. 201

6. *Ibid*, p. 201

7. Quoted in Ralph Raico, *Rethinking Churchill,* an essay in *The Costs of War: America's Pyrrhic Victories,* Edited by John V. Denson, p. 331

8. Latin for "power of the community," it means that local authorities have the right to suppress criminals without the help of nonlocal forces such as national military. The U.S. passed the Posse Comitatus Act in 1878 to prohibit the federal government from using military personnel to enforce state laws. This had been done extensively during the 1860s following the Civil War in the Reconstruction years (Like Versailles, Southern Reconstruction was also a harsh peace imposed on them by the North). After 911 all posse comatitus prohibitions were abolished by G.W. Bush, removing yet another check on federal power.

9. http://en.wikipedia.org/wiki/Treaty_of_Versailles

10. Ralph Raico, World War I: The Turning Point, an essay in The Costs of War: America's Pyrrhic Victories, Edited by John V. Denson, pp. 243-45

11. http://germanhistorydocs.ghi-dc.org/sub_document.cfm?document_id=3918

12. *The Papers of Woodrow Wilson, November 20, 1916—January 23, 1917,* Arthur S. Link, ed. (Princeton, N.J.: Princeton University Press, 1982), 40, p. 536, Quoted by Ralph Raico, *World War I: The Turning Point*

13. Robert Higgs, *How U.S. Economic Warfare Provoked Japan's Attack on Pearl Harbor*, The Independent Institute, May 1, 2006, http://www.independent.org/newsroom/article.asp?id=1930

14. Robert Stinnett, *Day of Deceit: The Truth about FDR and Pearl Harbor,* New York: Free Press, Touchstone ed. May 8, 2000, p. 416

15. *Ibid*, p. 8

16. *Ibid*, p. 9

17. *Ibid*

18. John V. Denson, Roosevelt and the First Shot: A Study of Deceit and Deception, an essay in Reassessing the Presidency, Edited by John V. Denson, p. 500

19. Quoted in *Ibid,* p. 512

20. See, Stephen Kinzer, All The Shah's Men: An American Coup and The Roots of Middle East Terror, John Wiley and Sons, July 18, 2003

21. Ivan Eland, *The Empire Has No Clothes: U.S Foreign Policy Exposed,* The Independent Institute, Oakland, CA, 2004, pp. 87-88

22. http://en.wikipedia.org/wiki/Sanctions_against_Iraq

23. Justin Raimondo, *The Evil of Sanctions,* The Free Market, April 1998, Volume 16, Number 4, http://mises.org/freemarket_detail.aspx?control=86

24. http://www.youtube.com/watch?v=R0WDCYcUJ4o

25. See Moroni 8: 8-12

26. Ether 8:22, Emphasis added

27. http://www.cnn.com/2012/01/23/world/meast/iran-sanctions-facts/

Chapter 9

Waging War on Civilians

Above all, don't target civilians. If you must fight, let the rulers and their loyal or hired retainers slug it out, but keep civilians on both sides out of it, as much as possible. The growth of democracy, the identification of citizens with the State, conscription, and the idea of a "nation in arms," all whittled away this excellent tenet of international law.

-Murray Rothbard

Prior to the 19th century, there existed in Europe a kind of code of conduct in matters of warfare. Monarchical kingdoms were less powerful than the democratic nations that exist today, making the coercive allocation of warfare resources much more difficult. War was generally conducted between quarreling sovereigns who employed mercenaries to carry out the conflicts. The costs of war were exacted from the kings' pocketbooks and thus greater care was taken to conserve men and resources. Battles were carefully and strategically waged in a manner that prioritized the employment of skillful maneuvers rather than focusing on the destruction of enemy garrisons. Because kings were the sole proprietors of the government, they had a vested interest in preserving the resources of their country and subjects. To be wasteful meant that their kingdoms may not be preserved for their future posterity. Civilians were essentially left alone and it was generally understood that those who did not wish to be involved were left unmolested. One 18th century writer put it this way:

> War became limited and circumscribed by a system of precise rules. It was definitely regarded as a kind of single combat between two armies, the civil population being merely spectators. Pillage, requisitions, and acts of violence against the population were forbidden in the home country as well as in the enemy country.[1]

With the advent of burgeoning democratic systems in Europe, these rules began to change. The French Revolution brought with it a shift in ideological philosophy. The concepts of nationalism, empire, group-think, and group hatred were employed by leaders to incite violent revolutions, ethnic cleansing, and genocide. The Reign of Terror that accompanied the revolution and the Napoleonic Wars paved the way for the indiscriminate bloodshed that characterizes the 20th century—the century of the State. This devolution toward total war was exacerbated throughout the war to prevent Southern independence, the American-Indian wars, and the Spanish-American war, which prepared the way for the ubiquitous carnage that accompanied WWI and WWII. Hans Hoppe points out—in his book, *Democracy: The God That Failed*—how the inception of total war correlates with democracy. He explains that because democratic governments are not privately owned, there is more incentive for war, conscription, and public spending. Those who run democratic governments have a higher time preference, meaning that they are primarily focused on the immediate future and not the long run. This high time preference exists because these leaders only have a limited amount of time before their terms expire, which creates a huge incentive to waste and spend as much as possible in the time allotted to them. Hoppe explains how this process relates to war as follows:

> From the viewpoint of those who prefer less exploitation over more and who value farsightedness and individual responsibility above shortsightedness and irresponsibility, the historic transition

from monarchy to democracy represents not progress but civilizational decline. Nor does this verdict change if more or other indicators are included. Quite to the contrary. Without question the most important indicator of exploitation and present-orientedness *not* discussed above is *war*. Yet if this indicator were included the relative performance of democratic republican government appears to be even worse, not better. In addition to the increased exploitation and social decay, the transition from monarchy to democracy has brought a change from limited warfare to total war, and the twentieth century, the age of democracy, must be ranked also among the most murderous periods in all of history.[2]

Keeping this concept in mind, we will review some of the wartime atrocities that have been committed by the two most democratic regimes of the 19th and 20th centuries—America and Britain. Some of our most touted leaders are some of the most brutal war criminals. These include: Abraham Lincoln, William McKinley, Winston Churchill, Franklin Delano Roosevelt, Harry Truman, and Linden B. Johnson. Throughout this chapter, we will touch on some of the worst of these atrocities committed by armies under the watch of these "great" leaders.

In 1863, the rules of the conduct of war were reaffirmed by the Geneva Convention, which was held in Geneva, Switzerland. These rules (which had long been acknowledged by the peoples of Europe) included certain prohibitions. Armies were not to attack defenseless civilian cities and towns, plunder innocents, or destroy property. In response to this, Lincoln issued General Order No. 100, which adopted the Lieber Code drafted by Columbia law professor Francis Lieber—a staunch Unionist and supporter of Otto Von Bismarck. The Lieber Code recognized the rules of war, yet left a clause in the fine print stating that there were certain situations where such rules could be exempted. This, of course, was left up to the discretion of the commander.[3] Needless to say, Lincoln and his generals—which included Sherman, Sheridan, and Grant—rationalized every kind of civilian abuse under a smokescreen of lip service to the Geneva rules. Our focus here will be predominantly the march of William Tecumseh Sherman toward Atlanta, wherein Southern civilians were raped, murdered and looted by animalistic and criminal soldiers of the Union.

As early as 1861, war began to be waged against the civilian populations of the South. Lincoln and his generals turned a blind eye as their men engaged in pillage, plunder, rape, murder, and burning of Southern towns and villages—including churches. Farms were destroyed, animals were slaughtered, barns and houses torched to the ground, and the rest was "foraged" by the Union army. Lincoln had no objections about waging war against civilians, and devised a strategy with the assistance of General Winfield Scott called the "Anaconda Plan" to choke the life out of the South. This included naval blockades of southern ports and inland waterways and embargoed such items as drugs and medicines.[4] This was the type of policy that killed over 500,000 Iraqi children, but it is difficult to determine the number of Southerners who perished under Lincoln's sanctions.

General Sherman—with Lincoln's blessing—burned and bombarded many Southern towns throughout his march to Atlanta. Under his oversight, Randolph, Tennessee was burned to the ground and a civilian who was suspected of being a guerilla fighter was beaten to death, though it was later found that he had been innocent.[5] Similarly, Vicksburg, Mississippi was also torched along with the surrounding farmland, which forced civilians "to resort to living in caves and eating rats, dogs, and mules."[6] In 1863, when Sherman entered Jackson, Mississippi, the town was indiscriminately bombed every five minutes for several days and nights, forcing those who were not killed to remain homeless and starving. This policy was expanded to several other towns and cities, some of which were never rebuilt after the war. Soldiers would rob unarmed civilians at gunpoint as towns were ransacked, burned, looted, and destroyed. In reference to Jackson, Sherman would later boast to Grant that, "The inhabitants are subjugated. They cry aloud for mercy. The land is devastated for 30 miles around."[7] Upon entering Meridian, Mississippi, Sherman and his men embarked on a path of destruction that he describes in his own words:

> For five days, ten thousand of our men worked hard and with a will in that work of destruction, with axes, sledges, crowbars, clawbars, and with fire, and I have no hesitation in pronouncing the work well done. Meridian…no long exists.[8]

By the time Sherman's army arrived in Atlanta, he had two years under his belt of waging war against civilians. Seasoned with the blood of the innocent, he and his men began a bombardment of Atlanta that would take the lives of many civilians, including women, children, and even slaves (those whom the Union army were purporting to save). The bombing left only 400 of the 4000 private homes that accompanied the city standing, leaving the surviving inhabitants to wander and beg for food. In fact, Sherman ordered the survivors out of the city with what they could carry—rendering many women and children homeless in the face of the oncoming winter.[9] The soldiers engaged in their usual looting, pillaging, and burning, which morbidly included the digging up of graves to find jewelry and other valuables. Sherman's cruelty was further extended, even up to the end of the war. In 1864, he resorted to the Leninist tactic of killing random civilians in order to instill fear into the remaining pockets of confederate resistance. He said to General Louis D. Watkins:

> Cannot you send over about Fairmount and Adairsville burn ten or twelve houses of known secessionists, kill a few at random, and let them know that it will be repeated every time a train is fired on from Resaca to Kingston?[10]

In addition to all of Sherman's antics of murder, carnage, theft and destruction, there is the deleterious sin of rape. DiLorenzo elucidates as follows:

Although it is oddly missing from most histories of Sherman's March, many eyewitness accounts of rape by Federal soldiers have been recorded. Many accounts emphasize that black women suffered the most and that many black men, in response, became just as bitterly opposed to the Federal army as any secessionist was. Civilized people not do publicize the names of rape victims, so we will never know the extent to which Sherman's army committed acts of rape. But the University of South Carolina library in Columbia, South Carolina, contains a large collection of letters and diaries of South Carolinians who wrote of their experiences during the war and Reconstruction. This collection contains hundreds of personal accounts of rape at the hands of Sherman's army.[11]

After the war was over, Sherman was given military command over the American frontier and had jurisdiction over everything west of the Mississippi. The U.S. government had initiated a war against the American Indian with a Hitlerian plan of extermination in order to build the subsidized transcontinental railroads. In chapter one, we mentioned Lincoln's neo-mercantilist economic policy that used wealth redistribution schemes to fund massive public works projects like railroads. The politically-connected railroad companies were paid by the government per mile of track they laid—thus giving them incentives to weave tracks aimlessly in a zigzag fashion rather than straight. The government largess even created an incentive to lay track on frozen ice and snow through the winter—resulting in the reconstruction of such tracks in the spring, thus enabling railroaders to profit twice. In regard to the Indian "problem," Sherman is quoted as saying that "we are not going to let a few thieving, ragged Indians check and stop the progress of the railroads."[12]

This "final solution to the Indian problem,"[13] proposed by the U.S. government was a direct fulfillment of a *Book of Mormom* prophecy that was shown to Nephi through the following vision:

And it came to pass that I beheld many multitudes of the Gentiles upon the land of promise; and I beheld the wrath of God, that it was upon the seed of my brethren; and they were scattered before the Gentiles and were smitten.[14]

The seed of his brethren spoken of here are those who are the descendants of Laman and Lemuel (some of the American Indian tribes). Let it not be assumed by the reader that Sherman, Sheridan, Grant, Custer, Chivington, *et al* were justified in their campaign of genocide against the Lamanites. Just because the Lord reveals a future event to a prophet does not mean that He necessarily condones it. For how could He condone acts of mass murder, rape, enslavement, mutilation, and dehumanization committed against His children? The holocaust conducted against the plains Indians was a despicable travesty that qualifies as one of the most reprehensible human rights atrocities in history. Sherman frankly admits to Ulysses S. Grant the agenda when while speaking of the Sioux he says that "we must act with vindictive earnestness against the Sioux, even to their extermination, men, women, and children."[15]

We shall see that this, indeed, was the case, and that the government actually *targeted* women and children. To illustrate this point, we will cite General John Milton Chivington's Sand Creek massacre in November of 1864, wherein his 700 troops brutally murdered over one hundred peaceful Cheyenne and Arapaho although their leader—Black Kettle—had been promised "that as long as the United States flag flew above him no soldier would fire upon him."[16] On his march toward Sand Creek, Chivington conscripted a rancher (he was pulled out of his bed against his will) named Robert Bent to act as his guide. Bent tells the following story of the massacre in his own words:

I saw the American flag waving and heard Black Kettle tell the Indians to stand around the flag, and there they were huddled—men, women, and children. This was when we were within fifty yards of the Indians. I also saw a white flag raised. These flags were in so conspicuous a position that they must have been seen. When the troops fired, the Indians ran, some of the men into their lodges, probably to get their arms…. I think there were six hundred Indians in all. I think there were thirty-five braves and some old men, about sixty in all… the rest of these men were away from the camp, hunting…. After the firing the warriors put the squaws and children together, and surrounded them to protect them. I saw five squaws under a bank for shelter. When the troops came up to them they ran out and showed their persons to let the soldiers know they were squaws and begged for mercy, but the soldiers shot them all. I saw one squaw lying on the bank whose leg had been broken by a shell; a soldier came up to her with a drawn saber; she raised her arm to protect herself, when he struck, breaking her arm; she rolled over and raised her other arm, when he struck, breaking it, and then left her without killing her. There seemed to be indiscriminate slaughter of men, women, and children. There were some thirty or forty squaws collected in a hole for protection; they sent out a little girl about six years old with a white flag on a stick; she had not proceeded but a few steps when she was shot and killed. All the squaws in that hole were afterwards killed, and four or five bucks outside. The squaws offered no resistance. Every one I saw dead was scalped. I saw one squaw cut open with an unborn child, as I thought, lying by her side. Captain Soule afterwards told me that such was the fact. I saw the body of White Antelope with the privates cut off, and I heard a soldier say he was going to make a tobacco pouch out of them. I saw one squaw whose privates had been cut out…. I saw a little girl about five years of age who had been hid in the sand; two soldiers discovered her, drew their pistols and shot her, and then pulled her out of the sand by the arm. I saw quite a number of infants in arms killed with their mothers.[17]

In a sick display of morbidity, some of the troops mutilated the bodies the day after the massacre—taking scalps and even cutting off the private parts of women *and* children for trophies. In fact most of the victims *were* women and children, as there were 105 of the former compared to only 28 men.[18] The *Book of Mormon* documents a similar degeneration of the bloodthirsty Nephites during Mormon's time. In an epistle to his son Moroni, he observes:

> And now I write somewhat concerning the sufferings of this people. For according to the knowledge which I have received from Amoron, behold, the Lamanites have many prisoners, which they took from the tower of Sherrizah; and there were men, women, and children. And the husbands and fathers of those women and children have they slain; and they feed the women upon the flesh of their husbands, and the children upon the flesh of their fathers; and no water, save a little, do they give unto them. And notwithstanding this great abomination of the Lamanites, it doth not exceed that of our people in Moriantum. For behold, many of the daughters of the Lamanites have they taken prisoners; and after depriving them of that which was most dear and precious above all things, which is chastity and virtue—And after they had done this thing, they did murder them in a most cruel manner, torturing their bodies even unto death; and after they have done this, they devour their flesh like unto wild beasts, because of the hardness of their hearts, and they do it for a token of bravery.[19]

This American barbarism continued through 1898 as we embarked on our first imperial war against Spain. Although the war was to "free" Cuba and the Philippines from Spanish aggression, we became the aggressors in the end. Hawaii was unconstitutionally annexed as a halfway point to the Philippines, and the latter was seized to set up a trading station with China. The unsuspecting Filipinos had unknowingly traded Spanish imperialism for American imperialism, and resisted when they realized they weren't being granted their independence. In response, the U.S. Army butchered some 200,000 of them—including men, women, and children. William McKinley and Teddy Roosevelt were the overseers of the mass murder. In a sycophantic rant, Teddy Roosevelt had this to say about the Filipino "savages":

> Of course, our whole national history has been one of expansion ... That the barbarians recede or are conquered, with the attendant fact that peace follows their retrogression or conquest, is due solely to the power of the mighty civilized races which have not lost the fighting instinct, and which by their expansion are gradually bringing peace into the red wastes where the barbarian peoples of the world hold sway.[20]

President McKinley—who ruled the Philippines as a *de facto* dictator without the consent of Congress—declared in a fit of pietism "that we could not leave them to themselves—they were unfit for government."[21] This conclusion he reached after he had prayed to "Almighty God," who—according to McKinley's works—apparently doesn't accept Filipinos as human beings. The ensuing carnage sickens the stomach much like the account of the Sioux. Concentration camps were established and those who were found outside of the gulags were threatened with the confiscation of their food and the destruction of other personal property. About 20,000 insurgents were killed by American guns, and over 200,000 Filipino civilians died as a result of malnutrition, disease, and/or massacre.[22] One officer put it this way:

> Our men have been relentless, have killed to exterminate men, women, and children, prisoners and captives, active insurgents and suspected people, from lads of ten up, an idea prevailing that the Filipino was little better than a dog.[23]

Another wrote to a reporter that:

> We exterminated the American Indians, and I guess most of us are proud of it, or, at least, believe the end justified the means; and we must have no scruples about exterminating this other race

standing in the way of progress and enlightenment, if it was necessary.[24]

The late 1800s were a time in American history when industry was producing so much that there was fear among business interests that if markets were not spread oversees then prices would have to fall, which was something called the "overproductionist" theory. In fact, prices had been falling consistently after the Civil War to about the 1890s—this is a natural result of the free market and is the best scenario for consumers. Falling prices are only a bane for inefficient businessmen who can't keep up with their more innovative competitors. The market has natural mechanisms for weeding out those who can't compete. However, the tradition of the Republicans was to prop up politically-connected businesses at the expense of more efficient businesses. This was usually accomplished by tariffs, but with the advent of Spanish aggression in Cuba and the Philippines, the Republicans saw a chance to set up American coaling stations in the West Indies in order to penetrate Asian markets. The Filipino "dogs" "standing in the way of progress and enlightenment" were, in reality, only a threat to protectionist businessmen who couldn't compete with falling prices.

We have already discussed Winston Churchill's hunger blockade that he imposed upon the German people, but what of his other war crimes that have been omitted from establishment history books? Churchill's bellicose personality was well-known among his contemporaries. He absolutely loved war. "All his life he was most excited—on the evidence, only really excited—by war," Raico says, "He loved war as few modern men have—he even 'loved the bangs,' as he called them, and he was very brave under fire."[25] Unfortunately, he was also unscrupulous as to the collateral damage of some his policies, and along with the starvation of the Germans, he engaged in other war crimes during WWII that resulted in the deaths of hundreds of thousands of civilians.

One instance that has received little press was the Churchillian ordered attack on a *French* Naval fleet off the coast of Algeria. After the

German invasion of France, Churchill ordered their "ally" to surrender their fleet to Britain. When they refused, he issued the injunction (against the advice of his Naval officers) to open fire on the French— killing 1500 sailors. He did this out of the fear that the French fleet wouldn't be true to their word to scuttle their own ships if faced with German defeat, which they did in a later event that proved the Prime Minister wrong.[26] Churchill's most brutal war crimes included the deliberate bombing of German cities and the targeting of civilians. The resultant carnage of this policy was the extermination of around 600,000 Germans and 70,000 French—more than the total amount of American deaths during the Civil War. Keep in mind that these numbers represent mostly *civilian* men, women, and children; indicting Churchill as a mass murderer.

Churchill's head bomber—Arthur "Bomber" Harris—opined fatuously that, "In Bomber Command we have always worked on the assumption that bombing anything in Germany is better than bombing nothing."[27] Although Churchill told the House of Commons that most of the targets were military, "the aim was to kill as many civilians as possible."[28] Harris would offer more transparency in a later statement that revealed the motives for the indiscriminate attacks. "The aim of the Combined Bomber Offensive," he said, "should be unambiguously stated [as] the destruction of German cities, the killing of German workers, and the disruption of civilized life throughout Germany."[29] Raico illuminates the carnage that erupted across Germany as follows:

> The campaign of murder from the air leveled Germany. A thousand-year-old urban culture was annihilated, as great cities, famed in the annuls of science and art, were reduced to heaps of smoldering ruins. There were high points: the bombing of Lubeck, when that ancient Hanseatic town "burned like kindling"; the 1000-bomber raid over Cologne, and the following raids that somehow, miraculously, mostly spared the great Cathedral but destroyed the rest of the city, including thirteen Romanesque churches; the firestorm that consumed Hapsburg and killed some 42,000 people.

No wonder that, learning of this, a civilized European like Joseph Schumpeter, at Harvard, was driven to telling "anyone who would listen" that Churchill and Roosevelt were destroying more than Ghengis Khan.[30]

Churchill's murderous barrage continued though the 1945 attacks on Dresden, when air raids senselessly killed hordes of innocent refuges attempting to escape the Red Army. The bombardment lasted for three days and nights, resulting in at least 30,000-recorded deaths— but in reality probably many more. It is ironic that many conservatives hail Churchill as a war hero although he killed hundreds of thousands more than the terrorists who attacked America on 9/11/2001. It seems as though many of us are deceived by the satanic philosophy that the ends justify the means. The sad and egregious truth behind these atrocities is that most of these people were innocent and had nothing to do with Nazism. We are forced to acknowledge that this "great" statesman—heralded by many in and outside of the LDS Christian faith—was, in reality, a despicable war criminal.

The United States Air Force was no less despicable in the way they conducted the war against Japan. Many Americans are unaware that prior to the dropping of the atomic bomb that ended the war, the USAAF launched a series of firebombing campaigns on over sixty Japanese cities that murdered more than 500,000 civilians. With the recent addition of the B-29 Bomber, the United States was well-equipped for the massive assault on unarmed women, children, and the elderly. General Henry Arnold had just given control over the air raids to General Curtis LeMay—a belligerent person who was adept at getting things done curtly and efficiently. On the night of 9 March, 1945, LeMay launched an offensive against the wooden city of Tokyo that leveled 267,171 buildings, killed over 100,000 civilians, and left 1,008,005 homeless.[31] William W. Ralph explains how LeMay toppled Tokyo and other major Japanese cities as follows:

Thus on the night of 9 March 1945, 325 Superfortresses attacked residential Tokyo for the purpose of starting a conflagration that would wipe out as much of the city as possible. Lead crews firebombed an 'X' in the middle of the 10 square mile target area, and the rest of the armada followed, dropping 1665 tons of incendiary bombs on the Japanese capital. The target area contained an average population of 103,000 people per square mile. The Asakusa war, one of the most densely populated areas of the world, contained 135,000 people per square mile. Bombs of jellied gasoline rained down on the city for three house, and by 3:30 a.m. a firestorm literally like none other was churning across the city, whipped by its own high winds, leaping effortlessly across firebreaks, flowing down the streets. People who were not immediately consumed by the fire spontaneously combusted, died inhaling heated air, or were trampled to death in the panic. Many of those who found cover in shelters and canals met similarly gruesome fates, and were baked, drowned, and boiled. The fire was so intense that it had burned itself out by daybreak. But those few hours were enough to claim nearly 16 square miles of the city and approximately 100,000 lives—mostly women, children, and the elderly. According to the United States Strategic Bombing Survey, it was 'the greatest disaster ever visited upon any city.'

But the mood in the Marianas was a different one. The attack was viewed as a rousing success by LeMay, Norstad, and Arnold. LeMay, knowing of plans to attack the six cities, immediately followed the raid with attacks on Nagoya (2 square miles destroyed), Osaka (8 square miles destroyed), Kobe (3 square miles destroyed), and Nagoya again (3 square miles destroyed). After all five raids were completed, the USAAF had destroyed 31.9 square miles of the four largest Japanese cities. In total, 9373 tons of bombs were dropped. In just five missions, the USAAF had inflicted destruction equal to 41% of the total destruction of German cities over the course of the war. And this had been accomplished with less than

1% of the total bomb tonnage dropped on Germany. During the entire four-city campaign, only 22 bombers were lost.[32]

As if over a half-million Japanese civilians deaths were not enough, in order to force an unconditional surrender the U.S. dropped atomic bombs on Hiroshima and Nagasaki in August of 1945—killing an additional 200,000 innocents. Harry Truman contended the preemptive strike was needed to save an estimated 500,000 Americans *if* a later invasion was needed. Raico explains that, "these (the half-million), supposedly, are the lives that would have been lost in the planned invasion of Kyushu in December, then in the all-out invasion of Honshu the next year, if that was needed. But the worst-case scenario for a full-scale invasion of the Japanese home islands was forty-six thousand American lives lost."[33] The figures put forth by the government were exaggerated greatly, and it should be noted that diplomatic negotiations would have brought the war to an end, but the Japanese didn't want to unconditionally surrender, and when one considers what happened to Germany at Versailles (crippling sanctions, unrealistic reparations, mass starvation, runaway inflation, *etc.*) it's hard to blame them. Truman didn't have to drop the bomb and was condemned by high-ranking officials—including both General McArthur and General Eisenhower. Dissent even came from Truman's own chief of staff, Admiral William D. Leahy, who lamented that:

> The use of the barbarous weapon at Hiroshima and Nagasaki was of no material assistance in our war against Japan . . . My own feeling was that in being the first to use it, we had adopted an ethical standard common to the barbarians of the Dark Ages. I was not taught to make wars in that fashion, and wars cannot be won by destroying women and children.[34]

In addition to the 200,000 Japanese murdered there were hundreds of thousands harmed by radiation poisoning. Thirty-three schools were destroyed, which trapped thousands of children alive. This insidious act was of the utmost belligerence and is terrorism that even modern day extremists can't match. Truman—in an attempt to justify the genocide—contended that Hiroshima was a military and industrial target, but in reality it was neither. Raico again clarifies:

> *Pearl Harbor* was a military base. Hiroshima was a *city*, inhabited by some three hundred thousand people, which contained military elements. In any case, since the harbor was mined and the U.S. Navy and Air Force were in control of the waters around Japan, whatever troops were stationed in Hiroshima had been effectively neutralized.[35]

And quoting from the U.S. Strategic Bombing Survey we discover that, "all major factories in Hiroshima were on the periphery of the city and escaped serious damage."[36] Obviously, the civilian population took the brunt of the damage. Leo Szilard—a world renounced physicist—made an interesting assertion concerning this:

> If the Germans had dropped atomic bombs on cities instead of us, we would have defined the dropping of atomic bombs on cities as a war crime, and we would have sentenced the Germans who were guilty of this crime to death at Nuremberg and hanged them.[37]

Indeed, Truman and Churchill are no better than their German counterparts who were also engaging in genocide. Whether the genocide is administered via a nuclear bomb, air strikes, gas chambers, or gulags, the result is the same—mass murder. It is alarming that many Latter-day Saints—who have the *Book of Mormon* as their guide—still believe in the mythology that WWII was a "good war." Perhaps many (the author included) have fathers or grandfathers who valiantly served their country in that war. However, we can still honor the soldiers while denouncing the politicians who orchestrated the war, as many with a sensitive conscience must do. J. Reuben Clark—when addressing the church during the 1946 General Conference—had this to say in regard to the atomic bombings:

> Then as the *crowning savagery of the war*, we Americans wiped out hundreds of thousands of civilian population with the atom bomb in Japan, few if any of the ordinary civilians being any more responsible for the war than were we, and perhaps most of them no more aiding Japan in the war than we were aiding America. Military men are now saying that the atom bomb was a mistake. It was more than that: *it was a world tragedy.* Thus we have lost all that we gained during the years from Grotius (1625) to 1912. And the worst of this atomic bomb tragedy is not that not only did the people of the United States not rise up in protest against this savagery, not only did it not shock us to read of this wholesale destruction of men, women, and children, and cripples, but that it actually drew from the nation at large a general approval of *this fiendish butchery.*[38]

It seems as though the 20th century has been the century of "fiendish butchery," for we discover that this civilian warfare has been perpetuated and has continued through the Vietnam War until the present. During that ominous conflict, there was an elite unit known by the appellation of "Tiger Force." Made up of approximately forty-five paratroopers, this unit was created to outperform the Vietcong guerillas, and by 1968 its parent battalion was even rewarded the Presidential Unit Citation by LBJ. However, after almost sixty years, the truth behind this unit's brutality towards civilians is coming out of the woodwork. Dennis Stout—a military journalist—was an eyewitness to many atrocities committed by these soldiers. He recalls viewing the slaughter of unarmed men, women, and children frequently—often involving mothers with crying children. In one instance he saw a platoon round up thirty-five women and children into a pasture and indiscriminately execute them. He witnessed in another instance "22 paratroopers rape and execute a woman," he said, "and a medic pump swamp water into the heart of a prisoner before he was fatally shot by the soldiers."[39]

This savagery was not just limited to Tiger force. On the morning of February 8, 1968, a platoon of soldiers from company B, 1st Battalion, 35th Infantry, 4th Infantry Division, came upon a settlement in the Quang Nam province. The company medic—20-year-old Jamie Henry—had just retired to a hut and lit a smoke when he heard a lieutenant's voice on the radio. The man had rounded up 19 civilians and was asking what he should do with them. The commander's voice responded with this retort: *kill anything that moves.* A few seconds later, Henry emerged from the hut and witnessed the brutal massacre. Appalled, he would later return home and publish an account of the slaughter—for which he was branded a traitor. None of the perpetrators were ever brought to justice.[40]

Henry was an eyewitness to a myriad of other atrocities committed by company B in the fall of 1967. His platoon had captured a 12-year-old boy during a rainstorm. When the soldiers who caught him asked the men who wanted to kill him there were two men who volunteered. One kicked the boy in the stomach and the other took him behind a rock and executed him in cold blood. Three days later, an old man was apprehended who was too slow to keep pace with the march up a steep hill. He was grabbed by a couple of paratroopers and thrown off the hill onto a pile of rocks. A few days later, Henry witnessed his men using a Vietnamese man for target practice after it had been decided that they would kill the man for sport. Henry recalled another incident, "Back at base camp on Oct. 23," he said, "members of the 1st Platoon told him they had ambushed five unarmed women and reported them as enemies killed in action."[41] In fact, all of the civilians that were murdered by company B were reported likewise.

Perhaps the most well-known attack on civilians during the war was the infamous My Lai massacre, carried out by Charlie Company, First Battalion, 20th Infantry Regiment, 11th Infantry Brigade, 23rd Infantry Division. These 140 men arrived in the village of My Lai on the morning of March 16, 1968 expecting—as had been told them by a commanding officer—that all they would encounter would be enemy combatants. These soldiers had been fighting the 48th Vietcong infantry battalion for two months in guerilla-style warfare, accompanied by the paranoia of not being able to easily distinguish friend from foe. Demoralized and seeking for revenge, the men were perplexed when they instead found hundreds of unarmed civilians in My Lai. They opened fire, killing anywhere from 300 to 500 innocent civilians including men, women, and children. The U.S. government actually brought charges against twenty men involved in the massacre. The foremost among these was Lieutenant William Calley—who was given a life sentence and then subsequently pardoned by President Nixon, ultimately spending a mere four and a half months in a military prison.[42]

Conclusion

It is estimated that civilian casualties during the Vietnam War were approximately 195,000-430,000 South Vietnamese, and 50,000-65,000 North Vietnamese.[43] In addition to these, there were 58,000 American servicemen who were also killed, marking the event as a true American travesty. Most of these civilians had nothing to do with the Vietcong or the communists and were simply in the wrong place at the wrong time. It is precisely for this reason—collateral damage in civilian form—that the *Book of Mormon* does not justify wars of aggression. And we find Mormon—in an epistle to his son Moroni—condemning the brutal tactics employed by the Nephites, which are, sadly, not much different than those employed in our day. The Nephites were raping, murdering, mutilating, torturing, and even engaging in cannibalism. They were executing innocent women and after depriving them of their virtue they would devour their flesh as a "token of bravery." Looking back through history, we see the many atrocities committed by American armies against Southerners, the Native Americans, the Filipinos, the Germans, the Japanese, the Vietnamese, and now the Iraqis, (See Chapter 11, *Waging War on Ideologies: A Dangerous Delusion*) Afghans, and Iranians. Are we any different than the barbaric and uncivilized Nephites during Mormon's time? Perhaps Mormon's condemnation applies to us as well:

O my beloved son, how can a people like this, that are without civilization—(And only a few years have passed away, and they were a civil and delightsome people.) But O my son, how can a people like this, whose delight is in so much abomination—How can we expect that God will stay his hand in judgment against us?[44]

Chapter Nine Notes and Sources

1. Guglielmo Ferrero, *Peace and War*, Quoted in Hans Herman Hoppe, *Democracy, The God That Failed*, Transaction Publishers, New Brunswick, New Jersey, 2001, pp. 34-35

2. *Ibid*, p. 69

3. DiLorenzo, *The Real Lincoln*, e-book, p. 190

4. *Ibid*, pp. 193-94

5. *Ibid*, p. 195

6. *Ibid*, p. 198

7. Quoted in *Ibid*, p. 198-99

8. Quoted in *Ibid*, p. 199

9. *Ibid*, p. 200

10. Quoted in *Ibid*, p. 201

11. *Ibid*, p. 202

12. Thomas J. DiLorenzo, *The Feds versus the Indians*, The Free Market, January 1998, Vol. 1, Num. 16, http://mises.org/freemarket_detail.aspx?control=99

13. *Ibid*

14. 1 Nephi 13:14

15. Thomas J. DiLorenzo, *The Feds versus the Indians*, The Free Market, January 1998, Vol. 1, Num. 16, http://mises.org/freemarket_detail.aspx?control=99

16. Dee Brown, *Bury My Heart at Wounded Knee, An Indian history of the American West*, Open Road Integrated Media, New York, e-book, 2013, p. 371

17. U.S. Congress. 39th. 2nd Session. Senate Report 156, pp. 73,96, quoted in *Ibid*, pp. 373-77

18. *Ibid*, pp. 378-80

19. Moroni 9:7-10

20. Quoted in Richard Drinnon, Facing West: The Metaphysics of Indian -Hating and Empire-building, New York, 1980

21. Quoted in Joseph Stromberg, The Spanish-American War as Trial Run, an essay in The Costs of War: America's Pyrrhic Victories, edited by John V. Denson, p. 186

22. *Ibid,* 188

23. Quoted in *Ibid*

24. Quoted in Drinnon, *Facing West,* pp. 314-15

25. Raico, Great Wars and Great Leaders, A Libertarian Rebuttal, p. 58

26. *Ibid,* p. 89

27. Quoted in *Ibid,* p. 90

28. *Ibid*

29. Quoted in *Ibid,* p. 91

30. *Ibid,* p. 91

31. William W. Ralph, *War In History 2006, Vol. 13(4):495-522,* Sage Publications, 2006, p. 495

32. *Ibid,* p. 513

33. Ralph Raico, Harry S. Truman: Advancing the Revolution, an essay in Reassessing the Presidency, Edited by John V. Denson, p. 579

34. William D. Leahy, *I Was There,* (New York: McGraw-Hill 1950), p. 441, Quoted in *Ibid,* p. 580

35. Denson, Reassessing the Presidency, p. 578

36. Quoted in *Ibid,* p. 579

37. Quoted in *Ibid,* p. 585

38. J. Reuben Clark, Conference Report, 1946, pp. 86-88, quoted in *Prophets, Principles, and National Survival,* compiled by Jerreld L. Newquist, Publishers Press, Salt Lake City, UT, 1964, p. 471

39. The Blade, *Witness to Vietnam atrocities never knew about investigation,* http://www.toledoblade.com/special-tiger-force/2003/11/08/Witness-to-Vietnam-atrocities-never-knew-about-investigation.html

40. Nick Turse and Deborah Nelson, *Civilian Killings Went Unpunished,* Los Angeles Times, http://www.latimes.com/news/la-na_vietnam6aug06,0,2056752.story#axzz2o9tpugPR

41. Nick Turse and Deborah Nelson, *Story of Vietnam Massacre is Finally Out,* Los Angeles Times, Tuesday, August 8, 2008, http://seattletimes.com/html/nationworld/2003182584_2vietnam08.html

42. http://www.pbs.org/wgbh/americanexperience/features/introduction/mylai/

43. http://en.wikipedia.org/wiki/Vietnam_War_casualties

44. Moroni 9:11-14

Chapter 10

Amalickiah and False Flag Operations

The question was how we should maneuver them into the position of firing the first shot without allowing too much danger to ourselves.

-Secretary of War Henry L. Stimson

Amalickiah was the perfect model for our modern-day scheming leaders. In his story, we have the classic tale of the lust for power and the justifying of any means to obtain it. We are told that Amalickiah was a "very subtle man to do evil" and had "laid the plan in his heart to dethrone the king of the Lamanaites."[1] In other words, he had conjured a premeditated plan to orchestrate a *coup d'etat* and establish himself as a dictator. He dissented from the Nephites after attempting an unsuccessful coup of their government and joined the Lamanites with a small band of his followers. He gained favor with the king of the Lamanites through flattery and so was given command of the portion of the king's army that was still loyal. The other portion was rebelling— lead by a man named Lehonti—against the king's attempts to force the armies to fight a war against the Nephites.

Amalickiah was given orders to locate Lehonti and compel his armies to go against the Nephites. However, when he arrived at mount Antipas where Lehonti's men were gathered, he had something else in mind. Lehonti and his men were "determined" that "they would not be subjected to go against the Nephites."[2] Amalickiah used their determination against them, for we learn that "it was his intention to gain favor with the armies of the Lamanites, that he might place himself at their head and dethrone the king and take possession of the kingdom."[3] He proceeded to make a deal with Lehonti in which he promised to yield up his armies (the ones obedient to the king) into their hands if he (Lehonti) would make him a second leader over the armies of the Lamanites. He allowed Lehonti's men to come and surround his own men the next morning, who "pled with Amalickiah that he would suffer them to fall in with their brethren, that they might not be destroyed."[4]

Having weaseled his way into the position of second in military command, Amalickiah was now ready to get rid of Lehonti—who had already served his purpose and was no longer needed. This was easily accomplished by one of his servants administering poison to the chief leader, which caused his death and allowed Amalickiah—in the tradition of the Lamanites—to take his place. He then marched with his newly acquired armies toward the land of Nephi (the land belonging to the Lamanites). When the king came out to meet him, he supposed that Amalickiah had been obedient to his commands by raising such a great army to go against the Nephites. However, the king was disappointed in his assumption, for when he raised Amalickiah's servants from their reverential bow he was stabbed to death. When this happened, the real servants of the king fled and the servants of Amalickiah raised the following cry: "Behold, the servants of the king have stabbed him to the heart, and he has fallen and they have fled; behold, come and see."[5]

Amalickiah—in a great display of acting—"pretended to be wroth, and said: Whosoever loved the king, let him go forth, and pursue his servants that they shall be slain."[6] This attempt of Amalickiah to get rid of the eyewitnesses to the king's murder failed, for we learn that these servants escaped the pursuers and joined the people of Ammon. Although the *Book of Mormon* does not specify, it is not unreasonable to surmise that part of Amalickiah's anti-Nephite propaganda campaign consisted of allegations that they were harboring terrorists who had murdered the Lamanite king. At any rate, Amalickiah was successful in his design to overthrow the king and usurp the kingdom. He was able to convince the queen by the false testimonies of his servants that the king's servants were the guilty parties. She was not only convinced, but she found so much favor with Amalickiah that she became his wife, which further cemented his rule. Not satisfied with only the Lamanite kingdom, Amalickiah immediately began to incite the Lamanites to go against the Nephites, and perhaps he used those "terrorists" who slew the king as a pretext for war. The means used are irrelevant, for we learn that his true desire was "to overpower the Nephites and to bring them into bondage."[7]

When attempting to explain Isaiah to his ignorant brothers, Nephi tells us that he "did liken all scriptures unto us, that it might be for our profit and learning."[8] In light of Nephi's counsel, we have to ask ourselves: why did the Lord have Mormon include this piece on Amalickiah? Was it just to give us an interesting read or is it a direct warning about similar men in our day? It is easy to discern the more commonly known tyrants who have usurped power in the pattern of Amalickiah; the Stalins, Maos, Hitlers, Mussolinis, *et al.* But what of the less obvious tyrants who have plunged their subjects into wars using deceit and false flag operations? The Lord gives us a clue in this regard for we learn that Amalickiah was a Nephite by birth that eventually dissented over to the Lamanites. The fact that he tried to overthrow the Nephite government first implies that he did not care what side he was on. He wanted to be on whatever side would help him accomplish his designs. This clue from the *Book of Mormon* should assist latter-day readers in discerning the Amalickiah-type men who have been and may still be in our midst—even in America.

It will be the subject of this chapter to discuss the presidents of this nation that, like Amalickiah, have used false flag operations to initiate wars of aggression. For those readers not familiar with the term *false flag,* we will offer the following explanation:

Covert, military, or paramilitary operations designed to deceive in such a way that the operations appear as though they are being carried out by other entities, groups or nations than those who actually planned and executed them.[9]

The men discussed herein will include Abraham Lincoln, William McKinley, Woodrow Wilson, Franklin Roosevelt, and Linden Johnson. The subjects discussed will be the catalysts that each administration used to get the American public to support certain wars. Shamefully—in the case of Wilson and FDR—innocent civilians were sacrificed and used as pawns in their game. The first event we will examine is the deliberate reinforcing of Ft. Sumter that manipulated the South into firing the first shot.

We discussed previously in this book that America's first real dictator was none other than Abraham Lincoln. His first official act of presidential dictatorship was the issuing of secret executive orders to reinforce the Southern forts Sumter and Pickens. Fort Sumter was located in Charleston Harbor and was in a key location for the enforcement of the Morrill Tariff signed into law by President Buchanan. Its location in the harbor also provided a strategic defensive position against invasion. South Carolina was in the process of secession as a result of the tariff, which raised the tariff rate on the South to 47%, but had gifted Fort Sumter to the federal government upon its coming into the Union. This created a tense situation. President Buchanan issued a verbal pledge that no efforts would be made to reinforce the Fort but General Winfield Scott pressed Buchanan to commandeer all the forts of the South, including Fort Pickens in Pensacola Bay, Florida. After some negotiations between Buchanan and U.S. Senator Stephen Mallory, a formal truce was entered into with the North, understanding that if reinforcements were sent to Ft. Pickens then the South would fire on the fort. Lincoln was inaugurated shortly thereafter and issued secret executive orders to reinforce Fort Pickens on March 4, 1861, which violated that truce. The South took Lincoln's covert action as an overt act of war but offered no retaliation.[10]

Meanwhile, Fort Sumter had been occupied by Northern Major Robert Anderson (on his own accord) and a small contingent of men, which further strained relations between the North and the South. Confederate President Jefferson Davis construed this as a belligerent act and formally declared that any attempt to further reinforce the fort would result in the South firing upon Anderson and his men. Again, President Buchanan promised that no such actions would be taken and that eventually the Fort would be evacuated and abandoned. However, when Lincoln took office he held a secret cabinet meeting to discuss the desirability of reinforcement. The diary of Attorney General Edward Bates reveals that he was willing to evacuate the fort despite the colluding opinions of the others. He notes that, "The Naval men have convinced me fully that the thing can be done, and yet as the doing of it would be almost certain to begin the war."[11] Six days later, Lincoln called another cabinet meeting regarding Fort Sumter and was met with several opposing opinions concerning the reinforcement of the fort, as they felt it would further aggravate Southern relations. The men present were Secretary of Treasury Salmon P. Chase, Secretary of War Simon Cameron, Secretary of the Navy Gideon Welles, and Attorney General Edward Bates.[12]Lincoln ignored almost all counsel from his cabinet and by the 29th of March plans were being made which led to the issuance of secret executive orders to send troops and Naval ships to Fort Sumter around April 6th. The rationale for this reinforcement was that Major Anderson and his troops were "starving," even though he had made arrangements with local merchants for food provisions. Lincoln sent eight ships, with fourteen hundred men and twenty-six cannons—without congressional approval—to supply Anderson with "food." Anderson was warned by Southern General P.G.T. Beauregard previously to evacuate the Fort after Governor Francis Pickens of South Carolina received an official notice from Lincoln through Robert Chew that reinforcements were coming. Anderson refused to leave, but desperately wanted to avoid a conflict as evidenced by a letter confiscated by the mail delivery a day earlier wherein he stated that "my heart is not in the war which I see is to be thus commenced."[13] Anderson also knew reinforcements were coming because of a letter he received from Secretary of War Cameron. However, his response (partially contained in the above quote) never made it back to Cameron.[14]

When the ships arrived in the harbor, the South opened fire upon Fort Sumter for thirty-six hours. The ships never returned any fire and just drifted in the harbor as Anderson and his men were bombarded. After the firing ceased, Anderson surrendered and the South sent a doctor in to tend to any wounded. Luckily, no one was injured. Confederate soldiers removed their hats in salute to the brave Major and his small garrison who had endured such an onslaught with no assistance. The ships removed out of the harbor and the ordeal was over. Lincoln had—through unconstitutional means—sent ships that placed Major Anderson deliberately in harm's way and then offered him no help when the firing started. For this treasonous act alone he should have been impeached. However, he used the incident as a justification to invade the South, again acting without congressional approval. Congress officially never declared war, yet Lincoln—through cunning—connived the South into firing the first shot anyway. Lincoln then commenced in becoming America's first dictator. One of his most ardent supporters—Arthur M. Schlesinger, Jr.—documents some of constitutional abuses he was guilty of as follows:

> Lincoln chose nevertheless to begin by assuming powers to act independently of Congress. Fort Sumter was attacked on April 12, 1861. On April 15, Lincoln summoned Congress to meet in special session—but not until July 4. He thereby granted ten weeks to bypass Congress, ruled by decree, and set the nation irrevocably on the path to war. On April 15, he called out state militia to the number of seventy-five thousand. Here he was acting on the basis of a statue. From then on he acted on his own. On April 19, he imposed a blockade on rebel ports, thereby assuming authority to take actions hitherto considered as requiring a declaration of war. On May 3, he called for volunteers and enlarged the army and navy, thereby usurping the power confided to Congress to raise armies and maintain navies. On April 20, he ordered the Secretary of

Treasury to spend public money for defense without congressional appropriation, thereby violating Article I, section 9, of the Constitution. On April 27, he authorized the commanding general of the army to suspend the writ of *habeas corpus*—despite the fact that the power of suspension, while not assigned explicitly to Congress, lay in that article of the Constitution devoted to the powers of Congress and was regarded by commentators before Lincoln as a congressional prerogative. Later he claimed the *habeas corpus* clause as a precedent for wider suspension of constitutional rights in time of rebellion or invasion—an undoubted stretching of the original intent.[15]

Perhaps the smoking gun that squarely places blame on Lincoln for initiating aggression toward the South is found in the diary of his close friend—Senator Orville H. Browning—who writes that Lincoln:

> …told me that the very first thing placed in his hands after his inauguration was a letter from Major Anderson announcing the impossibility of defending or relieving Sumter. That he called the cabinet together and consulted General Scott—that Scott concurred with Anderson, and the cabinet, with the exception of PM General Blair were for evacuating the Fort, and all the troubles and anxieties of his life had not equaled those which intervened between this time and the fall of Sumter. *He himself conceived the idea*, and proposed sending supplies, without an attempt to reinforce giving notice of the fact to Governor Pickens of S.C. *The plan succeeded. They attacked Sumter—it fell, and thus, did more service than it otherwise could.*[16]

Lincoln needed a pretext for war and was willing to use mendacious means to force the South into firing the first shot—even if it meant sacrificing Major Anderson and his men. Lincoln was ethically challenged, to say the least—especially when one considers the true reason he desired war; to preserve his precious tariff. In a private meeting with Colonel John B. Baldwin, Lincoln refused to issue a written proclamation to the State of Virginia (which wanted to remain in the Union) that he would not force the seceding States back into the Union. Although Baldwin mentioned that Lincoln seemed impressed with the sincerity of Virginia—who also promised that it would endeavor to bring back the seceding States if no coercion was used—Lincoln lamented that if he took such a course, "What then, would become of my tariff?"[17] Our next event happened on the evening of 15 February, 1898, when the U.S.S. Battleship *Maine* exploded and sunk into Havana Harbor, off the coast of Cuba. Of the 355 servicemen on board, the harbor claimed two officers, 222 sailors, and 28 marines, leaving only 103 survivors. The vessel—one of America's first steel ships—was sent into the harbor by President William McKinley in an effort to pressure the Spanish government into relenting on Cuba. Although the occupiers showed no hostility toward the ship during its stay in the harbor, the American press placed the blame squarely on Spanish shoulders. This "yellow journalism" was promulgated by William Randolph Hearst and Joseph Pulitzer, whose newspaper articles would incite the American public against the Spaniards regardless of the lack of evidence that they were responsible. The war cry was accompanied by the slogan, "Remember the Maine, to hell with Spain!"[18] It was surmised that the Spanish had attached a remote mine to the hull of the ship and detonated it from the shore. However, Spain conducted its own investigation and determined that the explosion was caused by internal combustion.

Conclusive evidence does not exist for either case, but the probabilities lean much more toward vindicating Spain. In any case, McKinley was able to petition Congress for the $50 million wanted for military intervention in Cuba and the Philippines. An ultimatum was sent to Spain in April of 1898, followed by a Naval blockade, which culminated in a Spanish declaration of war against the United States. The stage was set for America's first overseas military adventure and imperialistic disaster that took the lives of hundreds of thousands of innocent Filipinos. The war hawk Teddy Roosevelt—who was the undersecretary of the Navy—had been foaming at the mouth for a conflict just days after the explosion. He cabled Commodore George Dewey with the following communiqué, "Keep in full coal. In the event of declaration of war with Spain, your duty will be to see that the Spanish squadron does not leave the Asiatic coast and then offensive operations in Philippine Islands."[19]

Roosevelt got his war, and McKinley oversaw the butchery of the Filipinos as mentioned in the previous chapter. Whether this event qualifies as a false flag is fuzzy, but one thing is clear: the sinking of the *U.S.S. Maine* served as a catalyst for American intervention in places where she didn't belong, and planted the seedlings of the American empire. It is also interesting to note that Operation Northwoods (1962), which was detailed in a declassified Joint Chiefs of Staff document that outlines a plan for a staged Cuban attack on U.S. citizens, called for a "Remember the Maine" incident to incite a war with Cuba.[20] Finally, in 1976, a formal investigation of the cause of the Maine's demise was conducted by Hyman Rickover of the U.S. Navy. He and his team concluded that a coal dust fire probably caused the explosion, though his assessment was disputed and still is today.[21]

Almost twenty years later, America was again on the brink of entering another war, even a "war to end all wars." Winston Churchill was anxious to have the United States as an ally and the American anglophiles were desirous to assist their British counterparts. Woodrow Wilson was no exception, and when German U-boats began sinking British merchant ships (The British *Falaba* on March 28, 1915), opportunities began presenting themselves. The Germans were engaging merchant ships because they were carrying munitions of war (without the knowledge of the passengers) and contraband to British armies. German hostilities toward these vessels were, in part, retribution for Churchill's illegal hunger blockade that starved hundreds of thousands of German civilians. The most famous of these attacks was the sinking of the *Lusitania*—a British passenger ship carrying both British and American patrons. The ship was torpedoed on May 7, 1915 by a German U-boat, resulting in 1,195 British casualties and 124 American, which served to increase U.S. support for the English and stir America against Germany.

There are some interesting facts surrounding the sinking of this vessel—the fastest merchant ship of its day—which point to collusion between Churchill and Wilson undertaking an effort to use the incident as a false flag, as Churchill opined, "In the hopes especially of embroiling the United States with Germany."[22] The German embassy issued a warning to the American government about the dangers of traveling aboard the *Lusitania*, because it carried munitions of war and was therefore a legitimate German target. Wilson ignored these warnings and refused to allow the information to be published and actually encouraged Americans to travel aboard British passenger ships. Appalled, Wilson's secretary of state—William Jennings Bryan— resigned over the incident after a futile attempt to reason with the stubborn president. Bryan had pleaded with Wilson, "Germany has a right to prevent contraband going to the Allies, and a ship carrying contraband should not rely upon passengers to protect her from attack—it would be like putting women and children in front of an army."[23]

This is precisely what happened—the torpedo struck the starboard bow and ignited the explosives on board, which caused the ship to sink in just eighteen minutes and sent hundreds of women and children to a watery grave. Although substantive evidence is lacking to officially indict Churchill in the conspiracy, there are plenty of historians who concur with the premise. One such is Patrick Beesly, who wrote a history of British Naval Intelligence during WWI and opined that:

> I am reluctantly driven to the conclusion that there was a conspiracy deliberately to put the *Lusitania* at risk in the hope that even an abortive attack on her would bring the United States into the war. Such a conspiracy could not have been put into effect without Winston Churchill's express permission and approval.[24]

Another historian, John Denson, explains how Churchill changed captains at the last minute and placed speed restrictions on the cruiser as follows:

> On this fateful voyage, the British Admiralty, under Churchill's leadership, changed captains, substituting Captain William Turner for the usual captain. As the *Lusitania* drew near to its final destination, orders came from the British Admiralty to the military escort ship, the *Juno*, to abandon its usual mission, thereby leaving the ocean liner without protection from submarines. The *Lusitania* was not told that it was now alone, nor was it told that a German submarine was directly in its path—a fact known by the Admiralty. Finally, the Admiralty ordered Captain Turner to reduce his speed, thereby making the *Lusitania* an easy target for torpedoes.[25]

Finally, an LDS author also concurred with the conspiracy premise and documents the information in one of his books. PhD Jack Monnett chronicles the following succinct arguments in favor of conspiracy as follows:

> (1.) That merchant and other ships were considered war ships because of England's dictum to use them as such—in fact the *Lusitania* was registered in the British Navy as an auxiliary cruiser.
>
> (2.) That the *Lusitania* was owned by J.P. Morgan and that instructions had been given to fill much of the ocean-liner with explosive primers and ammunition (an estimated three tons).
>
> (3.) That the German embassy had sent announcements to fifty major newspapers warning Americans not to sail on the *Lusitania* and that the United States State Department had ordered the newspapers not to publish them.[26]

The tragedy of the *Lusitania,* whether the result of an actual conspiracy or not, served as the perfect catalyst to involve America in an overseas war—a war that cost millions of lives, allowed the Bolsheviks to easily overthrow Czarist Russia, and fueled the fire of Nazism, which led to WWII and the Cold War. If the American people had taken a stand against the warmongering Wilson administration and pushed for the foreign policy advocated by Washington to "avoid entangling alliances" then perhaps much of the blood and carnage of the 20th century could have been avoided. At any rate, Woodrow got his war and Winston got his alliance.

In a previous chapter, we mentioned Roosevelt's eight-point plan recommended and instituted by Lieutenant Commander Arthur H. McCollum to provoke a Japanese assault a year prior to the "surprise attack" on Pearl Harbor. This included plans for an oil embargo, Naval provocations, and the freezing of Japanese assets that strong-armed Japan into initiating an attack. There is much more to this story than most of us have heard and it was not until the last couple of decades that much of this information has surfaced. This is due to the fact that many of the Naval officers who have published their testimonies have had their families do so after their deaths to avoid trouble from the government. There is ample evidence that now affirms FDR's complicity in a conspiracy to provoke the Pearl Harbor attack as an excuse for America to enter the war against Germany via the "back door." FDR unilaterally pledged American involvement to Winston Churchill (who was made Prime Minister in 1940), and King George VI without even consulting Congress. His policies led to the sacrifice of all those who bravely died at Pearl Harbor and deliberately misled Admiral Kimmel and General Short in regard to intelligence that was intercepted from Japanese "purple code." All of these allegations and more can easily be proven, indicting FDR as a true traitor to his country.

When King George VI and his wife came to the United States, they visited the president at his home in Hyde Park, New York. A meeting commenced between the two in which the president "secretly promised the king full American support for the British Empire."[27] Roosevelt set up a U.S. Navy-patrolled zone in the Atlantic and even made plans to sink German U-boats preemptively. The king's biographer, John W. Wheeler-Bennett "concludes that these agreements served as the basis for the destroyer deal as well as for the Lend-Lease agreement made much later."[28] It is imperative for the reader to note that Lend-Lease was a foreign aid program that gave millions of dollars' worth of military support to England, France, and Russia prior to American entry in the war. This obviously enraged the Germans, as the Americans were supposed to be "neutral" antecedent to their entry. This program also led to the Cold War because of the massive buildup of the Soviet military-industrial-complex by American taxpayers and corporations.[29]

Prior to Churchill's appointment to prime minister in 1940, he and Roosevelt were sending coded communications that included secret plans to involve the United States in the war. These were intercepted by Tyler Kent—a code clerk working at the American embassy in England—and discussed with Captain Archibald Ramsay—a member of British parliament. The bellicose Churchill, upon becoming prime minister, immediately ordered the arrests of Kent and Ramsay. Although Kent was an American citizen, he received no immunity from FDR and was tried secretly in a British court, and subsequently served seven years in prison, while Ramsay was held without trial in a British prison until September 1944. These men, whose only crime was to stumble onto communiqués that were being sent illegally (it was against protocol for FDR to send messages to anyone other than the head of British government) were denied the writ of *habeas corpus*.[30] Perhaps if the real criminals—Roosevelt and Churchill—had instead been thrown into prison then the world could have avoided a costly war.

Roosevelt and Churchill had an inside man who helped to orchestrate the alliance between the US and Britain. This man, who was a close friend to Churchill, was named William Stephenson and was known by the code name Intrepid. This story is well document in the book *A Man Called Intrepid*.[31] Stephenson was placed at the head of a secret organization, financed by the Royal Family, in the heart of New York City at the Rockefeller Center. This organization served to fuel the fire for American involvement in the war by perfidious means such as false propaganda and the creation of pseudo documents. Roosevelt kept in contact with Intrepid through a lawyer, Ernest Cuneo, whose code name was Crusader. Two false documents created by this organization are worthy of note. Stephenson provided a false map allegedly obtained from a German spy that revealed details for a planned German invasion of South America, which Roosevelt used in a national radio speech addressed to the American people. The other document was fabricated and given to Hitler just three days prior to the Pearl Harbor attack. It detailed false American plans to preemptively invade Germany and served as a pretext for Hitler's declaration of war against the United States.[32]

The Latter-day Saint reader shouldn't be surprised that such misleading "rumors" were used to start this unconstitutional war, for we learn that the prophet Moroni saw these things by vision over sixteen hundred years before they transpired:

> Yea, it [the *Book of Mormon*] shall come in a day when there shall be heard of fires, and tempests, and vapors of smoke in foreign lands; And there shall also be heard of *wars, rumors of wars,* and earthquakes in divers places.[33]

Roosevelt took various deceptive measures prior to the Japanese attack that many historians (Roosevelt lovers and haters alike) now consider deliberately treasonous. As early as January of 1940 he ordered the Pacific Fleet moved from San Diego to Pearl Harbor—a position that made them much more vulnerable to attack. Over a year later, he announced that the fleet would remain there indefinitely. He also ordered several of the fleet's ships to the Atlantic where they would assist the British by delivering supplies and munitions of war—a further attempt to provoke the Germans. He relieved Admiral Richardson of his command when he brought complaints forward about these foolish orders, and replaced him with Admiral Husband E. Kimmel, who was later excoriated for his "incompetency" in defending Pearl Harbor. Roosevelt also refused negotiations with Japanese prince and Prime Minister Fumimaro Konoye, who was sent by Japan in a desperate attempt to seek peace diplomatically. Roosevelt's refusal to accept peace led to the replacement of Konoye with Tojo—who was much more militant. Roosevelt also gave ultimatums to Japan that required them to get their military presence out of China, further provoking the Japanese.[34]

In addition to these provocative maneuvers, Roosevelt withheld key information and intelligence from Admiral Kimmel, intelligence that could have saved countless lives at Pearl Harbor. Due to a solar storm that was brewing several million miles away in space, the U.S. was able to intercept seven Japanese messages between November 28th and December 6th, 1941. The storm bounced Japanese radio messages across the pacific directly to U.S. Navy intercept stations. It was learned from these intercepts that Japan intended to start a war, beginning with an attack on Pearl Harbor.[35] Most of these intercepts were withheld from Admiral Kimmel. Denson explains that:

> In fact, American cryptographers were decoding the military communications and sending them directly to Roosevelt; through directional radio finders, they were able to determine the exact location of the [Japanese] fleet all the way through their fateful journey. Roosevelt ordered all ships out of the North Pacific Ocean when he learned that the Japanese forces were in that area, and he did this to prevent any discovery of the Japanese presence there.[36]

Stinnett goes on to explain the "strange orders" given to the confused Kimmel:

> On orders from Washington, Kimmel left his oldest vessels inside Pearl Harbor and sent twenty-one modern warships, including his two aircraft carriers, west toward Wake and Midway. Those were strange orders, for they dispatched American forces directly into the path of the oncoming Japanese fleet of thirty submarines.[37]

Finally, from Kimmel's own book we learn that he felt he was intentionally "misled" by the Navy Department:

> The Navy Department thus engaged in a course of conduct, which definitely gave me the impression that intelligence from important intercepted Japanese messages were being furnished to me. Under these circumstances a failure to send me important information of this character was not merely withholding of intelligence. It amounted to an affirmative misrepresentation. I had asked for all vital information. I had been assured that I would have it. I appeared to be receiving it… Yet, in fact, the most vital information from the intercepted Japanese messages was withheld from me. This failure not only deprived me of essential facts. It misled me.[38]

The evidence that surrounds this act of "infamy" committed by FDR is extensively voluminous. There is not enough room to include everything in the short section concerning it in this chapter of this book. Suffice it to say that FDR not only had previous knowledge of the attacks, he also endeavored to cover his tracks by forming a Congressional commission to investigate how a surprise attack was allowed to be carried out on Hawaii. Admiral Kimmel and General Short were denied due process of law and were not allowed to submit any of their own evidence. In fact, they were both reduced in rank and eventually forced to disgracefully resign.[39] Their case was revisited in May of 1999 when a Senate resolution restored their credulity posthumously. The following is a summary of the investigation:

> Numerous investigations following the attack on Pearl Harbor have documented that then Admiral Kimmel and then Lieutenant General Short were not provided necessary and critical intelligence that was available, that foretold of war with Japan, that warned of imminent attack, including such essential communiqués as the Japanese Pearl Harbor Bomb Plot message of September 24, 1941,

and the message sent from the Imperial Japanese Foreign Ministry to the Japanese Ambassador in the United States form December 6—7, 1941, known as the Fourteen-Part Message.[40]

One smoking gun, of which there are many, is the diary of Secretary of War Henry Stimson—who contemplated how to maneuver the Japanese into firing the first shot:

> We face the delicate question of the diplomatic fencing to be done so as to be sure Japan is put in the wrong and makes the first bad move — overt move…The question was how we should maneuver them into the position of firing the first shot without allowing too much danger to ourselves.[41]

Just to get another perspective, we will also quote ten facts surrounding the "Day of Infamy" that were compiled by author Jack Monnett. They are:

(1)   Admiral James O. Richardson, Commander-in-Chief of the United States Fleet, was first given the Pearl Harbor command. He objected to the vulnerability of the location, the number of ships to be harbored, and the safety of his men and went directly to the President. He was relieved of his command.

(2)   On October 7, 1940, Lt. Commander Arthur H. McCollum of Naval Intelligence sent a memo to the President listing eight steps to take which would lead to an attack by Japan upon the United States. All were completed by the time of the attack on Pearl Harbor.

(3)   The memo called for a complete embargo on all trade with the United States and Japan and cessation of oil access from Holland—Japan's source of oil.

(4)   The intent of the President and his closest advisors was war in Europe against Germany. Japan, as one of the Axis Powers, was seen as the "back door" into the war. An October 18, 1941,

entry into the diary of Secretary of the Interior Harold Ickes reads, "For a long time I have believed that our best entrance into the war would be by way of Japan."

(5)   The Japanese war codes had been broken and deciphered prior to the attack. On September 24, 1941, Naval Intelligence in Washington, D.C. intercepted a message to Japan's consul-general located in Honolulu asking for the positioning of all naval ships docked at Pearl Harbor.

(6)   The November 25, 1941, diary entry of Secretary of War Henry Stimson reads that the President indicated that a Japanese attack would happen within a few days and asked, "...how we should maneuver them into the position of firing the first shot without too much danger to ourselves. In spite of the risk involved, however, in letting the Japanese fire the first shot, we realized that in order to have the full support of the American people it was desirable to make sure that the Japanese be the ones to do this so that there should remain no doubt in anyone's mind as to who were the aggressors."

(7)   On November 25, 1941, Winston Churchill communicated with President Roosevelt that the Japanese would strike America toward the end of the first week in December.

(8)   On November 26, 1941, two aircraft carriers docked at Pearl Harbor were sent out with fifty planes "as soon as possible" leaving the already vulnerable harbor further weakened in its defenses.

(9)   The New York Times article of December 8, entitled "Attack was expected," said that the United States knew of the attack a week earlier. (Secretary of State Cordell Hull had given the information to reporter Joe Lieb.)

(10)   Winston Churchill in writing later of the war said, "A Japanese attack upon the U.S. was a vast simplification of their problems and their duty. How can we wonder that they regarded the actual form of the attack, or even its scale, as incompletely less

important than the fact that the whole American nation would be united."[42]

Finally, we come to the year 1964, when LBJ found cause to plunge the United States into a bloody and disgraceful war. On August 2 of this fateful year, the *USS Maddox* supposedly engaged three North Vietnamese Navy torpedo boats during a signals intelligence patrol mission in the Gulf of Tonkin. It was alleged that the Vietnamese had fired the first shot in a wave of automatic machine gun fire. The *Maddox* then ostensibly returned fire by expending 280 three and five inch shells, and with the help of USN F-8 Crusader jet fighters, all three torpedo boats were damaged, killing four Vietnamese sailors and wounding six. It was alleged by the NSA that a second battle took place on August 4, which later was discovered to be a fabrication.[43]

In fact, this incident—known as the *Gulf of Tonkin incident*—was a complete anomaly. It didn't happen the way it was reported, yet Congress viewed it as the *casus belli* that justified the passage of the Gulf of Tonkin Resolution, which empowered President Johnson to assist any Southeast Asian country that was in danger of communist aggression. This was used as a pretext for Johnson to deploy troops in North Vietnam. However, what really happened on August 2 was that Captain Herrick of the *Maddox* ordered gun crews to fire on boats that approached within 10,000 yards. In fact, at 1505G the *Maddox* fired off three rounds to warn away the communists, which action was never reported by the Johnson Administration.[44] It was actually the Americans who had fired the first shot, which qualifies the United States as the aggressors of the Vietnam War. The August 4 incident never actually happened. Although it was claimed that the *Maddox* responded to Intel from sonar and radar signals that they were under attack by the Vietnamese, and had engaged and sunk two opposing ships, no wreckage, bodies, or any other evidence of a battle was discovered. Later reports and statements verify this premise. President Johnson himself admitted privately that, "For all I know, our Navy was shooting at whales out there." Secretary of State Robert S. McNamara—in a taped conversation of a meeting with President Johnson weeks after the Gulf of Tonkin Resolution passed—expressed doubts as to the validity of the attack. And in a 2003 documentary called the *Fog of War* he admitted frankly that the event never occurred.[45] Finally, in 2005, NSA historian Robert J. Hanyok concluded that the NSA purposefully distorted the Intelligence surrounding the August 4 event.[46]

Conclusion

The scriptures reveal that these types of false flag events will happen during the last days. The Lord, in His wisdom, has given us the account of Amalickiah—who engaged in a false flag event to murder the king of the Lamanites, usurped his kingdom, and then initiated a war with the Nephites. Amalickiah did this because he was obsessed with power and wanted to exercise unrighteous dominion over his subjects, much like government leaders of today. The scriptures are replete with warnings that the last days will be marked by wars and rumors of wars, and it is not unreasonable to assume that false flag events fall into the category of rumors (unfounded allegations) intended to start wars. There are also a myriad of examples throughout history that teach us that governments have been doing this for thousands of years. In fact, Hitler staged an attack on his own Reichstag building and blamed it on the Russians to use as a pretext to violate his nonaggression pact made with Stalin. This is simply the *modus operandi* of how oppressive governments function. In order for a person to see this in their own government, the blinders of nationalism have to be removed and intellectual honesty must guide their studies. Otherwise, there is a good chance that such a person will be deceived, and did the Lord not say that in the last days even "the very elect"[47] shall be deceived?

Chapter Ten Notes and Sources

1. Alma 47:4
2. Alma 47:6

3. Alma 47:8

4. Alma 47:15

5. Alma 47:26

6. Alma 47:27

7. Alma 48:4

8. 1 Nephi 19:23

9. http://en.wikipedia.org/wiki/False_flag

10. An essay *called Lincoln and the First Shot: A Study of Deceit and Deception,* by John V. Denson, in the book *Reassessing the Presidency,* Edited by John V. Denson, Mises Institute, 2001, pp. 237-240)

11. *Ibid,* p. 245

12. *Ibid,* pp. 246-247

13. *Ibid,* p. 262

14. *Ibid,* pp. 251, 263-264

15. *Ibid,* pp. 274-75

16. *Ibid,* p. 277

17. Denson, Reassessing the Presidency, pp. 259-60

18. http://en.wikipedia.org/wiki/USS_Maine_%28ACR-1%29

19. http://www.homeofheroes.com/wallofhonor/spanish_am/02_maine.html

20. http://www2.gwu.edu/~nsarchiv/news/20010430/northwoods.pdf

21. http://www.youtube.com/watch?v=s3aglqh-vog

22. Quoted in Raico, Great Wars and Great Leaders: A Libertarian Rebuttal, p. 67

23. Quoted in *Ibid,* p. 27

24. Quoted in *Ibid,* p. 67

25. Denson, Reassessing the Presidency, p. 484

26. Jack Monnett, *Awakening To Our Awful Situation; Warnings From the Nephite Prophets,* Nauvoo House Publishing, Heber City, UT, 2006, p. 143

27. Denson, Reassessing the Presidency, p. 485

28. *Ibid*

29. See Sutton, *National Suicide: Military Aid to the Soviet Union,* Arlington House, New Rochelle, N.Y., 1973

30. Denson, Reassessing the Presidency, p. 485-86

31. Stevenson, *A Man Called Intrepid: The Secret War* (New York: Ballantine, 1976)

32. *Ibid,* pp. 486-87

33. Mormon 8:29-30, Emphasis added

34. Denson, Reassessing the Presidency, pp. 491, 501

35. Stinnett, *Day of Deceit,* Chapter 4

36. Denson, Reassessing the Presidency, p. 503

37. Stinnett, *Day of Deceit,* p. 152

38. Kimmel as quoted in Denson, *Reassessing the Presidency,* p. 507

39. *Ibid,* p.515

40. Senate Congressional Record, p. 5878

41. Stimson, *Infamy, Pearl Harbor and Its Aftermath,* Oct. 16, 1941, pp. 275-76

42. Monnett, Awakening To Our Awful Situation, pp. 148-49

43. http://en.wikipedia.org/wiki/Gulf_of_Tonkin_incident

44. *Ibid*

45. http://www.youtube.com/watch?v=nwXF6UdkeI4

46. http://en.wikipedia.org/wiki/Gulf_of_Tonkin_incident

47. Joseph Smith—Mathew 1:22

Chapter 11

Betrayal at Yalta: Fruits of the Last "Good War"

Wherefore take heed, my brethren, that ye do not judge that which is evil to be of God, or that which is good and of God to be of the devil.

-Moroni

There is a myth that abounds in the lecture halls of American schools and universities, conservative think tanks, the mainstream media, and many American households; it is the myth of the last "good war." WWII is reverenced by liberals and conservatives alike as a grandiose crusade of right *vs.* wrong, in almost pietistic and sanctimonious rhetoric. Unfortunately, these good *vs.* evil semantics have even percolated into the vocabularies of Latter-day Saints who have scriptures that teach them to know better. The war that captain Moroni fought against the Lamanites can only be construed as defensive, while WWII was an aggressive war that ultimately resulted in the communistic enslavement of at least one-third of the world. We have already discussed the preemptive means Roosevelt employed to provoke the Japanese into firing the first shot—thereby allowing the U.S. to enter this "holy war"—but what of his antics in conducting it, specifically the special treatment of his ally "Uncle Joe" Stalin? The focus of this chapter will be to lay the "good war" myth to rest by exposing the fruits of it.

In the *Book of Mormon,* the prophet Moroni teaches us the way to judge whether something, or someone, is good or evil. He teaches us that we are all given the light of Christ, which is a built-in mechanism for discerning the true motives of people and policies, and the true meaning of doctrines and philosophies. There are various ways and means by which we can be deceived, yet if we are always on our guard then the light of Christ will help us to avoid deception. One particular method Satan uses to deceive us is to make us think that something is good, when in fact it is evil, and *vice versa*—as with jingoism. Perhaps in no subject has he been so successful in this endeavor than in that of war, for he has managed to convince the majority of the population that war (*i.e.* mass murder and catastrophic destruction) is actually a "good" thing. He tells us that we owe our allegiance to the state even when its actions are evil—causing us to partake of those evils; that to kill others is our duty, that war is good for the economy, that it brings us together in unity, that we need to sacrifice our freedoms for security, and other such nonsense. Thankfully, we have the *Book of Mormon* to help us see through this hazy smokescreen. Moroni expounds as follows:

> For behold, a bitter fountain cannot bring forth good water; neither can a good fountain bring forth bitter water; wherefore, a man being a servant of the devil cannot follow Christ; and if he follow Christ he cannot be a servant of the devil. Wherefore, all things which are good cometh of God; and that which is evil cometh of the devil; for the devil is an enemy unto God, and fighteth against him continually, and inviteth and enticeth to sin, and to do that which is evil continually. But behold, that which is of God inviteh and enticeth to do good continually; wherefore, every thing which inviteth and enticeth to do good, and to love God, and to serve him, is inspired of God. Wherefore take heed, my brethren, that ye do not judge that which is evil to be of God, or that which is good and of God to be of the devil.

The fruits of the Nephite war of defense against the Lamanites were peace, liberty, freedom of religion, the mass conversion of Lamanite POWs, and the restoration of Nephite lands and property. The fruits of WWII, however, were the enslavement of hundreds of millions of Eastern European peoples, a massive buildup of Soviet military power, the Cold War, and mass infiltration of Soviet spies into the American government (Elizabeth Bentley, Whittaker Chambers, Harry Dexter White, *et al*). The story we are going to tell here is one that will not be told in establishment schools, but it is nevertheless true. It begins in 1938 when Roosevelt made a secret military-information agreement with Stalin and Molotov. This agreement is summarized in a confidential State Department report (800.51 W 89.U.S.S.R./247) written by Soviet Union Ambassador Joseph E. Davies. Only four persons were privy to the Roosevelt-Stalin agreement; the President, the Secretary and Undersecretary of State, and Lieutenant Colonel Philip R. Faymonville—the liaison officer. Davies explains that he was authorized to seek the advice of a Mr. Sidney Weinberg—a New York banker—to decide how to financially aid the Soviets at extremely low interest rates. This was the beginning of the Lend-Lease program. Davies explains that:

> In January 1938, and prior to my departure for the Soviet Union, the President directed me to explore the possibility of *securing a liaison between the military and naval authorities of the United States and the Soviet Union* with a view to the inter-change of information as to the facts with reference to the military and naval situations of the United States and the Soviet Union vis-à-vis Japan and the general Far Eastern and Pacific problem.[2]

Roosevelt—who became somewhat infatuated with "Uncle Joe" Stalin—was eager for the U.S. to "familiarize" itself with the Soviet Union because of supposedly shared "similarity of purposes and necessities,"[3] whatever that means. Keep in mind that by this time Stalin had already executed and starved millions of kulaks. Why would the U.S.

want anything to do with such a monster? It turns out that not only did Roosevelt want to form an alliance with this miscreant, he actually gave him virtually *everything* he asked for while expecting *nothing* in return. Here is a list—compiled by Antony Sutton—of some of these war items that under the Lend-Lease program were given to the Soviet regime, which took priority even over American and Allied war fronts:

> 4700 tanks… requested 20,000 submachine guns—and were offered 98,220… 14,018 aircraft… [Including all types of bombers] 466,968 individual vehicles… combat vehicles included 1239 light tanks, 4957 medium tanks, about 2000 self-propelled guns, 1104 half-tracks, 2054 armored scout cars. The 2,293 ordinance vehicles included 1534 field-repair trucks and 629 tank-transporters. Trucks included 47,728 jeeps, 24,564 ¾-ton trucks, 148,664 1 ½-ton trucks, 182,938 2 ½-ton trucks… 32,200 motorcycles and 7,570 track-laying tractors with 3,216 spare tractor engines… A total of 325,784 tons of explosives was sent, which included 129,667 tons of smokeless powder and 129,138 tons of TNT. Wireless communication equipment included no less than 35,779 radio stations including… 705 radio direction finders, 528 radio altimeters, 800 radio compasses, and 63 radio beacons… Construction machinery valued at over $10 million included $5,599,000 worth of road- and aircraft-construction equipment, $2,459,000 in tractor-mounted equipment, $2,099,000 of mixers and pavers, and $635,000 of railroad-construction equipment. Railroad equipment included 1,900 steam locomotives, 66 diesel-electric locomotives, 9,920 flat cars, 1,000 dump cars, 120 tank cars, and 35 heavy-machinery cars, for a total of 13,041 railroad units. Other military items included 15 cableway bridges, 5 portable pipelines, 62 portable storage tanks, 100,000 flashlights with dry cells, and 13 pontoon bridges… naval and marine equipment included… 90 dry-cargo vessels, 10 oceangoing tankers, 9 Wye tankers, 3 icebreakers, 20 tugboats, 1 steam schooner, 2,398 pneumatic floats, 1 motor launch, and 2 floating repair shops. Combat ships sent to the Soviet Union included 46

110 foot submarine chasers, 57 65 ft. submarine chasers, 175 torpedo boats, 77 minesweepers, 28 frigates, 52 small landing craft, 8 tank-landing craft, 6 cargo barges. The marine-propulsion machinery included 3,320 marine diesel engines, 4,297 marine gasoline engines, 108 wooden gas engines, and 2,150 outboard motors, $254,000 worth of shafting and ship propellers, $50,000 worth of steering gear, 40 storage batteries for submarines, and parts and equipment (valued at $2,744,000) for marine-propulsion machinery. Special marine equipment included $1,047,000 worth of salvage stations and diving gear, $109,000 worth of jetting apparatus, a submarine rescue chamber, distilling apparatus valued at $36,000, and miscellaneous special shipping valued at $44,000. Also sent were trawling equipment for minesweepers valued at $3,778,000, mechanical and electrical equipment for tugboats valued at $545,000, and mechanical and electrical equipment for ferry boats valued at $1,717,000. A large quantity of naval artillery and ammunition included 1,849 Oerlikon guns and $2,692,000 worth of equipment for naval guns.[4]

Roosevelt's unnatural adulation for Stalin was perhaps a fascination of the great power he was able to wield, or that he a willing participant in FDR's pipe dream to abrogate war, and potentially borders, by the establishment of the United Nations. Stalin, however, wanted to use the UN as a tool to push international communism, something the naïve Roosevelt turned a blind eye to. In fact, Roosevelt was able to overlook and sweep under the rug a host of Soviet atrocities—including the 1939 Katyn Forest Massacre, when Russian forces took fifteen thousand captured Polish officers and executed them in cold blood. Roosevelt definitely knew of the incident, and tacitly suppressed a potential investigation of that mass murder.[5] Vigorously pushing the agenda of Soviet/American entente, Roosevelt went far beyond the restraints of reason by actually invoking Article 124 of the Russian constitution, which was a supposed guaranty of freedom of religion. The truth is that Roosevelt knew that right didn't exist in

Russia, as did everybody else, but still used the lie to advance the campaign for Soviet alliance in the war.[6]

At Casablanca—where Roosevelt and Harry Hopkins met with Churchill in 1943—the unconditional surrender of Germany and Japan was discussed. Roosevelt very much favored this policy, as did Stalin because it would give him great political advantage after the war was over. Germany had already tasted of the bitter fruit of the terms of unconditional surrender at Versailles and Japan was simply not willing to accept such terms.[7] At the November 1943 meeting held in Tehran, Iran, FDR capitulated to Stalin on virtually everything he asked for. Although Congress passed an act in 1940 granting independence to the Baltic States, Roosevelt acquiesced to Stalin in regards to Estonia, Latvia, Lithuania, and the eastern portion of Poland remaining under Soviet control. Churchill—who was also present at the meeting—agreed, along with Roosevelt, to Stalin's plan for Poland without even consulting the Polish people or its constitutional government. Marshal Stalin's plan was to annex all land east of the Curzon Line, ultimately seizing seventy thousand square miles of Polish territory.[8]

Roosevelt was promised by the shrewd Stalin that democratic elections would prevail in his newly acquired territories, which included Czechoslovakia and Yugoslavia. These elections, of course, were conducted "Soviet style," which meant that they were "free" to vote for Soviet occupation. The hypocritical Roosevelt—in writing to the Polish prime minister, Mikolajczyk—would promise (in spite of his agreement with Stalin) that "the United States stands unequivocally for a strong, free, and independent Polish state with the untrammeled right of the Polish people to order their internal existence as they see fit."[9] What he neglected to tell Mikolajczyk was that the Polish people had the right to self-government as long as it was sanctioned by the occupying Soviet dictatorship. Needless to say, less than two months after Yalta, the Soviets reneged on their promises to guarantee free elections.

Roosevelt had an immense desire to be respected and liked, and for some strange reason sought the deference of Stalin—the reprobate dictator who, prior to his rise to power, was a "fundraiser" (actually a bank robber) for the Bolsheviks and personally shot and killed 47 people. Yuri Maltsev—a former adviser in the Soviet government—relates an incident at Tehran that would have appalled most Americans had they known of it:

> In the midst of many toasts and jokes, Stalin proposed a toast to killing fifty thousand German officers and technicians as soon as they were captured. Churchill was aghast; he announced that the British would not sanction such butchery. Next, the great diplomat Franklin D. Roosevelt chimed in with a compromise: "We should settle on a smaller number, Shall we say 49,500?" When the president's son, Elliot, rose in agreement with Stalin's plan, Prime Minister Churchill left the table, surrounded by the laughter of Russians and Americans.10

By the time of the Yalta Conference in February 1945, most of the negotiations had already been settled upon, although clandestinely. Harry Hopkins—in a verbal display of "heartfelt compassion"—told Roosevelt that, "the Russians have given us so much at this conference that I don't think we should let them down."[11] Maltsev asks:

> What had Stalin given? He had agreed that in the new United Nations, the Soviet Union would have only three votes—one for the USSR, one for the Soviet Ukraine, and one for the Soviet White Russia—instead of sixteen votes, or one for each of the Soviet Republics.12

Roosevelt's pact with Stalin, much like the classic deal with the devil, was to sell his soul and his country for literally nothing in return. John T. Flynn—author of *The Roosevelt Myth*—asserts that Stalin's "policy was to commit himself to nothing, to admit nothing, and to demand and demand and demand."[13] Maltsev maintains that at a 1945 Yugoslavia Communist Delegation, Stalin toasted with Marshal Tito and other guests that "this war is not in the past; whoever occupies a territory also imposes on it his own social system."[14] Ironically, in the aftermath of WWII (the supposed crusade to free a few million Jews from Nazi aggression) an additional 800 million people were enslaved to one of the most despotic regimes in all of history, including many more Hebrews who were still persecuted by Stalin and his ilk. As there were only 170 million people in the Soviet Union prior to this time, FDR's naivety and blind persistence to his pipe dream of world peace through the United Nations actually assisted Stalin in the quadrupling of his subjects. One has to wonder what the Polio stricken president's motives were in pursuing such an odd alliance.

In recent years, G. Edward Griffin conducted an interview with a Russian defector named Alexander Contract. Contract—a Jew—became a bodyguard and secret agent for Nikita Khruschev (who was a member of the Communist Party under Stalin) when he was very young. He was wounded fighting on the front lines against the Germans, and during his recovery in the hospital he asked Khruschev for a special favor. Because his wound required months to heal, he asked if he could be moved to the Kremlin as a guard for Stalin. His request was granted and upon meeting Stalin—who learned that he spoke eleven dialects—was made his personal spy. He spied on everybody; members of the communist party, commissars, language interpreters, *et al.* When Roosevelt made his way to the Tehran conference, the Soviets started a rumor that Nazi spies were planning an assassination attempt on the president. This they did for the purpose of getting a meeting alone with the president without Churchill around. Stalin offered Roosevelt his protection and hospitality, which was accepted, and a meeting was set up in which only three people would be present; Roosevelt, Stalin, and Contract. Prior to the meeting, Stalin ordered Contract to get pictures of Nazi ghettos, concentrations camps, railways, bridges and crematoriums where Jews were being exterminated. He was to compile these pictures into a folder and present them to FDR.

Stalin told Contract that when the meeting started he would tell Roosevelt that he had a "tummy ache" and had to go to the bathroom. Contract was to then tell Roosevelt that he was a Jew, that Stalin didn't know he was a Jew, and then to take the folder out of his briefcase, show him the pictures, and ask him to consider what the Nazi's were doing to the Jews in Europe. He then pleaded with the president to bomb the ghettos, concentration camps, railways, bridges, and crematoriums where his people were being murdered. He told the president that his planes could fly from Italy to Russia, and that he would ask Stalin to refuel them so they could drop more bombs. FDR's curt reply was cold and calculated. He shoved the folder back to Contract and said, "I did not come here to help Jews, I came to help Uncle Joe."[15] We can see here the amorality with which Roosevelt conducted the war. He was not willing to bomb targets that were being used for the genocide of Jews, yet he offered no objections to Churchill's indiscriminate bombings of Dresden, or General LeMay's firebombing of Tokyo. Evidently, he had no true principles, and his main objective was the establishment of the United Nations, which was the "greater good" that justified the rampant murder throughout the war.

Another great tragedy of WWII was the communist subversion of China and her 450 million people. There had been a civil war raging in China since 1931 between nationalist and communist forces. The Nationalist Government of China was under the dictatorship of Chiang Kai-Shek, who was in favor of setting up a democratic constitution, restoring civil rights, and granting freedom of the press. The Nationalists' biggest threat to peace was the Chinese Communists in the northwest who were led by a man named Mao Tse-tung. Mao had agreed to meet with Chiang and discuss a peace settlement where he acquiesced to Chiang's proposal for establishing a democracy—although somewhat superficially. At any rate, prospects for peace were looking good until it came to the knowledge of the Kai-Shek regime that FDR and Churchill, "at Yalta had agreed to give Russia extensive property rights in Manchuria if the Soviets would join the war against Japan."[16]

The Chinese government, which was still fighting the Japanese invaders, had not even been consulted by the Allied forces. Manchuria was rich in agricultural resources, which proved to be a great boon to

Stalin—who began looting the area of its heavy industry in spite of a treaty he had made with Chiang that he would recognize the Nationalist Government if Chiang would give him "half ownership in the Manchurian railroads and the right to lease Port Arthur as a Russian Naval base."[17] Still, Chiang (realizing the mistake he made in negotiating with the Russian despot) continued endeavoring to set up a constitutional form of government. In a speech delivered in 1945 to the Preparatory Commission for Constitutional Government in Chungking, Chiang said the following:

> You will recall that in 1936 the Government decided to summon a National Assembly on November 12, 1937 for the inauguration of constitutional government and the termination of the period of political tutelage under the Kuomintang. On July 7, 1937, Japan suddenly made war on us, and the plan had to be shelved. However, the determination of the Kuomintang to realize constitutional government remained as strong as ever. Had it not been for the recommendation of further postponement by the People's Political Council, the National Assembly would have been convened during 1940 in accordance with another Government decision. This year, on the first of January, on behalf of the Government, I announced that the National Assembly will be summoned before the close of the year, unless untoward and unexpected military developments should in the meanwhile intervene.18

Unfortunately, Chiang's dream of Constitutional Government was not realized due to American meddling. U.S. diplomats who saw the UN as an organization that would preserve world peace decided that Chiang's Nationalists were more of a threat than the Red Chinese and so denounced his resistance against them. They saw Mao and his communists as "potentially peaceful" and claimed that they "had no territorial ambition."[19] An interesting assumption on the part of U.S. diplomats who were under the influence and tutelage of a myriad of communist agents scattered throughout Washington. A popular myth among Americans is that the UN is a peacekeeping organization with only the noblest intentions. However, the truth is that most of the Undersecretaries of the UN during that epoch were communists or communist sympathizers who "would not" be biased when choosing sides in a conflict.[20] In fact, the bias was so bad that Chiang couldn't convince the U.S. that he was justified in retaking territory that had been seized by the communists.

Ignoring all demands from Washington, Chiang reciprocated after the Reds had continually violated the truce, and led a counterattack in Manchuria in the summer of 1946. Chiang was determined to subdue the communists and resume his plans to establish a constitutional form of government. However, the State Department put the kibosh on his designs by issuing three unconditional cease-fires, slapping him with a U.S. embargo on all aid to China, and disarming 39 anti-Communist divisions stationed in China.[21] Needless to say, the Communists gained the upper hand, and by 1947 Nationalist morale was wasting away. At around this time, a man named General Albert C. Wedemeyer was sent to Asia by President Truman to investigate what was happening in China. Upon his return, he issued a report that came to be known as the Wedemeyer Report. W. Cleon Skousen explains the findings of the report as follows:

> He [Wedemeyer] indicated that not only had the interests of free China been violated, but the self-interests of the United States and her Allies had been subordinated to the whims of the Communists. He recommended prompt and voluminous aid to the Nationalist Government and predicted that the situation could still be salvaged if help were provided in time.22

Wedemeyer's report was not only disregarded, it was filed away in the depths of the State Department and not to surface again for about two years—by which time it was too late for Chiang. By 1949, the Communists had taken over and were setting up the People's Republic of China, forcing Chiang to flee to Formosa with what was left of his ragged armies. In an audacious move that drove the knife yet deeper into Chiang's back, the U.S. State Department held a meeting in October of that year where it was decided that foreign aid would be offered to Mao Tse-tung. Among those present at the meeting were Philip Jessup (State Department), Dr. John Leighton, and Harold Stassen. Skousen outlines the policies decided upon as follows:

(1) European aid should be given priority over Asia.

(2) Aid to Asia should not be started until after a "long and careful study."

(3) Russian Communists should be considered "not as aggressive as Hitler" and "not as apt to take direct military action to expand their empire."

(4) Communist China should be recognized by the U.S.

(5) Britain and India should be urged to follow suit in recognizing the Chinese Communists.

(6) The Chinese Communists should be allowed to take over Formosa.

(7) The Communists should be allowed to take over Hong Kong from Britain if the Communists insisted.

(8) Nehru (Prime Minister of India) should not be given aid because of his "reactionary and arbitrary tendencies."

(9) The Nationalist blockade of China should be broken and economic aid sent to the Communist mainland.

(10) No aid should be sent to Chiang or to the anti-Communist guerillas in South China.[23]

Secretary of State Dean Acheson made a statement three months after the conference that U.S. protection could not be afforded to South Korea or Formosa, leaving former allies defenseless in the wake of aggressive Communist empire expansion.[24] This policy—along with the Lend-Lease program, the betrayal of Eastern bloc nations at Yalta, and the ensuing Chinese betrayal—led directly to the Cold War. It should not surprise the reader that the first place the communists choose to attack was South Korea. Churchill and Roosevelt had already capitulated to Soviet occupation of North Korea during the Yalta meeting, and Stalin was licking his chops at South Korea. U.S. troops occupied the newly created Republic up to the 38th parallel, whose 96,000 native troops were no match for their Northern counterparts consisting of 187,000 men assisted by Russian military might. The UN mandated that both the Russians and the Americans withdraw their troops—however, on June 25, 1950 the Northern Red Korean Army invaded Seoul, which inaugurated the Korean War. The Soviets—who were absent from the UN Security Council—were mandated to retreat while Truman authorized General Douglas MacArthur to send U.S. troops in from Japan to repeal the Red threat. Thus the Cold War had begun.[25]

General MacArthur was subsequently given command of the UN forces and prepared a surprise attack on the communists. The U.S. Navy would launch an invasion at Inchon, where 29 ft. tides gave the Korean Communists a false sense of security. MacArthur would lead U.S. and UN forces in a sweeping victory. However, when he pursued the retreating army to the North, the United States government would begin to intervene. Intelligence was withheld from MacArthur, which stagnated his progress, yet, regardless of this neglect, his armies managed to push the North Koreans close to the Yalu River. Just as the war seemed to be approaching its end, the Chinese sent an army of one million communists across the river, which pushed MacArthur and his troops back to the 38th parallel. MacArthur was appalled when he learned that he would not be able to retaliate with air strikes and would be relegated to "limited" warfare. He was also not allowed to bomb the Yalu Bridge, which the Chinese were using to funnel in troops and supplies to kill his men, neither was he allowed to destroy the Manchurian Railroad, which brought supplies to the bridge. He learned that the State Department was diverting supplies to Europe at his expense, and that Chiang Kai-shek had offered to send thousands of troops from Formosa to assist and was flatly denied by the U.S.

government. Skousen explains MacArthur's actions over the next few months:

> Over a period of four months General MacArthur watched the slaughter resulting from these stalemate policies. Finally, he could contain himself no longer. He violated a presidential gag order dated December 6, 1950, and answered a written inquiry from Congressman Joseph W. Martin concerning the inexplicable reverses which UN forces were suffering in Korea. The General's letter giving recommendations for the winning of the war was read in Congress April 5, 1951, and five days later, President Truman ordered MacArthur summarily withdrawn from all commands.[26]

MacArthur's sudden dismissal from military command very well could have delayed the duration of the war and cost the United States more casualties. The policy of "Communist Containment" was adopted, which pitted the U.S and UN forces against the communists—perpetuating a physical war that could not be won. The armistice didn't come until 1953 upon the death of Stalin. This foreign entanglement had cost the United States $20 billion and 135,000 casualties, while the South Koreans lost over a million, with another million wounded or maimed and nine million homeless.[27] How ironic that MacArthur was inhibited by communist agents who had infiltrated the State Department and communist sympathizers in the UN while attempting to defend the South Koreans against communist aggressors. The Vietnam debacle was also a consequence of communist control of Indochina and was another war in which the United States was not allowed to win. It seems as though the U.S. government has created its own enemies by allying with the Russians, building up their military with foreign aid, and then fighting against those same weapons that were sent in the first place while not being allowed to win physical conflicts against them. The whole thing is absurd. Yet, if we had just followed the advice of the "wise men" of the founding generation by avoiding "entangling alliances," preemptive war, and wars of aggression, then millions of lives could have been saved, enemies would not have been created, and millions more could have been spared lives of slavery suffered behind the Iron Curtain.

Conclusion

Indeed, the last "good war" was not good at all. It was, in fact, a worldwide abomination accompanied by a slew of political corruption and collusion. Fraught with deceit, espionage, and betrayal, it consigned millions to the clutches of despotic tyrants and despicable states. It inaugurated a thirty-year war marked by hysteria and fear of an enemy that was created and built up by American industry, corporations, and tax dollars. It led to the CIA creation of al-Qaeda in an effort to suppress a Soviet invasion of Afghanistan in 1979—the same al-Qaeda that became the new "boogie-man" after the fall of the Red empire. Perhaps worst of all, the last "good war" has deceived millions of Americans into justifying and legitimizing mass murder. Many have mentally capitulated to the lie that Hiroshima and Nagasaki were justified in order to save lives. Many others would vindicate General LeMay's firebombing of Tokyo, Churchill's butchery in Dresden, the savagery of Operation Keelhaul, or the millions of French, German, Belgium, and Russian civilians that were killed, maimed, or otherwise abused. Perhaps they would rationalize that these are the costs of war, yet in doing so they fail to see the true casualties of war: *morality, humanity, civilization, and Christianity.*

Chapter Eleven Notes and Sources

1. Moroni 7: 11-14
2. Sutton, *National Suicide*, p. 80-81, Emphasis added
3. Ibid
4. *Ibid*, pp. 82-84

5. Yuri N. Maltsev and Barry Dean Simpson, Despotism Loves Company: The Story of Roosevelt and Stalin, an essay in Reassessing the Presidency, Edited by John V. Denson, p. 530

6. *Ibid,* p. 531-32

7. *Ibid,* p. 536

8. Arthur Bliss Lane, *I Saw Poland Betrayed,* Western Islands, Boston, LA, 1948, p. 41, Arthur Bliss Lane was the United States Ambassador to Poland 1944-1947

9. *Ibid,* pp. 41-42

10. Denson, Reassessing the Presidency, p. 539

11. *Ibid,* p. 541

12. *Ibid*

13. Quoted in *Ibid,* p. 543

14. Quoted in *Ibid,* p. 542

15. G. Edward Griffin, I Was A Spy for Stalin, A Close-Up View of History, The Testimony of Alexander Contract, *http://www.youtube.com/watch?v=q-6c2sFuT0s&list=PL99FD142B65FF20E1*

16. W. Cleon Skousen, *The Naked Communist,* The Ensign Publishing Co., Salt Lake City, UT, 1958, pp. 179-80

17. *Ibid,* pp. 180-81

18. http://www.milestonedocuments.com/documents/view/chiang-kai-shek-speech-before-the-preparatory-commission-for-constitutional/text

19. Skousen, *The Naked Communist,* p. 182

20. See, G. Edward Griffin, *The Fearful Master, A Second Look At The United Nations,* Western Island Publishers, Boston and LA, 1964

21. Skousen, The Naked Communist, p. 183

22. *Ibid,* pp. 184-85

23. *Ibid,* pp. 187-88

24. *Ibid,* pp. 188-89

25. *Ibid,* pp. 189-90

26. *Ibid,* pp. 191-92

27. *Ibid,* p. 193

Chapter 12

Waging War on Ideologies: A Dangerous Delusion
No nation could preserve its freedom in the midst of continual warfare.
-James Madison

Perhaps in no other activity does government deceive its subjects more than in war. It is bad enough when a state declares war on a nation or another state, but worse yet when aggression is waged upon ideologies, or abstractions. A nation or country is a real, tangible place with real people and real things. Ideas—such as poverty and terror—are conceptions and perceptions in our minds, and as such are intangible and incorporeal. A war waged on a nation usually always comes to an end (even though countries like the U.S. prefer to leave occupying soldiers in place long after the conflict is over); however, a war declared on an idea can last indefinitely. In George Orwell's epic novel *1984,* Big Brother and the Party continually brainwash their subjects with the phrase, "perpetual war for perpetual peace." This misleading maxim— fraught with nanny-state doublespeak—is used by the government as a fear-mongering device to keep its constituents in continual terror and obedience. Big Brother is constantly engaging in false flag operations by bombing his own nation of Oceania and blaming it on East Asia or Eurasia. Of course, the slaves who reside in Oceania are kept in continual fear of these "enemies" and are obliged to submit to the draconian laws of the Party, which they believe are necessary for their own safety. In other words, they have given up their liberty for security. Each home is furnished with a television set (keep in mind the novel was written in 1948) with two-way screens. Every time big brother addresses Oceania all people are required to listen to the propaganda and there is hardly a corner of each house that the government is not able to keep under strict surveillance. Each person is issued a job by the State, and every morning is required to subject themselves to a two-minute hate speech about their supposed enemies, which include the two other nations, and any potential domestic political dissidents. Orwell's novel is both prolific and prophetic—for he managed to predict the almost exact situation American's find themselves in today, including the two-way televisions (skype *et al*). The War on Terror has been the vehicle that has brought this American plight on—a war declared against an abstraction in which enemy combatants are vaguely defined, thereby granting the government the power to potentially label anyone a "terrorist."

In this novel, Orwell describes the bureaucratic agency that oversees the rehabilitation of political dissidents as the *Ministry of Love*. This ministry engages in the compulsory reeducation and "healing" of those who are "sick" (*i.e.*, those who disagree with Big Brother). Dissidents are kidnapped by the government and subjected to "treatment" (torture) until they are "persuaded" to love Big Brother (i.e., the welfare, warfare, big government spy-state). Citizens are encouraged to spy on their neighbors and report any signs of disaffection with the Party or its platform. In America today there exists a precursor to Orwell's Ministry of Love, it is called the Department of Homeland Security. Created in response to the September 11th attacks, this cabinet is directly controlled by the Commander-in-Chief, and has morphed into a bureaucratic monstrosity with over 200,000 employees. With a purported purpose of providing security from terrorists, this agency mostly engages in the destruction of God-given rights such as are found in the 1st, 4th, 5th, and 6th Amendments. DHS controls several smaller agencies that do its dirty work. One of these—The Transportation Security Agency (TSA)—engrosses itself in the groping, probing, and irradiation of innocent persons seeking to fly on airplanes. TSA employees reserve the "right" to isolate and screen any person they deem to be a threat. Screening procedures include pat down searches, radioactive photographs that reveal private parts, and the occasional body cavity search. These are violations of the 4th Amendment law against "unreasonable searches and seizures" and actually do not help any of us become safer. As Benjamin Franklin once said, "those who would give up essential liberty, to purchase a little temporary safety, deserve neither liberty, nor safety."[1]

Security is, in fact, a grand illusion. It does not and cannot exist in this mortal world. We live in a world of continual uncertainty, whether we are referring to economics, safety, or longevity. The government cannot guarantee anyone's safety, regardless of how many billions of dollars Congress pours into the DHS, wars of aggression, or airport strip searches. The fact is that the government has grossly failed in this department, 9/11/2001 and 9/11/2011 being ample evidence of its incompetency. How ironic that a nation with the most powerful military in the world could not even defend its own Department of Defense building on the fateful morning of 9/11/2001. How ironic that NORAD—whose reaction time was usually within minutes—lethargically delayed its response until it was too late. Yet, the absurd argument put forth by the government goes like this, "because we failed miserably on 9/11 to protect you, we need to adopt draconian legislation giving us more power to protect you for your own good." Yet, history teaches us (especially the Russian part), that granting government more power only results in the destruction of liberty and, in many cases, life (about 120 million persons have been killed by their own governments during the 20th century). How many have Islamic terrorists killed, and even then how many of those were pawns of corrupt governments? We Americans must ask ourselves; are we exempt from the lessons of history?

Another agency under the tutelage of the DHS is the Federal Emergency Management Agency (FEMA). FEMA was allegedly created to assist civilians with natural disasters, yet the survivors of Hurricane

Katrina were anything but "assisted" by this militant association. Guns were confiscated, food rationed with starvation rampant, and human beings were herded into "safe" areas and treated like prisoners. This organization is a violation of the *Posse Comitatus* Act of 1878, which prohibited federal U.S. military personnel from acting like domestic policemen on U.S. soil. There is, in fact, nothing Constitutional about FEMA or the DHS, who have been training domestic police as paramilitary troops in order to centralize power in the general government and create a behemoth police state complete with check points, warrantless searches, and indefinite detention. This all serves to create the illusion of security, though in reality it only gives us another whole set of terrorists to worry about—namely, the U.S. government. Billy Joe Armstrong—lead singer of Green Day—begged a question in one of his songs that neoconservatives who support the American police state should ask themselves; "is the cop or am I the one who's really dangerous?"

The National Security Agency (NSA), is perhaps the most invasive into the personal lives of American citizens. Burdened with the task of collecting intelligence, this leviathan bureaucracy engages in the mass surveillance of American phone conversations, and—through subversive software—their computer data. They can track credit card and bank transactions, online purchases, Facebook activity, Google accounts, and a myriad of other violations of privacy. A gross infraction of the 4th Amendment mandate ensuring "the right of the people to be secure in their persons, houses, papers, and effects," this domestic spying is most reprehensible. It is shameful what the government is able to get away with in the name of "national security."

The USA Patriot Act (passed in the wake of 9/11 by a terrified House and Senate) served to annihilate the remnants of the Bill of Rights protection against unwarranted searches and seizures, cruel and unusual punishment, and indefinite detention. This legislation granted the police the power to arrest without a warrant or even probable cause, and to detain indefinitely without trial (a violation of *habeas corpus*) on the grounds that the suspect *might* be a terrorist. Although many Americans offer the inane argument that "you shouldn't be worried if you have nothing to hide," that assertion is problematic. Because the term *terrorist* is an abstraction the government can precede the word with any adjective they choose. For example, what is stopping them from inserting the word Christian, or right-wing extremist, or domestic, or radical, or revolutionary, or fringe in front of the word terrorist? The answer is nothing except the "good will" of those who are wielding such illegitimate power. This is the reason why the War on Terror is so dangerous to liberty. They may as well have declared war on the Boogieman, Count Dracula, Yosemite Sam, or any other entity that we can only imagine in our heads. The word *terrorist* is not a single person, nation, or thing, it is virtually anything the government wants it to be. George W. Bush—when addressing a joint session of Congress nine days after the fall of the Twin Towers—himself asserted that this war would not end until an utter impossibility would be accomplished; the eradication of terrorism. He said, "Our war on terror begins with al Qaeda, but it does not end there. It will not end until every terrorist group of global reach has been found, stopped, and defeated."[2]

This logic is based upon a flawed assumption. It is not only *impossible* to accomplish such a global task, there is also no moral justification for it. Other regimes the world over can handle expunging a few ragged terrorists living in caves without assistance, yet the United States does not ask to assist, they take military control of the nation and set up a puppet government while accusing them of harboring enemy combatants. Meanwhile, they arrest and detain suspects all over the world and bring them to Guantanamo Bay off the coast of Cuba to torture them. Do they learn to love the *Big Brother* that is the United States government within this Cuban *Ministry of Love*, or are they simply executed? No one will ever know because they are not permitted to have a public trial. They become anomalies, ghosts, never to seen by their families and friends again as they vanish into the memory hole of this Orwellian nightmare that is unfolding before our eyes.

Finally, we come to the most egregious piece of legislation signed into law by a president who reneged on his campaign promises to bring the troops home, close Guantanamo, and sunset the Patriot Act. On December 31 2011, President Obama signed the National Defense Authorization Act (NDAA), which gave the president *Big Brother*-like powers to bomb and kill American citizens without trial. Thankfully, this can only be done off of American soil for now, but it's just a matter of time before this ghastly behemoth comes to roost at home. Before and since the drafting of this legislation, the president has murdered thousands with drone strikes, although the administration asserts a lowly number—all top al Qaeda leaders, of course. The official line is that great care is taken to avoid civilian casualties, but the evidence suggests that this rhetoric is bogus. It is estimated that about 50 to 100 civilians are killed by every drone that strikes an official target, which has probably resulted in thousands of deaths of both innocents and bad guys. American citizens who have been taken out include Anwar al-Awlaki and his sixteen year-old son—Abdulrahman al-Awlaki—who were killed in Yemen in 2011, Samir Khan—also killed in Yemen—and Jude Mohammed, killed in Pakistan.[3] More appalling still, is that the Obama administration asserted that this power to murder American citizens without trial is "constitutional" in response to lawsuits brought forth by the American Civil Liberties Union and the Center for Constitutional Rights. The official government statement by Paul E. Werner—a trial lawyer in the Justice Department—is riddled with legal drivel. He said that the targeting of Anwar Al-Awlaki was "subject to exceptionally rigorous interagency legal review and determined to be lawful."[4] Exceptionally *rigorous interagency legal review?* Could he be any more vague? Let's be honest here, this was a Soviet-style kangaroo court in which the defendant was not present and the President—apparently assisted by a few agencies—was the judge, jury and executioner. The real tragedy here is that the 4th, 5th, and 6th Amendments are dead, which relegates the United States to a police state where the government decides who has rights and who does not and hardly resembles the republic founded by Jefferson and others in which God-given inalienable rights existed before any federal government. We now live in a society where a person is considered guilty until proven innocent, instead of the other way around.

So, how did we get into this mess? The answer is war. War is the gateway to tyranny and is the vehicle government uses to terrorize its subjects into submission. To comprehend this concept, it is essential to understand the lies that the government used to initiate the Gulf War and its sequel—the subsequent invasion of Iraq in March of 2003. By 1988, the eight-year war between Iraq and Iran had finally ended, leaving Iraq's oil reserves depleted just in time for Kuwait to begin tapping into oil that was unquestionably on Iraqi soil. At least for the moment, the American government ignored the aggression that ensued against the smaller country. U.S. Ambassador to Iraq April Glaspie told Saddam on July 25, 1990 regarding the border dispute between the two countries that, "the instruction we had during this period was that we should express no opinion on this issue and that the issue is not associated with America."[5] Despite the promise of noninterference, the United States and Kuwait launched a massive propaganda campaign against the Iraqi regime.

With the help of a fifteen-year-old girl named Nayirah—who was later discovered to be a member of the Kuwaiti Royal Family—the U.S. government was able to drum up support for an Iraqi invasion, even though Saddam had been our former ally against communism. Nayirah asserted that she saw Iraqi soldiers "come into the hospitals with guns, and go into the rooms where ... babies were in incubators. They took the babies out of the incubators, and left the babies on the cold floor to die."[6] Even though Nayirah's story was a fabrication, the U.S. launched an invasion of Iraq just three months later. With no official declaration from Congress, the U.S. inaugurated a bombing campaign that lasted for seventy-four days. In fact, the British and American air raids continued for another month *after* the capitulation of Saddam. The bombings were an inhumane tragedy reminiscent of General LeMay's firebombing of Tokyo. In just one night (Mar. 9), the Anglo-American shelling left over 100,000 dead, including Palestinian and Kuwaiti civilians. These unfortunate casualties were trapped by depleted uranium on what was aptly named the "Highway of Death"—a stretch of land between Kuwait and Basra.[7]

After thirteen years of sanctions that left more than 500,000 children dead and the Iraqi economy devastated, Bush Jr. and his cronies began to beat the war drums once again. Only this time they had in their arsenal a "Pearl Harbor-like event" that provided a pretext for war, even though Saddam and his regime had absolutely nothing to do with the 9/11/2001 attacks. The lack of evidence linking Saddam to the twin tower attacks was later admitted by the State Department, but the damage had already been done. The administration made the outlandish claims that Saddam was preparing to manufacture nuclear weapons, was hoarding chemical and biological weapons, and was planning on using them on Americans. The propaganda phrase that echoed throughout the Bush Cabinet when U.N. inspectors failed to verify the allegations was "we don't want the smoking gun to be a mushroom cloud." The weapons of mass destruction (WMD) rumors were continually propagated by a regime desperate to start a war, even though weapons inspectors were coming up empty handed. The State Department on September 12, 2002 concurred with "a new report released on September 9, 2002 from the International Institute for Strategic Studies, an independent research organization," which concluded that, "Saddam Hussein could build a nuclear bomb within months if he were able to obtain fissile material." However, IAEA (International Atomic Energy Agency) Director General Mohammed ELBaradei, replied with the following statement in *Time Magazine:*

> I hope the U.S. does not know anything we do not know. If they do, they should tell us. If they are talking about indigenous capability, Iraq is far away from that. If Iraq has imported material hidden, then you're talking about six months or a year. But that's a big if [...]. I think it's difficult for Iraq to hide a complete nuclear-weapons program. They might be hiding some computer studies or [research and development] on one single centrifuge. These are not enough to make weapons.[8]

Similar allegations were made in regard to Iraq's stockpile of chemical and biological weapons, with similar results. There weren't many left over from Iraq's long conflict with Iran (fought with weapons that were made by materials that were sold by American corporations), and with the subsequent UNSCOM (United Nations Special Commission) inspections that took place between 1991 and 1998 there wasn't much room to manufacture any more. Although there was a discrepancy between how many weapons were produced prior to 1991 and how many had been destroyed, there was doubt that those that remained would be viable or usable. In fact, after seven years of inspections and Intelligence gathering, there was no evidence found to support the premise that Iraq's chemical and biological weapons were any kind of threat to the United States.[9] Further testimony from Hans Blix—the man in charge of inspections—verifies that "more than 400 inspections covering more than 300 sites" were conducted, without notice, and with prompt access provided.[10] Senator Carl Levin of the Senate Armed Services Committee also asserted—in addition to Blix's testimony—that "1,750 experts have visited 1,200 potential WMD sites and have come up empty handed."[11] The WMD myth was just that—a myth; perpetuated by a sycophantic regime hell bent on a path of war and destruction.

In fact, the Bush regime had plans to topple the Hussein regime long before the March 2003 invasion. As early as 2001, two CIA operatives over a forty-five day training period laid out a plan to oust Saddam. This covert operation was named DB/Anabasis, DB being the agency cryptonym for Iraq. The two operatives were a Cuban-American named Luis, and John Maguire—a former member of the Boston city SWAT team. They were both involved in covert CIA ops during the 1980s. Maguire had previously been a gunrunner to the Nicaraguan contras when they were fighting the Sandinista government, and was later stationed in Afghanistan where he assisted Ahmed Shah Massoud's Northern Alliance against the Russian invaders. In the spirit of the

Rooseveltian provocation of the Japanese, Bush signed and authorized project Anabasis on February 16, 2002:

> Anabasis was a no-holds barred covert action. It called for installing a small army of paramilitary CIA officers on the ground inside Iraq; for elaborate schemes to penetrate Saddam's regime; recruiting disgruntled military officers with buckets of cash; for feeling the regime with disinformation about internal descent in ways that would cause Saddam to lash out, most likely through mass executions; for disrupting the regime's finances and supply networks; for sabotage that included blowing up railroad lines and communications towers, and for targeting the lives of key regime officials. It also envisioned staging a phony incident that could be used to start a war. A small group of Iraqi exiles would be flown into Iraq by helicopter to seize an isolated military base near the Saudi border. They then would take to the airwaves and announce a coup was under way. If Saddam responded by flying troops south, his aircraft would be shot down by U.S. fighter planes patrolling no-fly zones established by UN edict after the first Persian Gulf War. A clash of this sort could be used to initiate a full-scale war.[12]

Luis and Maguire headed to Iraq and began implementation of the Anabasis project about a year before the official U.S. invasion. After a successful meeting with Kurdish authorities who were willing to cooperate, Maguire slipped behind enemy lines and discovered that the battered Iraqi armies had no desire to fight with the United States. Happily, he reported back to Cheney that an invasion of Iraq might even be seen as a mission of "liberation" rather than occupation. Meanwhile, back in the U.S., official disinformation was being spread about the Iraqi purchase of aluminum tubes. The CIA—suspecting the tubes were being used for uranium centrifuge—seized an Asian shipment in Jordan and after inspection determined that they were the same tubes Iraq had used previously for artillery rockets.[13] Furthermore, allegations that Iraq had purchased "yellow cake" uranium from Niger were similarly debunked by U.S. Intelligence analysts, who concurred with French Intelligence that hard evidence of such a purchase was lacking.[14] In short, the Bush administration had plunged the U.S. into a war based on nothing but rumors and fabricated lies.

What were the fruits of this war? Although the exact amounts of military and civilian casualties have not yet been determined accurately, we know that at least 4500 American military personnel and possibly hundreds of thousands of civilians have died. Other casualties of this war have been the lost rights mentioned earlier in this chapter and the morality of Americans in general. We have morphed into a nation of sadistic killers obsessed with warfare and war-culture. We love our violent video games, television shows, and movies that glorify black ops, guerilla warfare, police brutality, and secret assassination missions. We love to worship our gods of military steel as we arrogantly assume that our nation is too powerful to fall, and that we deserve to be the policemen of the world. We cheerfully submit to our airport pat downs, police-conducted unwarranted roadside car searches, and the "benevolent" and ubiquitous NSA spying that pervades our personal lives. We have acquiesced to the Bush doctrine of waterboarding and other methods of torture that have been proven to be inaccurate in obtaining intelligence.[15] We have engaged in the collective hatred of entire groups and civilizations just on mere suspicion. Most perniciously, we have capitulated to a fear-mongering government by supporting its iconoclastic War on Terror, which is, in reality, just a war against American citizens and the rest of the world. Ron Paul—a lone voice crying in the wilderness against the war in 2003—wrote this in his diary in regard to the invasion of Iraq:

> This is truly a historic event. Yes, we have flaunted the rules of engaging in war and ignored the advice of our Founders regarding an interventionist foreign policy. But this pre-emptive strike far surpasses any previous military strike by the United States in sheer arrogance. At least in the past we picked sides and chose allies in ongoing wars. We're starting this war, and will set a standard for the

entire world to follow. Attack anyone we disapprove of, anyone who might have weapons, and anyone who might strike us at a later date. We are opening a Pandora's Box, and can be certain that others will use it as a justification to strike—maybe even against the U.S., since we have let the world know that this attack on Iraq is only the beginning. Several other nations have been forewarned about a potential U.S. strike. Others will view our actions as a Pearl Harbor type attack against a nation unable to defend itself, that has not committed aggression against us. Iraq's crime is they are too slow in following UN resolutions, while we ignore the will of the UN when it pleases us. The world is about to get a lot more dangerous, and it's all so unnecessary. The inexplicable need to go abroad in search of monsters to destroy has prompted us to accept a foreign policy better suited to a tyrant than a constitutional republic. The odds of a worldwide conflict involving many nations have risen, as the chaos from this naked act of aggression materializes. The consequences of this assault will be unpredictable and horrendous.[16]

The fruits of the War on Terror are not only civil liberties lost at home, but include the aggregate loss of liberties worldwide. When the Lord revealed to Joseph Smith that He suffered the Constitution to be "established ... for the rights and protection of *all* flesh,"[17] He didn't just mean American citizens. The Lord loves *all* of His children, not just those who reside in the Promised Land. Notwithstanding, because of the acquiescence of the American people to the ludicrous notion that liberty should be exchanged for security, the president of the United States—one man—has been given the authority to hunt down and kill any person he deems a threat, whether citizen or noncitizen; without due process, substantive evidence, or any other pretext except that the person *might* be a terrorist. This lone ranger has the power to declare war on any sovereign nation that he or his Intel cronies deem a threat to national security—without Congressional approval, and without discretion. The War on Terror has given the office of president a Caesar-like mantle by providing him with a *carte blanche* to declare war on any person, nation, or thing he desires, without checks and balances. As a nation, we have descended far beyond the slippery slope of tyranny by ceding our individual sovereignty to a predatory state, replacing Christianity with demagoguery and statolatry, and by capitulating to the repugnance of the jingoistic dogma of killing in the name of 'Merica.

Other ill effects of this deleterious War on the Boogiemen have been the despicable treatment of POWs at Abu Ghraib prison, where the U.S. military held Iraqi detainees. War crimes that were committed there include the following; murder, rape, extreme humiliation such as stripping detainees naked and urinating on them, pouring phosphoric acid on detainees, sodomizing detainees with a baton, leashing detainees and dragging them across cold floors, forcing the detainees to engage in sexual acts, and hanging detainees up by their wrists for extended periods of time.[18] As if these nefarious crimes are not enough, U.S. military also engaged in the mass slaughter of innocent Iraqi men, women, and children via the indiscriminate bombing of civilian neighborhoods. Keep in mind that some of these "targets" were nowhere close to Iraqi military establishments or industrial centers. In April of 2003, a U.S. bomb hit a neighborhood where General Ali Hassan al-Majid—AKA "Chemical Ali"—was alleged to be. Not only was this target not eliminated, the explosion managed to kill twenty-three innocents, including children. When a grandfather pulled his grandson out of the wreckage he was not able to resuscitate the infant who had not even reached the age of two. Abed Hassan Hamoodi—who had lost ten members of his family in the blast—put a pertinent question to the warmongering American president: "How would President Bush feel if he had to dig his daughters from out of the rubble?"[19]

Another deplorable tactic employed by the U.S. military in Iraq was the use of cluster munitions, which are explosives that are dropped or launched, and then subsequently eject smaller sub munitions, some of which explode later when disturbed. These highly indiscriminate and noxious weapons have been dropped by the military into heavily populated areas. Higgs elucidates a few of the ensuing atrocities committed by the bomblets:

> (In the Karbala-Hillah area alone, U.S. teams had destroyed by late August last year more than thirty-one thousand unexploded bomblets "that landed on fields, homes, factories and roads … many were in populated areas on Karbala's outskirts.") The toll among children, whose natural curiosity draws them to the interesting-looking bomblets, has been heavy. Khalid Tamimi and four other members of his family were walking on a footpath in Baghdad when his brother, seven-year-old Haithem, spotted something interesting, picked it up and examined it, then threw it down. The bomblet's explosion killed Haithem and his nine-year-old cousin Nora, and seriously wounded Khalid, as well as the children's mothers, Amal and Mayasa.[20]

Other atrocities, even more villainous, include the deliberate bombing of Iraqi hospitals and subsequent sniping of civilians who were endeavoring to access medical centers and makeshift facilities—sometimes with others who were wounded. Higgs continues:

> According to Dahr Jamail's report in The Nation, "two soccer fields in Fallujah have been converted to graveyards." Jamail also reported that "the Americans have bombed one hospital, and, numerous sources told us, were sniping at people who attempted to enter and exit the other major medical facility." Snipers also shot ambulances braving the dangerous streets to bring the wounded to makeshift places of medical assistance.[21]

There is absolutely nothing civilized, patriotic, or "liberating" about this war that was supposedly fought to establish a free government in Iraq. Indeed, operation "Iraqi Freedom" would be more aptly named operation "Iraqi enslavement and oppression," and the conditions that have been foisted upon the Iraqi people in consequence of our presence there can be summarized into one word; *barbarism*. In this day and age of highly technologically-advanced weaponry combined with the amorality of the satanic doctrines of secular humanism and social Darwinism that teach "survival of the fittest," we are forced to come to one disparaging conclusion: *America has become a nightmare.* The U.S government has engaged in the following since the Civil War; war crimes, torture, mass propaganda schemes, mass murder, firebombing, indiscriminate shelling, starvation of children, nuclear bombing, forced repatriation, the establishment of gulags on American soil, and the destruction of Natural Rights emanating from God and established as Supreme U.S. Law since the time of the Founders. It is we Americans who have destroyed our own Constitution and are currently creating a milieu of geopolitical chaos around the globe by our constant intervention and meddling in affairs that are none of our business. This hubris—if not brought to an end by an uprising from within the American masses against corruption—will eventually end like the empire of our Roman predecessors; in a collapse from the inside that will leave us susceptible to real foreign powers such as Russia and China. As the lessons of history teach us, the welfare-warfare state is simply not sustainable for extended periods of time.

This *pseudo*-war was happily continued and expanded by Barrack Obama, who deployed 30,000 troops to Afghanistan after he promised to bring them home. Some have asserted that Obama and the CIA were instrumental in ousting Hosni Mubarak—president of Egypt since 1981—because he opposed "the current US-UK plan to organize a block of Sunni Arab states such as Egypt, Saudi Arabia, Jordan, and the Gulf states — under a US nuclear umbrella and shoulder to shoulder with Israel — for purposes of confrontation and war with Iran, Syria, Hezbollah, and their Shiite and radical allies."[22] The next intervention—the US-UK-UN backing of the removal of Muammar Gaddafi of Libya—was seen by many as a CIA coup reminiscent of Mohammad Mosadegh's ousting in 1953. One writer offers the following explanation:

The uprisings in the border countries of Tunisia and Egypt gave the west a convenient opportunity to overthrow Gaddafi while making it appear to be a continuation of the "Arab Spring." "The CIA's early involvement with Libyan rebels, along with early support for the rebels by French and British intelligence, indicates that the Libyan rebellion was not based on events of neighboring Tunisia and Egypt, but was designed to authorize the rebels to move when a favorable situation presented itself, wrote Wayne Madsen in The Illegal War on Libya. Western intelligence agencies worked on the ground manipulating Libyans, orchestrating protests and assembling a ragtag collection of renegades, traitors and western collaborators, who could be counted on to form a friendly, subservient government after Gaddafi was ousted.

Although the west claims that al-Qaeda is the preeminent terrorist organization that must be eradicated, it supported anti-Gaddafi rebels, many of whom were affiliated with al-Qaeda. Indeed, al-Qaeda fighters were easily recruited to do the dirty work in retaliation against Gaddafi, who always considered al-Qaeda as one of his enemies and provided the west with intelligence about it before and after 9/11. The Obama administration supplied two thousand al-Qaeda "irregulars with weapons and other support in rebel-controlled eastern Libya." Thus, when it came to destabilizing Libya and removing Gaddafi, the U.S., and European interests had no compunction about arming and using "terrorist" forces to do their bidding.[23]

A year later, at the U.S. embassy located in Benghazi, U.S. ambassador Christopher Stevens and three other embassy staffers were killed in a wave of violence that erupted after an anti-Muslim video was released on YouTube, apparently by a U.S. filmmaker. The Obama administration gave lip service to the event by declaring that security for ambassadors would be heightened worldwide, yet many contend that the event was a cover-up. Stevens may have been in charge of a gunrunning operation that was supplying arms to the rebels in Syria via the Turks, although there is no hard evidence to prove it. Former Lt. Gen. and special forces commander William G. Boykin said the following in regard to the incident, "Now, with regards to supporting the rebels in Syria, I can't prove that there was a covert action program," said Boykin. "I've got a lot of information that says there was."[24] These Syrian rebels are being assisted by al-Qaeda and are working at ousting the president of Syria—Bashar al-Assad—whom the Obama administration has accused of using sarin gas against his own people. However, there is evidence that has surfaced which has implicated al-Qaeda in this crime, and it was determined that the rocket carrying the sarin gas did not have enough range to be fired from Syrian military positions and was probably fired by al-Qaeda. The Homeland Security Newswire reported as follows:

> In the report, titled "Possible Implications of Faulty U.S. Technical Intelligence," Richard Lloyd, a former United Nations weapons inspector, and Theodore Postol, a professor of science, technology and national security policy at the Massachusetts Institute of Technology, argue that the question about the rocket's range indicates a major weakness in the case for military action initially pressed by Obama administration officials. The administration eventually withdrew its request for congressional authorization for a military strike after Syria agreed to submit to the Chemical Weapons Convention, which bans the weapons. Polls showed overwhelming public opposition to a military strike, however, and it was doubtful Congress would have authorized an attack.[25]

For the time being, war hawks like McCain *et al* who advocate military action in Syria have been silenced, yet the government's war of aggression against U.S. citizens continues raging on. The burgeoning American police state—assisted by the wave of unconstitutional legislation that has been passed in the wake of 9/11—is beginning to rear its ugly head. The pseudo-*War on Drugs*—a war declared on a thing—is a vehicle being used by law enforcement to further encroach upon Natural Rights. Door-busting SWAT teams are trampling the Constitution under their feet as they trespass into houses with guns blazing to apprehend innocent people merely enjoying recreational drugs, while those who are addicted to harmful over-the-counter and prescription drugs are left unmolested. The idea that we as individuals cannot put into our bodies whatever we choose would've been considered a heresy to our Founding Fathers, and implies that we do not even own our bodies. The government's denial of this right of self-ownership has been enforced by its civil forfeiture laws, which allow it to confiscate and redistribute loot that is seized from drug-toting "criminals." As Christians—Latter-day Saints included—we should be suspicious concerning the justification of this policy that allows the government to steal property from those who are simply minding their own business. We must ask ourselves who the real criminals are in this scenario; those who are violating the Word of Wisdom (which was originally a suggestion and not a commandment, see D&C 89:2), or the violation of the commandments *thou shalt not trespass/steal/kill?* The answer seems obvious, yet many are deceived into thinking that the State is justified in its endeavors even when evil. They are not simply stealing, their crimes extend into assault and murder as well. John W. Whitehead—in his new book, *A Government of Wolves, The Emerging American Police State*—documents many of these unconstitutional abuses. Here are a few:

> In one drug raid, for instance, an unarmed pregnant woman was shot as she attempted to flee the police by climbing out a window. In another case, the girlfriend of a drug suspect and her young child crouched on the floor in obedience to police instructions during the execution of a search warrant. One officer proceeded to shoot the family dogs. His fellow officer, in another room, mistook the shots for hostile gunfire and fired blindly into the room where the defendant was crouched, killing her and wounding her child.[26]

In 2012 alone there were at least 50,000 such raids conducted against drug users. These SWAT teams are issued government costumes, which include Darth Vader-like helmets, paralyzing Taser guns, automatic machine guns, bullet-proof vests, and crowd-dispelling tear gas. In recent years, the Department of Homeland Security has been issuing federal grants for local law enforcement in the form of money or used military equipment. Thus, these grants are contributing to the steady building up paramilitary police all over the United States in violation of the Posse Comitatus Act. The question to ask here is what makes a government employee in a government-issued costume morally superior to the rest of us? And what gives them the right to break and enter, steal, abuse, and even kill in the name of the "War on Drugs?" If the Constitution is consulted on the matter then the authority of these wolves is found to be illegitimate. Nevertheless, that inspired document has been violated by our "beloved" political leaders. Whitehead continues with several stories of "tragic mistakes" made by law enforcement:

> ...an 88-year-old African-American woman was shot and killed in 2006 when policemen barged unannounced into her home, reportedly in search of cocaine. Police officers broke down Kathryn Johnston's door while serving a "no-knock" warrant to search her home on a run-down Atlanta street known for drugs and crime, prompting the woman to fire at what she believed to be the "intruders" in self-defense. The officers returned fire, killing the octogenarian. No cocaine was found.
>
> Police tasered and gunned to death Derek Hale, a decorated 25-year-old U.S. Marine who was talking to a woman and two children in front of a house in a Delaware neighborhood that police suspected was the home of an outlaw motorcycle gang member. Ordering Hale to place his hands in view, the police reportedly tasered him three times and fire three 40-caliber rounds into his chest, ultimately

leading to his death. Hale had no criminal or arrest record in Delaware, and witnesses insist that he was no threat to the police. In fact, after police tasered Hale the second time, one of the independent witnesses yelled at the police that what they were doing was "overkill," to which one of the officers responded, "Shut…up or we'll show you overkill."

Fifty-seven-year-old Alberta Spruill was getting ready for work on May 16, 2003, when a police raiding party in search of a drug dealer broke down the door of her Harlem apartment, tossed in a "flashbang" stun grenade and handcuffed her to a chair. After realizing their mistake—the man they wanted lived in the same building but had been arrested by a different police unit four days earlier—the police un-cuffed Ms. Spruill, checked her vital signs, and sent her to the Emergency Room. Spruill, however, who suffered from a heart condition, died on the way to the hospital.

Similarly, in Boston, thirteen heavily armed policemen in black fatigues smashed into the apartment of Acelynne Williams, a 75-year-old retired African-American preacher. Supposedly, they had been working off an anonymous tip that four Jamaican drug dealers lived somewhere in the apartment building. Williams died of a heart attack from the "shock and awe" of being visited by commando-like cops.

…Consider what happened to 7-year-old Aiyana Jones. At 12:40 a.m. on Sunday, May 16, 2010, a flash grenade was thrown through the Jones family's living room window, followed by the sounds of police bursting into the apartment and a gun going off. Rushing into the room, Charles Jones found himself tackled by police and forced to lie on the floor, his face in a pool of blood, his daughter, Aiyana's blood. It would be hours before Charles would be informed that his daughter, who had been sleeping on the living room sofa, was dead. According to news reports, the little girl was shot in the neck by the lead officer's gun after he allegedly collided with

Aiyana's grandmother during a police raid gone awry. The 34-year-old suspect the police had been looking for would later be found during a search of the building. Ironically, camera crews shadowing the police SWAT team for the reality television show "The First 48" (cop shows are among the most popular of the television reality shows) caught the unfolding tragedy on film.[27]

Conclusion

These and other despicable encroachments on human rights spoken of in this chapter are the effects of a government gone awry, and has subverted the God-condoned Constitution and replaced it with a blank check for tyranny. War has been the vehicle that has enabled the government to engage in this debauchery, which has been facilitated by the fear-mongering antics of the Machiavellians who sit in our judgment seats. The War on Terror, the War on Drugs, and even the War on Poverty are used by government as excuses to engage in all sorts of rights-violations and devastating economic interventions. These wars are perpetual, irrational, tyrannical, and can *never* be won. Logic tells us that it is completely impossible to totally eradicate all evil by destroying every single terrorist cell and drug dealer, and by locking up every drug user with rapists, serial killers, and child molesters. Not to mention the concomitant absurdity of attempting to end poverty by stealing and redistributing wealth. Obviously, the government cannot accomplish this. Since the inception of each of these wars poverty has increased, drug abuse and crime have escalated, and the war on terrorism has created more American enemies. Government has failed miserably in each of these endeavors and has proved its incompetence over and over again. No earthly power can abrogate all evil in the world—it was never meant to be done. God gives us opposition in all things for a wise purpose, and those who believe that such a task can be accomplished are stricken by the disease of hubris. A far more tenable argument is that this government is using these unrighteous wars to justify their attempts at seizing more power and authority. The *Book of Mormon* warned us about governments like these when Nephi—the son of Helamen—lamented that secret combinations had subjugated the Nephite government:

> And seeing the people in a state of such awful wickedness, and those Gadianton robbers filling the judgment-seats—having usurped the power and authority of the land; laying aside the commandments of God, and not in the least aright before him; doing no justice unto the children of men; condemning the righteous because of their righteousness; letting the guilty and the wicked go unpunished because of their money; and moreover to be held in office at the head of government, to rule and do according to their wills, that they might get gain and glory of the world, and, moreover, that they might the more easily commit adultery, and steal, and kill, and do according to their own wills.[28]

Chapter Twelve Notes and Sources

1. Benjamin Franklin, 1755 (Pennsylvania Assembly: Reply to the Governor, Tue, Nov 11, 1755),

2. Quoted in Monnet, Awakening To Our Awful Situation, p. 404

3. http://www.csmonitor.com/USA/USA-Update/2013/0522/Drone-strikes-Four-American-citizens-killed-in-drone-strikes-video

4. http://www.huffingtonpost.com/2013/06/07/drone-killings-american-citizens_n_3398294.html

5. Quoted in Monnett, Awakening to our Awful Situation, p. 390

6. Quoted in *Ibid*, p. 393

7. *Ibid*, p. 394

8. http://grassrootspeace.org/iraqweaponsn.html

9. *Ibid*

10. Quoted in Monnett, Awakening to our Awful Situation, p. 403

11. Quoted in *Ibid*, p. 404

12. Michael Isikoff and David Corn, *Hubris, The Inside Story of Spin, Scandal, and the Selling of the Iraq War,* Three Rivers Press, Copyright 2006, Chapter 1

13. *Ibid*, Chapter 3

14. http://en.wikipedia.org/wiki/Yellowcake_forgery

15. See Joost A.M. Meerloo M.D., *The Rape of the Mind,* Copyright by Author, 1956

16. Ron Paul, *A Foreign Policy of Freedom,* Copyright 2007, the Foundation for Rational Economics and Education, Inc., p. 254

17. D&C 101:77, Emphasis added

18. http://en.wikipedia.org/wiki/Abu_Ghraib_torture_and_prisoner_abuse

19. Robert Higgs, *Resurgence of the Warfare State, The Crisis since 9/11,* The Independent Institute, 2005, p. 185

20. Ibid

21. *Ibid*, p. 186

22. http://tarpley.net/2011/02/18/mubarak-toppled-by-cia-because-he-opposed-us-plans-for-war-with-iran/

23. https://web.archive.org/web/20140630233057/http://blacknewsexaminer.com/gaddafi/

24. http://cnsnews.com/news/article/former-special-forces-commander-was-us-running-guns-syrian-rebels-benghazi-cia-no

25. http://www.examiner.com/article/obama-was-likely-wrong-about-sarin-gas-attack-by-syria-s-assad

26. John W. Whitehead, *A Government Of Wolves, The Emerging American Police State,* copyright 2013 by John W. Whitehead, p. 65

27. *Ibid*, pp. 67-69

28. Helaman 7:4-5

Chapter 13

A Misunderstood Hero

I seek not for power, but to pull it down. I seek not for honor of the world, but for the glory of my God, and the freedom and welfare of my people.

-Captain Moroni

Captain Moroni is heralded by many in the church as a war hero, perhaps seen as an icon of the strong military type who commands obedience and respect and who always wins his battles. To Moroni, however, this type of perception would probably be offensive because he was a man of peace, not of war. His heart gloried in preserving his people's freedom and in maintaining the cause of liberty, not in the shedding of blood. He disliked power-seeking men and gloried in the God-granted rights and liberties of his people. Moroni was only obedient to God, not to the State. He would've never succumbed to the false rationale that subordinates are to execute every command of their superiors. He would never have to say at the judgment bar of God, "I was just doing my duty and obeying orders," especially if those orders meant bombing civilians, executing prisoners, or casting innocents into gulags. Had Moroni been asked by the government to do any of these things he would have rebuked the perpetrators who sit on their "thrones in a state of thoughtless stupor"[1] and would have threatened to cleanse the "inward vessel"[2] unless such orders were rescinded. He boldly wrote to Pahoran that he would lead a charge against the capital city of

Zarahemla unless the government repented and supplied men and provisions to his armies who were weakened from hunger and had suffered many casualties against the Lamanites. The State meant nothing to Moroni, except insofar as it remained a free government, but other than that he had no use for it. He put principle over politics, and he held liberty in the highest regard.

Mormon—who was laden with the task of abridging a thousand years of Nephite history—obviously had to sift through a myriad of records to find the most important things that relate to modern-day America. It is interesting to note that of all the Nephite heroes to choose from, Mormon named his son after Captain Moroni. Mormon—who was a "sober child"[3] at the age of ten, and was given command of the Nephite army at age fifteen—describes Moroni as "a man of a perfect understanding,"[4] and that "if all men had been, or were, or ever would be, like unto Moroni, behold, the very powers of hell would be shaken forever, yea, the devil would never have power over the hearts of the children of men."[5] What does Mormon mean by "perfect understanding?" There is a clue to this mystery in Pahoran's response to Moroni's epistle wherein he states that the "Spirit of God ... is also the spirit of freedom"[6]. Did Moroni spend the early years of his life in the study of the principles of liberty, and is this the only way to understand the true Spirit of God? Mormon included no account of Moroni before the age of twenty-five—does he know something he's not telling us? Perhaps Moroni understood that in order to comprehend the nature and disposition of God, and the nature of man, we must grasp the concept of individual freedom, which is at the root of the Gospel of Jesus Christ.

There is much more to this "strong and mighty man"[7] than being terrifying to his enemies, or a symbol of military might among the Mormon community. It is not a far cry to say that Moroni was of a type of man like Jefferson, Washington, or Henry—whom the Lord referred to as "wise men" raised up for the very purpose of establishing a free government. Yet, Captain Moroni was even better than Washington and Jefferson, because unlike them he did not exercise even the slightest degree of unrighteous dominion. Don't misunderstand—the former two were good men, but both violated the newly formed Constitution in trivial ways. Moroni—as far as we know—never laid a trade embargo, led an army against a group of whiskey tax evaders, or established a national bank. In fact, all he ever did was fight for liberty, never conscripting forces into his armies or punishing anyone except those who had sought to replace the free government with a king.

He was a man who was at the head of his armies as he led them to battle. How many modern generals have done the same? He was a man who held the sanctity of life in high regard. He could have easily slaughtered all those Lamanite guards who drank themselves into a stupor, yet he let them live during an operation to rescue many Nephite women and children POWs. He never plunged his men into battles that were suicide missions, and avoided engaging his men against the enemy when the odds were severely stacked in the enemy's favor. When Moroni's high regard for human life is compared to modern leaders, we are left to ponder the following; would Moroni have approved of Lincoln's willingness to sacrifice 600,000 Americans to save his precious tariff and mystical Union? Would he have tolerated McKinley and Roosevelt's massacre of 200,000 Filipino's in order to establish Chinese coaling stations? Or Wilson's restriction of freedom of speech and his withholding of vital information about the Lusitania's vulnerability? How would Captain Moroni view the bombing of Dresden, General LeMay's firebombing of Tokyo, the dropping of the nuclear bomb on Hiroshima and Nagasaki, the sacrifice of thousands of Americans and allied troops on the beaches of Normandy, or the deliberate withholding of crucial intelligence from Admiral Kimmel that could have saved countless lives at Pearl Harbor? Would he have acquiesced to FDR's executive order to establish Japanese internment camps, or Truman's forced repatriation of Soviet escapees back to the USSR? Would he have approved of FDR's entangling alliance with a ruthless dictator while supplying the malevolent reprobate with a staggering amount of dangerous resources? Would he have just stood back and watched as FDR and Churchill consigned 800 million Eastern Europeans into the clutches of Soviet tyranny? Would he have suffered General Eisenhower to oversee the imprisonment and mass execution of thousands in post-war Germany[8]? Or the indiscriminate killings of innocent civilians by Tiger Force and other units in the jungles of Vietnam? Indeed, would Captain Moroni support the War on Terror, *et al,* and remote drone bombings from Nevada basements, or accompanying legislation such as the Patriot Act and NDAA that destroy liberty? Would he condone torture at Guantanamo, or foreign nation-building, or policing the world? In light of all we know about this good man, we have to assume that the prevailing answer to the above queries is *no*. Moroni did not delight in the shedding of blood or the building up of political power and, therefore, would not have supported most of America's offensive legislative, economic, and military choices.

We are not told very much about Moroni other than of his valor under fire and his great desire to fight for the liberty of his people. Although the text declares that he was a man like unto Ammon and the sons of Mosiah, we are not informed on the details of his church activity and service. In fact—as far as we know—he was never a missionary, a high priest, or even a home teacher. Yet, Mormon declared that if all men where to emulate this man then the powers of hell would be subdued forever. To esteem Mormon's pronouncement as trivial would be a grave error, for the lesson contained therein is of the utmost import. What is that lesson? That Moroni was great because of his *love of liberty*, and only the principles of liberty will triumph over the devil—whose utmost desire is to destroy that liberty, dethrone God, and usurp power over all. Satan—despite all his pretended glory and pomp—is nothing but a kingman who is blinded by his insatiable appetite for power, puffed up by the delusion of his own brilliance, longing to lord over the wills of those whom he pretends to love, and who yearns for the masses to fall down and worship him. Moroni, on the other hand, is the antithesis of all that the devil promulgates—whose only desire was to "pull down"[9] all corrupted and usurped power.

Conclusion

We must realize that all earthly organizations are temporary and as such are trumped in importance when compared to eternal principles such as liberty. The Gods in the eternities do not use government to coerce themselves into continuing to live flawlessly in godhood, yet they live in perfect harmony with the principles that govern the broad expanse of heaven and they do so of their own volition. God Himself will force no person to heaven, but rather grants His children the gift of agency in all things. If His children choose to ignore those heavenly principles that govern the universe then He is saddened, but He *never* compels them into compliance. Perhaps Moroni understood that without individual liberty there would be no institution of religion or personal property rights. Indeed, without people like Moroni and Washington—who marched on the front lines of their armies—there would be no civilization at all. Without heroes like these, tyrants would gobble up the last vestiges of freedom, and all would be subject to the whims of deleterious dictatorships. The absence of such heroes in the modern era (excepting men like Ron Paul) has strengthened the grip of the Gadiantons who work to usurp power, and has placed us—as Mormon's son, Moroni opined—in "an awful situation"[10].

Perhaps what made Captain Moroni so great and his understanding so "sound" was his unrelenting vigilance and adherence toward eternal and immutable principles that are over *all* earthy organizations—including church and state—and his unyielding obedience to God Himself rather than political parties, social organizations, modern trends, synagogues, or demagogues. Perhaps this is the reason why the historian Mormon sifted through centuries of Nephite war history, dissensions, prophesying, and destruction: to reveal to us the great lessons of Moroni and his campaign for freedom. When we consider that the Lord chose this twenty-year war history (Alma 43-Helaman 1) out from among a thousand years of "wars and contentions," we are obliged to humble ourselves and ask the Lord what is to be learned from such an account. Consider that the seemingly most imperative themes of the *Book of Mormon* are as follows: (1) Christ and His atonement, (2) warfare, (3) missionary work, (4) secret combinations. Warfare is the <u>number two</u> theme within the *Book of Mormon*, a book which speaks to us from the dust concerning those who understood the eternal principles that condemn wars of aggression. Perhaps it's time to start listening to Captain Moroni's message—a message that cries out for nations to stop killing, maiming, torturing, and usurping in the name of jingoistic patriotism. Perhaps it's time to stop delighting in the shedding of blood by sending drones to bomb weddings in Yemen, killing untried American civilians, and bombing residential neighborhoods with depleted uranium, to stop bombing at all, in fact. Perhaps it's time to stop starving innocent children with economic sanctions, to stop engaging in unchecked national group hate, and to actually honor the Lord's commandment to love our neighbor. Indeed, it is time to start giving obeisance to Moroni's legacy of freedom, liberty, justice and—most importantly—*Peace*.

Notes and Sources Chapter Thirteen

1. Alma 60:7
2. Alma 60:23
3. Mormon 1:2
4. Alma 48:11
5. Alma 48:17
6. Alma 61:15
7. Alma 48:11
8. See, Giles MacDonogh, After The Reich, The Brutal History of the Allied Occupation, Basic Books, 2009
9. Alma 60:36
10. Either 8:24

Appendix A

Section 1a Daniel Webster, "The Draft is Unconstitutional"

Excerpt from a speech delivered before the House of Representatives on December 9, 1814

Let us examine the nature and extent of the power, which is assumed by the various military measures before us. In the present want of men and money, the Secretary of War has proposed to Congress a military conscription. For the conquest of Canada, the people will not enlist; and if they would, the treasury is exhausted, and they could not be paid. Conscription is chosen as the most promising instrument, both of overcoming reluctance to the service, and of subduing the difficulties of the exchequer. The Administration asserts the right to fill the ranks of the regular army by compulsion. It contends that it may now take one out of every twenty-five men, and any part, or the whole of the rest, whenever its occasions require. Persons thus taken by force, and put into an army, may be compelled to serve during the war, or for life. They may be put on any service, at home or abroad, for defense or for invasion, accordingly to the will and pleasure of the government. The power does not grow out of any invasion of the country, or even out of a state of war. It belongs to government at all times, in peace as well as in war, and it is to be exercised under all circumstances, according to its mere discretion. This, sir, is the amount of the principle contended for by the Secretary of War.

Is this, sir, consistent with the character of a free government? Is this civil liberty? Is this the real character of our Constitution? No, sir, indeed it is not. The Constitution is libeled. The people of this country have not established for themselves such a fabric of despotism. They have not purchased at a vast expense of their own treasure and their own blood a Magna Carta to be slaves. Where it is written in the Constitution, in what article or section is it contained, that you may take children from their parents, and parents from their children, and compel them to fight the battles of any war in which the folly or the wickedness of government may engage it? Under what concealment has this power lain hidden which now for the first time comes forth, with a tremendous and baleful aspect, to trample down and destroy the dearest rights of personal liberty? Who will show me any Constitutional injunction which makes it the duty of the American people to surrender everything valuable in life, and even life itself, not when the safety of their country and its liberties may demand the sacrifice, but whenever the purposes of an ambitious and mischievous government may require it? Sir, I almost disdain to go to quotations and references to prove that such an abominable doctrine has no foundation in the Constitution of the country. It is enough to know that that instrument was intended as the basis of a free government, and that the power contended for is incompatible with any notion of personal liberty. An attempt to maintain this doctrine upon the provisions of the Constitution is an exercise of perverse ingenuity to extract slavery from the substance of a free government. It is an attempt to show, by proof and argument, that we ourselves are subjects of despotism, and that we have a right to chains and bondage, firmly secured to our children and us by the provisions of our government....

If the Secretary of War has proved the right of Congress to enact a law enforcing a draft of men out of the militia into the regular army, he will at any time be able to prove, quite as clearly, that Congress has power to create a Dictator. The arguments which have helped him in one case, will equally aid him in the other, the same reason of a supposed or possible state necessity, which is urged now, may be repeated then, with equal pertinency and effect.

Sir, in granting Congress to power to raise armies, the people have granted all the means which are ordinary and usual, and which are consistent with the liberties and security of the people themselves, and they have granted no others. To talk about the unlimited power of the government consists as much in its means as in its ends; and it would be ridiculous and absurd constitution, which should be less cautious to guard against abuses in the one case than in the other. All the means and instruments, which a free government exercises, as well as the ends and objects which it pursues, are to partake of its own essential character, and to be conformed to tis genuine spirit. A free government with arbitrary means to administer it is a contradiction; a free government without adequate provisions for personal security is an absurdity; a free government with an uncontrolled power of military conscription, is a solecism, at once the most ridiculous and abominable that ever entered into the head of man....

Who shall describe to you the horror, which your orders of conscription shall create in the once happy villages of this country? Who shall describe the distress and anguish which they will spread over those hills and valleys, where men have heretofore been accustomed to labor, and to rest in security and happiness? Anticipate the scene, sir, when the class shall assemble to stand its draft, and to throw the dice for blood. What a group of wives and mothers and sisters, of helpless age and helpless infancy, shall gather round the theatre of this horrible lottery, as if the stroke of death were to fall from heaven before their eyes on a father, a brother, a son, or a husband. And in a majority of cases, sir, it will be the stroke of death. Under present prospects of the continuance of the war, not one half of them on whom your conscription shall fall will ever return to tell the tale of their sufferings. They will perish of disease or pestilence or they will their bones to whiten in fields beyond the frontier. Does the lot fall on the father of a family? His children, already orphans, shall see his face no more. When they behold him for the last time, they shall see him lashed and fettered, and dragged away from his own threshold, like a felon and an outlaw. Does it fall on a son, the hope and staff or aged parents? That hope shall fail them. On that staff they shall lean no longer. They shall not enjoy the happiness of dying before their children. They shall totter to their grave, bereft of their offspring and unwept by any who inherit their blood. Does it fall on a husband? The eyes that watch his parting steps may swim in tears forever. She is a wife no longer. There is no relation so tender or so sacred that by these accursed measures you do not propose to violate it. There is no happiness so perfect that you do not propose to destroy it. Into the paradise of domestic life you enter, not indeed by temptations and sorceries, but by open force and violence....

Nor is it, sir, for the defense of his own house and home that he who is the subject of military draft is to perform the task allotted to him. You will put him upon a service equally foreign to his interests and abhorrent to his feelings. With is aid you are to push your purposes of conquest. The battles, which he is to fight, are the battles of invasion— battles which he detests perhaps, and abhors, less from the danger and the death that gathers over them, and the blood with which they drench the plain, than from the principles in which they have their origin. Fresh from the peaceful pursuits of life, and yet a soldier but in name, he is to be opposed to veteran troops, hardened under every scene, inured to every privation, and disciplined in every service. If, sir, in this strife he fall—if, while ready to obey every rightful command of government, he is forced from his home against right, not to contend for the defense of his country, but to prosecute a miserable and detestable project of invasion, and in that strife he fall 'tis murder. It may stalk above the cognizance of human law, but in the sight of Heaven it is murder; and though millions of years may roll away, while his ashes and yours lie mingled together in the earth, the day will yet come when his spirit and the spirits of his children must be met at the bar of omnipotent justice. May God, in his compassion, shield me from any participation in the enormity of this guile.

Section 2a

Lysander Spooner on the Civil War, "No Treason"

Excerpt taken from Spooner's "No Treason: The Constitution of No Authority"
(1867)

Notwithstanding all this, that we had learned, and known, and professed, for nearly a century, these lenders of blood money had, for a long series of years previous to the war, been the willing accomplices of the slaveholders in perverting the government from the purposes of liberty and justice, to the greatest of crimes. They had been such accomplices *for a purely pecuniary consideration,* to wit, a control of the markets in the South; in other words, the privilege of holding the slave-holders themselves in industrial and commercial subjection to the manufacturers and merchants of the North (who afterwards furnished the money for the war). And these Northern merchants and manufacturers, these lenders of blood-money, were willing to continue to be the accomplices of the slave-holders in the future, for the same pecuniary considerations. But the slaveholders, either doubting the fidelity of their Northern allies, or feeling themselves strong enough to keep their slaves in subjection without Northern assistance, would no longer pay the price, which these Northern men demanded. And it was to enforce this price in the future — that is, to monopolize the Southern markets, to maintain their industrial and commercial control over the South — that these Northern manufacturers and merchants lent some of the profits of their former monopolies for the war, in order to secure to themselves the same, or greater, monopolies in the future. These — and not any love of liberty or justice — were the motives on which the North lent the money for the war. In short, the North said to the slave-holders: If you will not pay us our price (give us control of your markets) for our assistance against your slaves, we will secure the same price (keep control of your markets) by helping your slaves against you, and using them as our tools for maintaining dominion over you; for the control of your markets we will have, whether the tools we use for that purpose be black or white, and be the cost, in blood and money, what it may. On this principle, and from this motive, and not from any love of liberty, or justice, the money was lent in enormous amounts, and at enormous rates of interest. And it was only by means of these loans that the objects of the war were accomplished. And now these lenders of blood money demand their pay; and the government, so called, becomes their tool, their servile, slavish, villainous tool, to extort it from the labor of the enslaved people both of the North and South. It is to be extorted by every form of direct, and indirect, and unequal taxation. Not only the nominal debt and interest — enormous as the latter was — are to be paid in full; but these holders of the debt are to be paid still further — and perhaps doubly, triply, or quadrupled paid — by such tariffs on imports as will enable our home manufacturers to realize enormous prices for their commodities; also by such monopolies in banking as will enable them to keep control of, and thus enslave and plunder, the industry and trade of the great body of the Northern people themselves. In short, the industrial and commercial slavery of the great body of the people, North and South, black and white, is the price, which these lenders of blood money demand, and insist upon, and are determined to secure, in return for the money lent for the war.

This programme having been fully arranged and systematized, they put their sword into the hands of the chief murderer of the war, [undoubtedly a reference to General Grant, who had just become president] and charge him to carry their scheme into effect. And now he, speaking as their organ, says, "LET US HAVE PEACE. The meaning of this is: Submit quietly to all the robbery and slavery we have arranged for you, and you can have "peace." But in case you resist, the same lenders of blood money, who furnished the means to subdue the South, will furnish the means again to subdue you. These are the terms on which alone this government, or, with few exceptions, any other, ever gives "peace" to its people. The whole affair, on the part of those who furnished the money, has been, and now is, a deliberate scheme of robbery and murder; not merely to monopolize the markets of the South, but also to monopolize the currency, and thus control the industry and trade, and thus plunder and enslave the laborers, of both North and South. And Congress and the president are today the merest tools for these purposes. They are obliged to be, for they know that their own power, as rulers, so-called, is at an end, the moment their credit with the blood-money loan-mongers fails. They are like a bankrupt in the hands of an extortioner. They dare not say nay to any demand made upon them. And to hide at once, if possible, both their servility and crimes, they attempt to divert public attention, by crying out that they have "Abolished Slavery!" That they have "Saved the Country!" That they have "Preserved our Glorious Union!" and that, in now paying the "National Debt," as they call it (as if the people themselves, ALL OF THEM WHO ARE TO BE TAXED FOR ITS PAYMENT, had really and voluntarily joined in contracting it), they are simply "Maintaining the National Honor!" By "maintaining the national honor," they mean simply that they themselves, open robbers and murderers, assume to be the nation, and will keep faith with those who lend them the money necessary to enable them to crush the great body of the people under their feet; and will faithfully appropriate, from the proceeds of their future robberies and murders, enough to pay all their loans, principal and interest. The pretense that the "abolition of slavery" was either a motive or justification for the war, is a fraud of the same character with that of "maintaining the national honor." Who, but such usurpers, robbers, and murderers as they, ever established slavery? Or what government, except one resting upon the sword, like the one we now have, was ever capable of maintaining slavery? And why did these men abolish slavery? Not from any love of liberty in general — not as an act of justice to the black man himself, but only "as a war measure," and because they wanted his assistance, and that of his friends, in carrying on the war they had undertaken for maintaining and intensifying that political, commercial, and industrial slavery, to which they have subjected the great body of the people, both black and white. And yet these imposters now cry out that they have abolished the chattel slavery of the black man — although that was not the motive of the war — as if they thought they could thereby conceal, atone for, or justify that other slavery which they were fighting to perpetuate, and to render more rigorous and inexorable than it ever was before. There was no difference of principle — but only of degree — between the slavery they boast they have abolished, and the slavery they were fighting to preserve; for all restraints upon men's natural liberty, not necessary for the simple maintenance of justice, are of the nature of slavery, and differ >from each-other only in degree. If their object had really been to abolish slavery, or maintain liberty or justice generally, they had only to say: All, whether white or black, who want the protection of this government, shall have it; and all who do not want it, will be left in peace, so long as they leave us in peace. Had they said this, slavery would necessarily have been abolished at once; the war would have been saved; and a thousand times nobler union than we have ever had would have been the result. It would have been a voluntary union of free men; such a union as will one day exist among all men, the world over, if the several nations, so called, shall ever get rid of the usurpers, robbers, and murderers, called governments, that now plunder, enslave, and destroy them. Still another of the frauds of these men is, that they are now establishing, and that the war was designed to establish, "a government of consent." The only idea they have ever manifested as to what is a government of consent, is this — that it is one to which everybody must consent, or be shot. This idea was the dominant one on which the war was carried on; and it is the dominant one, now that we have got what is called "peace." Their pretenses that they have "Saved the Country," and "Preserved our Glorious Union," are frauds like all the rest of their pretenses. By them they mean simply that they have subjugated, and maintained their power over, an unwilling people. This they call "Saving the Country"; as if an enslaved and subjugated people — or as if any people kept in subjection by the sword (as it is intended that all of us shall be hereafter) — could be said to have any country. This, too, they call "Preserving our Glorious Union"; as if there could be said to be any Union, glorious or inglorious, that was not voluntary. Or as if there could be said to be any union between masters and slaves; between those who conquer, and those who are subjugated. All these cries of having "abolished slavery," of having "saved the country," of having "preserved the union," of establishing "a government of consent," and of "maintaining the national honor," are all gross, shameless, transparent cheats — so transparent that they ought to deceive no one — when uttered as justifications for the war, or for the government that has succeeded the war, or for now compelling the people to pay the cost of the war, or for compelling anybody to support a government that he does not want. The lesson taught by all these facts is this: As long as mankind continue to pay "national debts," so-called — that is, so long as they are such dupes and cowards as to pay for being cheated, plundered, enslaved, and murdered — so long there will be enough to lend the money for those purposes; and with that money a plenty of tools, called soldiers, can be hired to keep them in subjection. But when they refuse any longer to pay for being thus cheated, plundered, enslaved, and murdered, they will cease to have cheats, and usurpers, and robbers, and murderers and blood-money loan-mongers for masters.

Section 3a

William Graham Sumner, "The Conquest of the United States by Spain"

As Quoted in "We Who Dared To Say No To War," edited by Murray Polner and Thomas E. Woods, JR., copyright Polner and Woods, 2008, pp. 93-96

During the last year the public has been familiarized with descriptions of Spain and of Spanish methods of doing things until the name of Spain has become a symbol for a certain well-defined set of notions and policies. On the other hand, the name of the United States has always been, for all of us, a symbol for a state of things, a set of ideas and traditions, a group of views about social and political affairs. Spain was the first, for a long time the greatest, of the modern imperialistic states. The United States, by its historical origin, its traditions, and its principles, is the chief representative of the revolt and reaction against that kind of a state. I intend to show that, by the line of action now proposed to us, which we call expansion and imperialism, we are throwing away some of the most important elements of the American symbol and are adopting some of the most important elements of the Spanish symbol. We have beaten Spain in a military conflict, but we are submitting to be conquered by her on the field of ideas and policies. Expansionism and imperialism are nothing but the old philosophies of national prosperity, which have brought Spain to where she now is. Those philosophies appeal to national vanity and national cupidity. They are seductive, especially upon the first view and the most superficial judgment, and therefore it cannot be denied that they are very strong for popular effect. They are delusions, and they will lead us to ruin unless we are hardheaded enough to resist them. In any case the year 1898 is a great landmark in the history of the United States. The consequences will not be all good or all bad, for such is not the nature of societal influences. They are always mixed of good and ill, and so it will be in this case. Fifty years from now the historian, looking back to 1898, will no doubt see, in the course which things will have taken, consequences of the proceedings of that year and of this present one which will not all be bad, but you will observe that that is not a justification for a happy-go-lucky policy; that does not affect our duty today in all that we do to seek wisdom and prudence and to determine our actions by the best judgment which we can form…The original and prime cause of the war was that it was a move of partisan tactics in the strife of parties at Washington. As soon as it seemed resolved upon, a number of interests began to see their advantage in it and hastened to further it. It was necessary to make appeals to the public, which would bring quite other motives to the support of the enterprise and win the consent of classes who would never consent to either financial or political jobbery. Such appeals were found in sensational assertions that we had no means to verify, in phrases of alleged patriotism, in statements about Cuba and the Cubans that we now know to have been entirely untrue…There is another observation, however, about the war, which is of far greater importance: that is, that it was a gross violation of self-government. We boast that we are a self-governing people, and in this respect, particularly, we compare ourselves with pride with older nations. What is the difference after all? The Russians, whom we always think of as standing at the opposite pole of political institutions, have self-government, if you mean by it acquiescence in what a little group of people at the head of the government agree to do. The war with Spain was precipitated upon us headlong, without reflection or deliberation, and without any due formulation of public opinion. Whenever a voice was raised in behalf of deliberation and the recognized maxims of statesmanship, it was howled down in a storm of vituperation and cant. Everything was done to make us throw away sobriety of thought and calmness of judgment and to inflate all expressions with sensational epithets and turgid phrases. It cannot be denied that everything in regard to the war has been treated in an exalted strain of sentiment and rhetoric very unfavorable to the truth. At present the whole periodical press of the country seems to be occupied in tickling the national vanity to the utmost by representations about the war which are extravagant and fantastic. There will be a penalty to be paid for all this. Nervous and sensational newspapers are just as corrupting, especially to young people, as nervous and sensational novels. The habit of expecting that all mental pabulum shall be highly spiced, and the corresponding loathing for whatever is soberly truthful, undermines character as much as any other vice. Patriotism is being prostituted into a nervous intoxication that is fatal to an apprehension of truth. It builds around us a fool's paradise, and it will lead us into errors about our position and relations just like those that we have been ridiculing in the case of Spain… There is not a civilized nation that does not talk about its civilizing mission just as grandly as we do. The English, who really have more to boast of in this respect than anybody else, talk least about it, but the Phariseeism with which they correct and instruct other people has made them hated all over the globe. The French believe themselves the guardians of the highest and purest culture, and that the eyes of all mankind are fixed on Paris, whence they expect oracles of thought and taste. The Germans regard themselves as charged with a mission, especially to us Americans, to save us from egoism and materialism. The Russians, in their books and newspapers, talk about the civilizing mission of Russia in language that might be translated from some of the finest paragraphs in our imperialistic newspapers… The point is that each of them repudiates the standards of the others, and the outlying nations, which are to be civilized, hate all the standards of civilized men. We assume that what we like and practice, and what we think better, must come as a welcome blessing to Spanish-Americans and Filipinos. This is grossly and obviously untrue. They hate our ways. They are hostile to our ideas. Our religion, language, institutions, and manners offend them. They like their own ways, and if we appear amongst them as rulers, there will be social discord in all the great departments of social interest. The most important thing that we shall inherit from the Spaniards will be the task of suppressing rebellions. If the United States takes out of the hands of Spain her mission, on the ground that Spain is not executing it well, and if this nation in its turn attempts to be school-mistress to others, it will shrivel up into the same vanity and self-conceit of which Spain now presents an example. To read our current literature one would think that we were already well on the way to it. Now, the great reason why all these enterprises which begin by saying to somebody else, We know what is good for you better than you know yourself and we are going to make you do it, are false and wrong is that they violate liberty; or, to turn the same statement into other words, the reason why liberty, of which we Americans talk so much, is a good thing is that it means leaving people to live out their own lives in their own way, while we do the same. If we believe in liberty, as an American principle, why do we not stand by it? Why are we going to throw it away to enter upon a Spanish policy of dominion and regulation? My patriotism is of the kind which is outraged by the notion that the United States never was a great nation until in a petty three months' campaign it knocked to pieces a poor, decrepit, bankrupt old state like Spain. To hold such an opinion as that is to abandon all American standards, to put shame and scorn on all that our ancestors tried to build up here, and to go over to the standards of which Spain is a representative.

Section 4a

Murray N. Rothbard, "War, Peace, and the State"

As quoted in "Egalitarianism as a Revolt Against Nature and Other Essays."

William F. Buckley, Jr., has chided the libertarian movement for failing to use its "strategic intelligence" in facing the major problems of our time. We have, indeed, been too often prone to "pursue our busy little seminars on whether or not to demunicipalize the garbage collectors" (as Buckley has contemptuously written), while ignoring and failing to apply libertarian theory to the most vital problem of our time: war and peace. There *is* a sense in which libertarians have been utopian rather than strategic in their thinking, with a tendency to divorce the ideal system, which we envisage from the realities of the world in which we live. In short, too many of us have divorced theory from practice, and have then been content to hold the pure libertarian society as an abstract ideal for some remotely future time, while in the concrete world of today we follow unthinkingly the orthodox "conservative" line. To live liberty, to begin the hard but essential strategic struggle of changing the unsatisfactory world of today in the direction of our ideals, we must realize and demonstrate to the world that libertarian theory can be brought sharply to bear upon all of the world's crucial problems. By coming to grips with these problems, we can demonstrate that libertarianism is not just a beautiful ideal somewhere on Cloud Nine, but a tough-minded body of truths that enables us to take our stand and to cope with the whole host of issues of our day. Let us then, by all means, use our strategic intelligence. Although, when he sees the result, Mr. Buckley might well wish that we had stayed in the realm of garbage collection. Let us construct a libertarian theory of war and peace. The fundamental axiom of libertarian theory is that no one may threaten or commit violence ("aggress") against another man's person or property. Violence may be employed only against the man who commits such violence; that is, only defensively against the aggressive violence of another. In short, no violence may be employed against a non-aggressor. Here is the fundamental rule from which can be deduced the entire *corpus* of libertarian theory.

Let us set aside the more complex problem of the State for a while and consider simply relations between "private" individuals. Jones finds that he or his property is being invaded, aggressed against, by Smith. It is legitimate for Jones, as we have seen, to repel this invasion by defensive violence of his own. But now we come to a more knotty question: is it within the right of Jones to commit violence against innocent third parties as a corollary to his legitimate defense against Smith? To the libertarian, the answer must be clearly, no. Remember that the rule prohibiting violence against the persons or property of innocent men is absolute: it holds regardless of the subjective *motives* for the aggression. It is wrong and criminal to violate the property or person of another, even if one is a Robin Hood, or starving, or is doing it to save one's relatives, *or* is defending oneself against a third man's attack. We may understand and sympathize with the motives in many of these cases and extreme situations. We may later mitigate the guilt if the criminal comes to trial for punishment, but we cannot evade the judgment that this aggression is still a criminal act, and one, which the victim has every right to repel, by violence if necessary. In short, A aggresses against B because C is threatening, or aggressing against, A. We may understand C's "higher" culpability in this whole procedure; but we must still label this aggression as a criminal act, which B has the right to repel by violence.

To be more concrete, if Jones finds that his property is being stolen by Smith, he has the right to repel him and try to catch him; but he has *no* right to repel him by bombing a building and murdering innocent people or to catch him by spraying machine gun fire into an innocent crowd. If he does this, he is as much (or more of) a criminal aggressor as Smith is. The application to problems of war and peace is already becoming evident. For while war in the narrower sense is a conflict between States, in the broader sense we may define it as the outbreak of open violence between people or groups of people. If Smith and a group of his henchmen aggress against Jones and Jones and his bodyguards pursue the Smith gang to their lair, we may cheer Jones on in his endeavor; and we, and others in society interested in repelling aggression, may contribute financially or personally to Jones's cause. But Jones has *no* right, any more than does Smith, to aggress against anyone else in the course of his "just war": to steal others' property in order to finance his pursuit, to conscript others into his posse by use of violence, or to kill others in the course of his struggle to capture the Smith forces. If Jones should do any of these things, he becomes a criminal as *fully* as Smith, and he too becomes subject to whatever sanctions are meted out against criminality. In fact, if Smith's crime was theft, and Jones should use conscription to catch him, or should kill others in the pursuit, Jones becomes more of a criminal than Smith, for such crimes against another person as enslavement and murder are surely far worse than theft. (For while theft injures the extension of another's personality, enslavement injures, and murder obliterates, that personality itself.)

Suppose that Jones, in the course of his "just war" against the ravages of Smith, should kill a few innocent people, and suppose that he should declaim, in defense of this murder, that he was simply acting on the slogan, "Give me liberty or give me death." The absurdity of this "defense" should be evident at once, for the issue is not whether Jones was willing to risk death personally in his defensive struggle against Smith; the issue is whether he was willing to kill other people in pursuit of his legitimate end. For Jones was in truth acting on the completely indefensible slogan: "Give me liberty or give *them* death" surely a far less noble battle cry. The libertarian's basic attitude toward war must then be: it is legitimate to use violence against criminals in defense of one's rights of person and property; it is completely impermissible to violate the rights of *other* innocent people. War, then, is only proper when the exercise of violence is rigorously limited to the individual criminals. We may judge for ourselves how many wars or conflicts in history have met this criterion.

It has often been maintained, and especially by conservatives, that the development of the horrendous modern weapons of mass murder (nuclear weapons, rockets, germ warfare, *etc.*) is only a difference of *degree* rather than *kind* from the simpler weapons of an earlier era. Of course, one answer to this is that when the degree is the number of human lives, the difference is a very big one. But another answer that the libertarian is particularly equipped to give is that while the bow and arrow and even the rifle can be pinpointed, if the will be there, against actual criminals, modern nuclear weapons cannot. Here is a crucial difference in kind. Of course, the bow and arrow could be used for aggressive purposes, but it could also be pinpointed to use only against aggressors. Nuclear weapons, even "conventional" aerial bombs, cannot be. These weapons are *ipso facto* engines of indiscriminate mass destruction. (The only exception would be the extremely rare case where a mass of people who were all criminals inhabited a vast geographical area.) We must, therefore, conclude that the use of nuclear or similar weapons, or the threat thereof, is a sin and a crime against humanity for which there can be no justification.

This is why the old cliché no longer holds that it is not the arms but the will to use them that is significant in judging matters of war and peace. For it is precisely the characteristic of modern weapons that they cannot be used selectively, cannot be used in a libertarian manner. Therefore, their very existence must be condemned, and nuclear disarmament becomes a good to be pursued for its own sake. And if we will indeed use our strategic intelligence, we will see that such disarmament is not only a good, but the highest political good that we can pursue in the modern world. For just as murder is a more heinous crime against another man than larceny, so mass murder – indeed murder so widespread as to threaten human civilization and human survival itself – is the worst crime that any man could possibly commit. And that crime is now imminent. And the forestalling of massive annihilation is far more important, in truth, than the demunicipalization of garbage disposal, as worthwhile as that may be. Or are libertarians going to wax properly indignant about price control or the income tax, and yet shrug their shoulders at or even positively advocate the ultimate crime of mass murder? If nuclear warfare is totally illegitimate even for individuals defending themselves against criminal assault, how much more so is nuclear or even "conventional" warfare between States! It is time now to bring the State into our discussion. The State is a group of people who have managed to acquire a virtual monopoly of the use of violence throughout a given territorial area. In particular, it has acquired a monopoly of aggressive violence, for States generally recognize the right of individuals to use violence (though not against States, of course) in self-defense. The State then uses this monopoly to wield power over the inhabitants of the area and to enjoy the material fruits of that power. The State, then, is the only organization in society that regularly and openly obtains its monetary revenues by the use of *aggressive* violence; all other individuals and organizations (except if delegated that right by the State) can obtain wealth only by peaceful production and by voluntary exchange of their respective products. This use of violence to obtain its revenue (called "taxation") is the keystone of State power. Upon this base the State erects a further structure of power over the individuals in its territory, regulating them, penalizing critics, subsidizing favorites, *etc.* The State also takes care to arrogate to itself the compulsory monopoly of various critical services needed by society, thus keeping the people in dependence upon the State for key services, keeping control of the vital command posts in society and also fostering among the public the myth that *only* the State can supply these goods and services. Thus the State is careful to monopolize police and judicial service, the ownership of roads and streets, the supply of money, and the postal service, and effectively to monopolize or control education, public utilities, transportation, and radio and television. Now, since the State arrogates to itself the monopoly of violence over a territorial area, so long as its depredations and extortions go unresisted, there is said to be "peace" in the area, since the only violence is one-way, directed by the State downward against the people. Open conflict within the area only breaks out in the case of "revolutions" in which people resist the use of State power against them. Both the quiet case of the State unresisted and the case of open revolution may be termed "vertical violence": violence of the State against its public or vice versa. In the modern world, each land area is ruled over by a State organization, but there are a number of States scattered over the earth, each with a monopoly of violence over its own territory. No super-State exists with a monopoly of violence over the entire world; and so a state of "anarchy" exists between the several States. (It has always been a source of wonder, incidentally, to this writer how the same conservatives who denounce as lunatic any proposal for eliminating a monopoly of violence over a given territory and thus leaving private individuals without an overlord, should be equally insistent upon leaving *States* without an overlord to settle disputes between them. The former is always denounced as "crackpot anarchism"; the latter is hailed as preserving independence and "national sovereignty" from "world government.") And so, except for revolutions, which occur only sporadically, the open violence and two-sided conflict in the world takes place *between* two or more States, that is, in what is called "international war" (or "horizontal violence").

Now there are crucial and vital differences between inter-State warfare on the one hand and revolutions against the State or conflicts between private individuals on the other. One vital difference is the shift in geography. In a revolution, the conflict takes place *within* the same geographical area: both the minions of the State and the revolutionaries inhabit the same territory. Inter-State warfare, on the other hand, takes place between two groups, each having a monopoly over its own geographical area; that is, it takes place between inhabitants of different territories. From this difference flow several important consequences: (1) in inter-State war the scopes for the use of modern weapons of destruction is far greater. For if the "escalation" of weaponry in an intra-territorial conflict becomes too great, each side will blow itself up with the weapons directed against the other. Neither a revolutionary group nor a State combating revolution, for example, can use nuclear weapons against the other. But, on the other hand, when the warring parties inhabit different territorial areas, the scope for modern weaponry becomes enormous, and the entire arsenal of mass devastation can come into play. A second consequence (2) is that while it is *possible* for revolutionaries to pinpoint their targets and confine them to their State enemies, and thus avoid aggressing against innocent people, pinpointing is far less possible in an inter-State war. This is true even with older weapons; and, of course, with modern weapons there can be no pinpointing whatever. Furthermore, (3) since each State can mobilize all the people and resources in its territory, the other State comes to regard all the citizens of the opposing country as at least temporarily its enemies and to treat them accordingly by extending the war to them. Thus, all of the consequences of inter-territorial war make it almost inevitable that inter-State war will involve aggression by each side against the innocent civilians – the private individuals – of the other. This inevitability becomes absolute with modern weapons of mass destruction.

If one distinct attribute of inter-State war is inter-territoriality, another unique attribute stems from the fact that each State lives by taxation over its subjects. Any war against another State, therefore, involves the increase and extension of taxation-aggression over its own people. Conflicts between private individuals can be, and usually are, voluntarily waged and financed by the parties concerned. Revolutions can be, and often are, financed and fought by voluntary contributions of the public. But State wars can only be waged through aggression against the taxpayer. All State wars, therefore, involve increased aggression against the State's own taxpayers, and almost all State wars (*all*, in modern warfare) involve the maximum aggression (murder) against the innocent civilians ruled by the enemy State. On the other hand, revolutions are generally financed voluntarily and may pinpoint their violence to the State rulers, and private conflicts may confine their violence to the actual criminals. The libertarian must, therefore, conclude that, while some revolutions and some private conflicts *may* be legitimate, State wars are *always* to be condemned. Many libertarians object as follows: "While we too deplore the use of taxation for warfare, and the State's monopoly of defense service, we have to recognize that these conditions exist, and while they do, we must support the State in just wars of defense." The reply to this would go as follows: "Yes, as you say, unfortunately States exist, each having a monopoly of violence over its territorial area." What then should be the attitude of the libertarian toward conflicts between these States? The libertarian should say, in effect, to the State: "All right, you exist, but as long as you exist at least confine your activities to the area which you monopolize." In short, the libertarian is interested in reducing as much as possible the area of State aggression against all private individuals. The only way to do this, in international affairs, is for the people of each country to pressure their own State to confine its activities to the area, which it monopolizes, and not to aggress against other State-monopolists. In short, the objective of the libertarian is to confine any existing State to as small a degree of invasion of person and property as possible. And this means the total avoidance of war. The people under each State should pressure "their" respective States not to attack one-another, and, if a conflict should break out, to negotiate a peace or declare a cease-fire as quickly as physically possible. Suppose further that we have that rarity – an unusually clear-cut case in which the State is actually trying to defend the property of one of its citizens. A citizen of country A travels or invests in country B, and then State B aggresses against his person or confiscates his property. Surely, our libertarian critic would argue, here is a clear-cut case where State A should threaten or commit war against State B in order to defend the property of "its" citizen. Since, the argument runs, the State has taken upon itself the monopoly of defense of its citizens, it then has the obligation to go to war on behalf of any citizen, and libertarians have an obligation to support this war as a just one. But the point again is that each State has a monopoly of violence and, therefore, of defense only over its territorial area. It has no such monopoly; in fact, it has no power at all, over any other geographical area. Therefore, if an inhabitant of country A should move to or invest in country B, the libertarian must argue that he thereby takes his chances with the State-monopolist of country B, and it would be immoral and criminal for State A to tax people in country A *and* kill numerous innocents in country B in order to defend the property of the traveler or investor.

It should also be pointed out that there is no defense against nuclear weapons (the only current "defense" is the threat of mutual annihilation) and, therefore, that the State *cannot* fulfill any sort of defense function so long as these weapons exist.

The libertarian objective, then, should be, regardless of the specific causes of any conflict, to pressure States not to launch wars against other States and, should a war break out, to pressure them to sue for peace and negotiate a cease-fire and peace treaty as quickly as physically possible. This objective, incidentally, is enshrined in the international law of the eighteenth and nineteenth centuries, that is, the ideal that no State could aggress against the territory of another – in short, the "peaceful coexistence" of States.

Suppose, however, that despite libertarian opposition, war has begun and the warring States are not negotiating a peace. What, then, should be the libertarian position? Clearly, this reduces the scope of assault of innocent civilians as much as possible. Old-fashioned international law had two excellent devices for this: the "laws of war," and the "laws of neutrality" or "neutrals' rights." The laws of neutrality are designed to keep any war that breaks out confined to the warring States themselves, without aggression against the States or particularly the peoples of the other nations. Hence the importance of such ancient and now forgotten American principles as "freedom of the seas" or severe limitations upon the rights of warring States to blockade neutral trade with the enemy country. In short, the libertarian tries to induce neutral States to *remain* neutral in any inter-State conflict and to induce the warring States to observe fully the rights of neutral citizens. The "laws of war" were designed to limit as much as possible the invasion by warring States of the rights of the civilians of the respective warring countries. As the British jurist F.J.P. Veale put it: The fundamental principle of this code was that hostilities between civilized peoples must be limited to the armed forces actually engaged . . . It drew a distinction between combatants and noncombatants by laying down that the sole business of the combatants is to fight each-other and, consequently, that noncombatants must be excluded from the scope of military operations. In the modified form of prohibiting the bombardment of all cities not in the front line, this rule held in Western European wars in recent centuries until Britain launched the strategic bombing of civilians in World War II. Now, of course, the entire concept is scarcely remembered, the very nature of nuclear war resting on the annihilation of civilians. In condemning all wars, regardless of motive, the libertarian knows that there may well be varying degrees of guilt among States for any specific war. But the overriding consideration for the libertarian is the condemnation of any State participation in war. Hence his policy is that of exerting pressure on all States not to start a war, to stop one that has begun and to reduce the scope of any persisting war in injuring civilians of either side or no side. A neglected corollary to the libertarian policy of peaceful coexistence of States is the rigorous abstention from any foreign aid; that is, a policy of nonintervention between States (= "isolationism" = "neutralism"). For any aid given by State A to State B (1) increases tax aggression against the people of country A and (2) aggravates the suppression by State B of its own people. If there are any revolutionary groups in country B, then foreign aid intensifies this suppression all the more. Even foreign aid to a revolutionary group in B – more defensible because directed to a voluntary group opposing a State rather than a State oppressing the people – must be condemned as (at the very least) aggravating tax aggression at home.

Let us see how libertarian theory applies to the problem of *imperialism,* which may be defined as the aggression by State A over the people of country B, and the subsequent maintenance of this foreign rule. Revolution by the B people against the imperial rule of A is certainly legitimate, provided again that revolutionary fire be directed only against the rulers. It has often been maintained – even by libertarians – that Western imperialism over undeveloped countries should be supported as more watchful of property rights than any successor native government would be. The first reply is that judging what might follow the *status quo* is purely speculative, whereas existing imperialist rule is all too real and culpable. Moreover, the libertarian here begins his focus at the wrong end – at the alleged benefit of imperialism to the native. He should, on the contrary, concentrate first on the Western taxpayer, who is mulcted and burdened to pay for the wars of conquest, and then for the maintenance of the imperial bureaucracy. On this ground alone, the libertarian must condemn imperialism.

Does opposition to all war mean that the libertarian can never countenance change – that he is consigning the world to a permanent freezing of unjust regimes? Certainly not. Suppose, for example, that the hypothetical state of "Waldavia" has attacked "Ruritania" and annexed the western part of the country. The Western Ruritanians now long to be reunited with their Ruritanian brethren. How is this to be achieved? There is, of course, the route of peaceful negotiation between the two powers, but suppose that the Waldavian imperialists prove adamant. Or, libertarian Waldavians can put pressure on their government to abandon its conquest in the name of justice. But suppose that this, too, does not work. What then? We must still maintain the illegitimacy of Ruritania's mounting a war against Waldavia. The legitimate routes are (1) revolutionary uprisings by the oppressed Western Ruritanian people, and (2) aid by private Ruritanian groups (or, for that matter, by friends of the Ruritanian cause in other countries) to the Western rebels – either in the form of equipment or of volunteer personnel.

We have seen throughout our discussion the crucial importance, in any present-day libertarian peace program, of the elimination of modern methods of mass annihilation. These weapons, against which there can be no defense, assure maximum aggression against civilians in any conflict with the clear prospect of the destruction of civilization and even of the human race itself. Highest priority on any libertarian agenda, therefore, must be pressure on all States to agree to general and complete disarmament down to police levels, with particular stress on nuclear disarmament. In short, if we are to use our strategic intelligence, we must conclude that the dismantling of the greatest menace that has ever confronted the life and liberty of the human race is indeed far more important than demunicipalizing the garbage service. We cannot leave our topic without saying at least a word about the domestic tyranny that is the inevitable accompaniment of war. The great Randolph Bourne realized that "war is the health of the State." It is in war that the State really comes into its own: swelling in power, in number, in pride, in absolute dominion over the economy and the society. Society becomes a herd, seeking to kill its alleged enemies, rooting out and suppressing all dissent from the official war effort, happily betraying truth for the supposed public interest. Society becomes an armed camp, with the values and the morale – as Albert Jay Nock once phrased it – of an "army on the march."

The root myth that enables the State to wax fat off war is the canard that war is a defense *by* the State *of* its subjects. The facts, of course, are precisely the reverse. If war is the health of the State, it is also its greatest danger. A State can only "die" by defeat in war or by revolution. In war, therefore, the State frantically mobilizes the people to fight for *it* against another State, under the pretext that *it* is fighting for them. But all this should occasion no surprise; we see it in other walks of life. For which categories of crime does the State pursue and punish most intensely – those against private citizens or those against *itself?* The gravest crimes in the State's lexicon are almost invariably not invasions of person and property, but dangers to its *own* contentment: for example, treason, desertion of a soldier to the enemy, failure to register for the draft, conspiracy to overthrow the government. Murder is pursued haphazardly unless the victim be a *policeman,* or *Gott soll hüten,* an assassinated Chief of State; failure to pay a private debt is, if anything, almost encouraged, but income tax evasion is punished with utmost severity; counterfeiting the State's money is pursued far more relentlessly than forging private checks, *etc.* All this evidence demonstrates that the State is far more interested in preserving its own power than in defending the rights of private citizens.

A final word about conscription: of all the ways in which war aggrandizes the State, this is perhaps the most flagrant and most despotic. But the most striking fact about conscription is the absurdity of the arguments put forward on its behalf. A man must be conscripted to defend his (or someone else's?) liberty against an evil State beyond the borders. Defend his liberty? How? By being coerced into an army whose very *raison d'être* is the expunging of liberty, the trampling on all the liberties of the person, the calculated and brutal dehumanization of the soldier and his transformation into an efficient engine of murder at the whim of his "commanding officer?" Can any conceivable foreign State do anything worse to him than what "his" army is now doing for his alleged benefit? Who is there, 0 Lord, to defend him against his "defenders?"

Section 5a

Llewellyn H. Rockwell, Jr., "The Glory of War"

The bloom on the rose of war eventually fades, leaving only the thorns. By the time this takes place, most everyone has already begun the national task of averting the eyes from the thorns, meaning the awful reality, the dashed hopes, the expense, the lame, the limbless, the widows, the orphans, the death on all sides, and the resulting instability. The people who still take an interest are those who first took an interest in war: the power elite, who began the war for purposes very different from that which they sold to the public at the outset. Thus does the American public not care much about Iraq. It is not quite as invisible as other nations that were the subject of national obsessions in the recent past. Hardly anyone knows who or what is running El Salvador, Nicaragua, Haiti, Libya, Serbia, or Somalia, or any of the other formerly strategic countries that once engaged national attention. In fact, the president of Nicaragua, Enrique Bolanos (never heard of him, huh?) is visiting the White House next week in hopes of soliciting support for the upcoming election, which could prove to be dicey since the old US nemesis Daniel Ortega is running and gaining some support on a consistently anti-US platform. Should he win, one can imagine the White House swinging into high gear about how Nicaragua is harboring communists, or…terrorists, or maybe not. Maybe he will rule the country and never make a headline. It is all up to the state. Why the state goes to war is not a mystery — at least the general reasons are not mysterious. War is an excuse for spending money on its friends. It can punish enemies that are not going with the program. It intimidates other states tempted to go their own way. It can pave the way for commercial interests linked to the state. The regime that makes and wins a war gets written up in the history books. So the reasons are the same now as in the ancient world: power, money, glory. Why the bourgeoisie back war is another matter. It is self-evidently not in their interest. The government gains power at their expense. It spends their money and runs up debt that is paid out of taxes and inflation. It fosters the creation of permanent enemies abroad who then work to diminish our security at home. It leads to the violation of privacy and civil liberty. War is incompatible with a government that leaves people alone to develop their lives in an atmosphere of freedom. Nonetheless, war with moral themes — we are the good guys working for God and they are the bad guys doing the devil's work — tends to attract a massive amount of middle class support. People believe the lies, and, once exposed, they defend the right of the state to lie. People who are otherwise outraged by murder find themselves celebrating the same on a mass industrial scale. People who harbor no hatred toward foreigners find themselves attaching ghastly monikers to whole classes of foreign peoples. Regular middle class people, who otherwise struggle to eke out a flourishing life in this vale of tears, feel hatred well up within them and confuse it for honor, bravery, courage, and valor. Why? Nationalism is one answer. To be at war is to feel at one with something much larger than oneself, to be a part of a grand historical project. They have absorbed the civic religion from childhood — Boston tea, cherry trees, log cabins, Chevrolet — but it mostly has no living presence in their minds until the state pushes the war button, and then all the nationalist emotions well up within them. Nationalism is usually associated with attachment to a particular set of state managers that you think can somehow lead the country in a particular direction of which you approve. So the nationalism of the Iraq war was mostly a Republican Party phenomenon. All Democrats are suspected as being insufficiently loyal, of feeling sympathy for The Enemy, or defending such ideas as civil liberty at a time when the nation needs unity more than ever. You could tell a Republican nationalist during this last war because the words peace and liberty were always said with a sneer, as if they didn't matter at all. Even the Constitution came in for a pounding from these people. Bush did all he could to consolidate decision-making power unto himself, and even strongly suggested that he was acting on God's orders as Commander in Chief, and his religious constitutionalist supporters went right along with it. They were willing to break as many eggs as necessary to make the war omelet. I've got an archive of a thousand hate mails to prove it. But nationalism is not the only basis for bourgeois support for war. Long-time war correspondent Chris Hedges, in his great book *War is a Force that Gives Us Meaning* (First Anchor, 2003) argues that war operates as a kind of canvas on which every member of the middle and working class can paint his or her own picture. Whatever personal frustrations exist in your life, however powerless you feel, war works as a kind of narcotic. It provides a means for people to feel temporarily powerful and important, as if they are part of some big episode in history. War then becomes for people a kind of lurching attempt to taste immortality. War gives their lives meaning. Hedges don't go this far but if you know something about the sociology of religion, you can recognize what he is speaking of: the sacraments. In Christian theology they are derived from periodic ceremonies in the Jewish tradition that cultivate the favor of God, who grants our lives transcendent importance. We receive sacraments as a means of gaining propitiation for our sins, an eternal blessing on worldly choices, or the very means of eternal life. War is the devil's sacrament. It promises to bind us not with God but with the nation state. It grants not life but death. It provides not liberty but slavery. It lives not on truth but on lies, and these lies are themselves said to be worthy of defense. It exalts evil and puts down the good. It is promiscuous in encouraging an orgy of sin, not self-restraint and thought. It is irrational and bloody and vicious and appalling. And it claims to be the highest achievement of man. It is worse than mass insanity. It is mass wallowing in evil. And then it is over. People oddly forget what took place. The rose wilts and the thorns grow but people go on with their lives. War no longer inspires. War news becomes uninteresting. All those arguments with friends and family — what were they about anyway? All that killing and expense and death — let's just avert our eyes from it all. Maybe in a few years, once the war is out of the news forever and the country we smashed recovers some modicum of civilization, we can revisit the event and proclaim it glorious. But for now, let's just say it never happened. That seems to be just about where people stand these days with the Iraq War. Iraq is a mess, hundreds of thousands are killed and maimed, billions of dollars are missing, the debt is astronomical, and the world seethes in hatred toward the conquering empire. And what does the warmongering middle class have to say for itself? Pretty much what you might expect: nothing. People have long accused the great liberal tradition of a dogmatic attachment to peace. It would appear that this is precisely what is necessary in order to preserve the freedom necessary for all of us to find true meaning in our lives.

Do we reject war and all its works? We do reject them.

Section 6a

Ludwig Von Mises, "Peace is the Father of All Things"
An Excerpt take from Mises' book, Socialism, An Economic and Sociological Analysis, first published by Mises in 1951 and reprinted in 2009 by the Mises Institute, Chapter III, "The Social Order and the Political Constitution," pp. 69-70.

The domination of the principle of violence was naturally not restricted to the sphere of property. The spirit which put its trust in might alone, which sought the fundamentals of welfare, not in agreement, but in ceaseless conflict, permeated the whole of life. All human relations were settled according to the 'Law of the Stronger', which is really the negation of law. There was no peace; at best there was a truce.

Society grows out of the smallest associations. The circle of those who combined to keep the peace among themselves was at first very limited. The circle widened step by step through millennia, until the community of international law and the union of peace extended over the greatest part of humanity, excluding the half savage peoples who lived on the lowest plane of culture. Within this community the principle of contract was not everywhere equally powerful. It was most completely recognized in all that was concerned with property. It remained weakest in fields where it touched the question of political domination. Into the sphere of foreign policy it has so far penetrated no further than to limit the principles of violence by setting up rules of combat. Apart from the process of arbitration, which is recent development, disputes between states are still, in essentials, decided by arms, the most usual of ancient judicial processes; but the deciding combat, like the judicial duels of the most ancient laws, most conform to certain rules. All the same, it would be false to maintain that in the intercourse of states, fear of foreign violence is the one factor that keeps the sword in its sheath. Forces that have been active in the foreign policy of states through millennia have set the value of peace above the profit of victorious war. In our time even the mightiest warlord cannot isolate himself completely from the influence of the legal maxim that wars must have valid reasons. Those who wage war invariably endeavor to prove that theirs is the just cause and that they fight in defense or at least in preventive-defense; this is a solemn recognition of the principle of Law and Peace. Every policy that has openly confessed to the principle of violence has brought upon itself a world-coalition, to which it has finally succumbed.

In the Liberal Social Philosophy the human mind becomes aware of the overcoming of the principle of violence by the principle of peace. In this philosophy for the first time humanity gives itself an account of its actions. It tears away the romantic nimbus with which the exercise of power had been surrounded. *War, it teaches, is harmful, not only to the conquered but to the conqueror. Society has arisen out of the works of peace; the essence of society is peacemaking. Peace and not war is the father of all things. Only economic action has created the wealth around us; labor, not the profession of arms, brings happiness. Peace builds, war destroys. Nations are fundamentally peaceful because they recognize the predominant utility of peace. They accept war only in self-defense; wars of aggression they do not desire. It is the princes who want war, because thus they hope to get money, goods, and power. It is the business of the nations to prevent them from achieving their desire by denying them the means necessary for making war.*

The love of peace of the liberal does not spring form philanthropic considerations, as does the pacifism of Bertha Suttner and of others of that category. It has none of the woebegone spirit that attempts to combat the romanticism of blood lust with the sobriety of international congresses. Its predilection for peace is not a pastime, which is otherwise compatible with all possible convictions. It is *the* social theory of Liberalism. Whoever maintains the solidarity of the economic interests of all nations, and remains indifferent to the extent of national territories, and national frontiers; whoever has so far overcome collectivist notions that such an expression as 'Honor of the State' sounds incomprehensible to him; that man will nowhere find a valid cause for wars of aggression. Liberal pacifism is the offspring of the Liberal Social Philosophy. That Liberalism aims at the protection of property and that it rejects war, are two expressions of one and the same principle.

Section 7a

Laurence M. Vance, "Should a Christian Join the Military?"

An article published in Vance's book entitled,"War, Christianity, and the State," copyright 2013 by Laurence M. Vance, pp. 283-292

Christian enthusiasm for war is at an all-time high.

Gullible Christians have not just tolerated the state's nebulous crusade against "evil," they have actively promoted both it and the overgrown U.S. Military establishment. Because the Republican Party is in control of the federal government instead of the "ungodly" Democrats, because President Bush is the commander in chief instead of the "immoral" Bill Clinton, and because the "enemy" is the easily-vilifiable Muslim infidel, many Christians, who certainly ought to know better given the history of state-sponsored persecution of Christians, "heretics," and other religious groups over the past two thousand years, have come to view the state, and in particular its coercive arm, the military, as sacrosanct.

For far too long Christians have turned a blind eye to the U.S. Global Empire of troops and bases that encircles the world. Many Christians have willingly served as cannon fodder for the state and its wars and military interventions. Christians who haven't died (wasted their life) for their country in some overseas desert or jungle increasingly perpetuate the myth that being a soldier in the U.S. Military is a noble occupation that one can wholeheartedly perform as a Christian.

The Question

The question of whether a Christian should join the military is a controversial one in some Christian circles. By a Christian I don't just mean someone who accepts the title by default because he was born in "Christian" America or "Christian" Europe. In this respect, everyone but Jews and atheists could be classified as Christians. The mention of a Christian in this article should be taken in the narrower sense of someone who professes to believe that Jesus Christ is the Savior (Luke 2:11) and that the Bible is some kind of an authority (Acts 17:11). It is true that this may be too broad a definition for some Christians, and it is also true that many who profess to be Christians hold defective views on the person of Christ and the nature of the Atonement. But for the purposes of this article, the "broadness" of this definition and the permitting of these "defects" do not in any way affect the question: Should a Christian join the military? In fact, the narrower one's definition of what constitutes a real Christian, the stronger the case can be made against a Christian joining the military. The idea that there are certain things Christians should not do is not only scriptural (1 Corinthians 6:9—11; Galatians 5:19—21), it is readily acknowledged by Christians and non-Christians alike. Christians have historically applied this idea to occupations as well. But it is not just unlawful occupations like pimp, prostitute, drug dealer, and hit man that Christians have shied away from. Most Americans — whether they be atheist or theist — would have a problem with those occupations as well. Everyone knows that there are also certain lawful occupations that Christians frown upon: bartender, exotic dancer, casino card dealer, *etc.* This prohibition is also usually extended to benign occupations in not so benign environments. Therefore, a clerk in a drug store or grocery store is acceptable, but a clerk in liquor store or an X-rated video store is not. Likewise, most Christians would not work for an abortion clinic, for any amount of money, whether in the capacity of a doctor or a secretary. In other places of employment, however, a Christian might have no problem with being employed, only with working in a certain capacity. This explains why some Christians might not wait tables in restaurants that forced them to serve alcohol, but would feel perfectly comfortable working for the same restaurant in some other capacity, like a bookkeeper or janitor.

The larger question of whether a Christian (or anyone opposed to the federal leviathan) should work for the state is not at issue. Someone employed by the state as a teacher, a mailman, a security guard, or a park ranger is providing a lawful, moral, non-aggressive, non-intrusive service that is in the same manner also provided by the free market. Thus, it might be argued that working for the BATF, the CIA, the FBI, or as a regulation-enforcing federal bureaucrat is off limits, whereas these other occupations are not. The question then is which of these two groups the U.S. Military belongs in. Given the actions of the U.S. Military since Sherman's state-sponsored "total war" against Southerners and Indians the host of twentieth-century interventions, subjugations, and "liberations," and the current debacle in Iraq, it should be obvious.

The question before us then is whether a Christian should join the military. Although my remarks are primarily directed at the idea of Christian being a professional soldier (a hired assassin in some cases) for the state, they are also applicable to serving in the military in any capacity.

To save some people the trouble of e-mailing me to ask if I have ever been in the military, I will say now that, no, I have never been in the military. For some strange reason, many Americans think that if you have not "served" your country in the military then you have no right to criticize it. There are three problems with this attitude.

First of all, this is like saying that if you have not "served" in the Mafia then you have no right to criticize John Gotti. It reminds me of fellow travelers in the 1950s, 1960s, and 1970s saying that if you have not lived in the Soviet Union then you have no right to criticize it. So no, I am not a veteran, but I have family members who were in the military and have lived near military bases and been intimately associated with military personnel since I was ten years old. No, I am not a veteran, but I am a student of history ("Those who cannot learn from history are doomed to repeat it" — George Santayana), and was born with enough common sense to know government propaganda when I see it. I can also read above a tenth-grade level, which is about all it takes to compare the wisdom of the Founding Fathers with the drivel from Bush, Cheney, Wolfowitz, Powell, and Rumsfeld.

Secondly, some of the most vocal critics of the military have been in the military, like USMC Major General Smedley Butler. So it is not just non-veterans who are critics of the military.

The third problem with the knee-jerk reaction to this article and me because I have never been in the military is that it is misplaced indignation. I am only examining the question of whether a Christian should join the military. Criticism of the military is not my direct purpose.

Another objection to an article of this nature is that if it were not for the U.S. Military then no one would have the freedom right now to write anything. But if the military exists to defend our freedoms, and does not just function as the force behind an aggressive, interventionist U.S. foreign policy, then why are our troops scattered across150 different regimes of the world? Why doesn't the military control our borders? Why do we need a Department of Homeland Security if we already have a Department of Defense? Why, with the biggest military budget ever do we have less freedom in America now than at any time in history? The U.S. Military could not even defend the Pentagon. The case could even be argued that U.S. Military intervention is the cause for much of the anti-American sentiment in the world. So, like Brad Edmonds, I don't owe and still do not owe the military anything. I trust in God Almighty to keep me safe from a nuclear attack, not the U.S. Military.

The Commandments

Using the Ten Commandments (Exodus 20:3—17) as a guide, it is my contention that the military is no place for a Christian. As a Christian under the authority of the New Testament, I am perfectly aware that the Ten Commandments are in the Old Testament and were originally given to the nation of Israel. But I am also cognizant that the Apostle Paul said: "Whatsoever things were written aforetime were written for our learning" (Romans 15:4) after he had just recited many of the Ten Commandments (Romans 13:8—9).

1. Thou shalt have no other gods before me (Exodus 20:3).

The state has historically been the greatest enemy of Christianity. Yet, many Christians in the military have made the state their god. Members of the military are totally dependent on the state for their food, clothing, shelter, recreation, and medical care. They are conditioned to look to the state for their every need. But the state demands unconditional obedience. Shoot this person, bomb this city, blow up this building — don't ask why, just do it because the state tells you to. The soldier is conditioned to believe that whatever he does is right because it is done in the name of the state. The state's acts of aggression are regarded as acts of benevolence. Then, once the benevolent state is viewed as never doing anything wrong, it in essence becomes the all-seeing, all-knowing, omniscient state, since it would take absolute knowledge to know for certain that the person shot, the city bombed, or the building blown up "deserved" it.

2. Thou shalt not make unto thee any graven image (Exodus 20:4).

The state has an image that it expects its citizens to reverence and pledge allegiance to. This is especially true of people serving in the military. Perhaps the most famous picture of the flag is the raising of the flag by U.S. troops at Iwo Jima on February 23, 1945. But there is another picture of the flag that has occurred thousands of times that the state does its best to suppress: the picture of the flag-draped coffin of a life wasted in the service of one of the state's needless wars. Foreigners who object to our intervention in their country and our military presence across the globe burn American flags in protest. But they are not protesting because we are capitalists who believe in liberty, freedom, and democracy and they do not share our values. Christians in the military must reverence what has often justly come to be viewed by most of the world as a symbol of oppression. They must also pledge their allegiance to it. Christians blindly recite the Pledge of Allegiance without even bothering to find out where it came from, what its author intended, and how the state uses it to instill loyalty to the state in the minds of its youth. Never mind that the author was a socialist Baptist minister, Francis Bellamy (1855—1932), who was forced to resign from his church in Boston because of his socialist ideas (like preaching on "Jesus the Socialist"). Never mind that the idea for Bellamy's pledge of allegiance was taken from Lincoln's oath of allegiance imposed on Southerners after the successful Northern invasion of the Southern states. Never mind that "republic for which" the flag "stands" was, in Bellamy's eyes, "the One Nation which the Civil War was fought to prove." The Pledge is an allegiance oath to the omnipotent, omniscient state. There is nothing inherently wrong with the United States having a flag, but it has been made into a graven image that no Christian, in the military or otherwise, should bow down to.

3. Thou shalt not take the name of the LORD thy God in vain (Exodus 20:7).

The state will tolerate God and religion as long as He and it can be used to legitimize the state. God's name is taken in vain when it is used to justify the state's wars and military interventions. Some Christians in the military envision themselves as modern-day crusaders warring against the Muslim infidel. Indeed, the president even termed his war on terrorism "this crusade." Others, all the way up to the commander in chief, invoke the name of God or His words in Scripture to give authority to their unconstitutional, unscriptural, and immoral military adventures. When a young Christian man (or woman, unfortunately) leaves home and joins the military he often learns to take God's name in vain in ways that he never could have imagined. There is a reason the old expression is "cuss like a sailor," not cuss like a mechanic, an accountant, or a fireman. Singing "God Bless America" while cognizant of the abortions, promiscuity, and pornography that curse America is taking God's name in vain. Likewise, military chaplains asking God to bless troops on their missions of death and destruction are taking God's name in vain. Many Christians were upset a few years ago when the 9th U.S. Circuit Court of Appeals (which covers Alaska, Arizona, California, Hawaii, Idaho, Montana, Nevada, Oregon, and Washington) tried to strike out the phrase "under God" from the Pledge of Allegiance (which was only added in 1954). They should have cheered instead, for even though the two federal judges (the decision was 2-1) who made the ridiculous ruling that the inclusion of the phrase "under God" was an unconstitutional "endorsement of religion" ought to have their heads examined, America is not a nation "under God," and to say that it is (as when one recites the Pledge of Allegiance), is the epitome of using God's name in vain.

4. Remember the Sabbath day, to keep it holy (Exodus 20:8).

Although the Sabbath day is technically the Jewish seventh day (Saturday) and not the Christian first day (Sunday), the basic principle is still the same. Christians the world over set aside the first day of the week to attend church services. Christians in the military are often deployed to some strange city or remote country for months at a time and are therefore forced to violate the precept of "not forsaking the assembling of ourselves together" (Hebrews 10:25). Defense consultant Josh Pollack, in his "Saudi Arabia and the United States, 1931-2002," has documented that during the early decades of the American troop presence in Saudi Arabia, Air Force chaplains were forbidden to wear Christian insignia or hold formal services. During the First Gulf War of Bush the Elder, the importation of Bibles for Christian troops was discouraged, and no alcohol was permitted to U.S. troops in accordance with Islamic Law.

5. Honor thy father and thy mother (Exodus 20:12).

It used to be thought that following one's father into the military was a noble thing that honored him. Thankfully, this is not so much the case anymore. Is it honoring to one's father and mother for a Christian to accept the state's amoral values that are taught in the military and reject the values learned from a Christian upbringing? The temptations in the military for a Christian young person away from home for the first time are very great. Joining the military is one of the surest ways for a

Christian to dishonor his parents by associating with bad company and picking up bad habits. This is not to deny that some Christians who are well grounded in the Scriptures live an exemplary life while in the military and are a positive force for good. But see the next point.

6. Thou shalt not kill (Exodus 20:13).

This is perhaps the greatest reason for a Christian not to join the military. But there is a difference between killing and murdering. Under certain conditions, a Christian would be entirely justified in taking up arms to defend himself, his family, and his property against an aggressor. If America was attacked, Christians could in good conscience kill and maim enemy invaders. However, when was the United States ever in danger from Guatemala, Vietnam, Indonesia, Grenada, Panama, Kosovo, Cuba, Haiti, Afghanistan, Iraq, North Korea, or any of the other places where the United States has intervened militarily? How then can a Christian justify killing any of them on their own soil? The old adage, "Join the army, meet interesting people, kill them," is now just "join the army and kill them" since you can't meet anyone at 10,000 feet before you release your load of bombs. The U.S. Military turns men into callous killers. The D.C. sniper, Lee Harvey Oswald, and Timothy McVey all learned how to kill in the military. When a Christian in the military is faced with an order to kill, bomb, or destroy someone or something halfway around the world that he has never met or seen, and is no real threat to him, his family, or his country, there is really only one option: "We ought to obey God rather than men" (Acts 4:29).

7. Thou shalt not commit adultery (Exodus 20:14).

Human nature being what it is, the forcing of men and women together, especially for extended periods on Navy ships, has been the source of many broken marriages and unwanted pregnancies. Christians in the military also face incredible temptations when they are deployed overseas. In his seminal work *Blowback: The Costs and Consequences of American Empire*, Chalmers Johnson has described the network of bars, strip clubs, whorehouses, and VD clinics that surround U.S. bases overseas. The former U.S. naval base at Subic Bay in the Philippines "had no industry nearby except for the 'entertainment' business, which supported approximately 55,000 prostitutes and a total of 2,182 registered establishments offering 'rest and recreation' to American servicemen." At the annual Cobra Gold joint military exercise in Thailand: "Some three thousand prostitutes wait for sailors and marines at the South Pattaya waterfront, close to Utapao air base." The prohibition in this commandment applies equally as well to men who are not married, for "whosoever looketh on a woman to lust after her hath committed adultery with her already in his heart" (Matthew 5:28).

8. Thou shalt not steal (Exodus 20:15).

Through its system of forced revenue collection (the income tax), the state is guilty of stealing untold trillions of dollars from working Americans. Very little of that money is spent for constitutionally authorized purposes. One of the largest expenditures of the state is its bloated military budget. Training, feeding, housing, transporting, paying, and arming thousands of troops all over the planet is a very expensive undertaking. Robert Higgs has estimated the true military budget in fiscal year 2004 to be about $695 billion. Besides being the recipient of stolen money, a Christian in the military may have to steal the lives of the sons and daughters of parents he has never met. He may have to steal land in foreign countries to build bases on. He certainly steals the resources of the countries he bombs. Christians in the military should heed the words of the Apostle Paul: "Let him that stole steal no more: but rather let him labour, working with his hands the thing which is good, that he may have to give to him that needeth" (Ephesians 4:28).

9. Thou shalt not bear false witness against thy neighbour (Exodus 20:16).

The state is the greatest bearer of false witness that there has ever been. The latest round of lies concerns the war in Iraq. Continual government lies about Iraq's supposed weapons of mass destruction, aluminum tubes, chemical and biological weapons, threat to the United States, tie to al Qaeda, and link to the September 11th attacks are the rule rather than the exception. The Christian in the military is supporting a lie and living a lie when he devotes his time and energy to supporting a U.S. war machine based on deception, disinformation, falsehood, and lies.

10. Thou shalt not covet (Exodus 20:17).

Young people generally join the military for the wrong motive. Bored, indecisive, in trouble, unemployed, seeking to get away from home — these are some of the reasons why young men and women join the military. But perhaps the greatest reason young people join the military today is because of covetousness. Recruitment slogans all emphasize how much money an enlistee can earn towards his college education. Then there are enlistment bonuses, free medical care, commissary and exchange shopping privileges, the lucrative retirement program, and the future "veterans preference" to help get that government job after retirement. But aside from money, some people covet an increase in prestige ("The few, the proud, the Marines"). Others covet the power that powerful weapons bring. Some Christian young people join the military because they are patriotic, loyal Americans who have been conditioned to think that they owe the state something ("Ask not what your country can do for you, but what you can do for your country"). Their patriotism is noble, but misdirected.

The Conclusion

Should a Christian join the military? Should anyone join the military? The U.S. Military, although officially called the Department of Defense, is the state's arm of aggression. If it limited itself to controlling our borders, patrolling our coasts, and protecting our citizens instead of intervening around the globe and leaving death and destruction in its wake then perhaps it might be a noble occupation for a Christian. But as it is now, the military is no place for a Christian.

The argument that you have to become one of them to win them is fallacious. No one would think of becoming a pimp or a prostitute in order to convert them to Christianity. The fact that a Christian is compared to a soldier (2 Timothy 2:3) is no more a scriptural endorsement of Christians in the military than God being compared to "a mighty man that shouteth by reason of wine" (Psalm 78:65) is an endorsement of drunkenness.

When the nation of Israel rejected the LORD and desired a king "like all the nations" (1 Samuel 8:5), God described "the manner of the king that shall reign over them" (1 Samuel 8:9):

And he said, this will be the manner of the king that shall reign over you: He will take your sons, and appoint them for himself, for his chariots, and to be his horsemen; and some shall run before his chariots.

And he will appoint him captains over thousands, and captains over fifties; and will set them to earn his ground, and to reap his harvest, and to make his instruments of war, and instruments of his chariots.

And he will take your daughters to be confectionaries, and to be cooks, and to be bakers.

And he will take your fields, and your vineyards, and your olive yards, even the best of them, and give them to his servants.

And he will take the tenth of your seed, and of your vineyards, and give to his officers, and to his servants.

And he will take your menservants, and your maidservants, and your goodliest young men, and your asses, and put them to his work.

He will take the tenth of your sheep: and ye shall be his servants.

And ye shall cry out in that day because of your king which ye shall have chosen you; and the LORD will not hear you in that day.

Nevertheless the people refused to obey the voice of Samuel; and they said, Nay; but we will have a king over us;

That we also may be like all the nations; and that our king may judge us, and go out before us, and fight our battles (1 Samuel 8:11—20).

Christians should remember that "the weapons of our warfare are not carnal" (2 Corinthians 10:4), and that we wield "the sword of the spirit, which is the word of God" (Ephesians 6:17).

That criticizing the military or recommending that Christians don't join it is seen as being un-American or traitorous shows just how effective the state has been with its propaganda. The United States is the greatest country on earth for a Christian to live in, but in spite of its military, not because of it.

Appendix B

Selected Writings From Fellow Saints, Section 1b
**Jeremy Ashton, "Open Letter to Mormons Regarding Ron Paul:
An LDS View of War"**
*Jeremy Ashton is the cofounder of LDS Liberty (www.ldsliberty.org) where he
dedicates his time and efforts to "advancing the cause of liberty in light of the restored
gospel. The following is an article that was published on lewrockwell.com in February
of 2008.*

Certainly, he who taught that to inherit eternal life we must "love
thy neighbor as thyself" would be deeply concerned with the destruction
of life so rampant in the world today. Since we live in a time of "wars
and rumors of wars," it is of supreme importance that we gain gospel
insight into the just causes for supporting war.

Much of the *Book of Mormon* is devoted to war, which was a
continual plague in ancient America. When were the followers of Christ
justified in taking part in this destruction of life? Alma 43:47 states "And
again, the Lord has said that: Ye shall defend your families even unto
bloodshed. Therefore for this cause were the Nephites (*i.e.* the followers
of Christ) contending with the Lamanites (*i.e.* those who were attacking
the Nephites), to defend themselves, and their families, and their lands,
their country, and their rights, and their religion." In Alma 48:14 we read
"Now the Nephites were taught to defend themselves against their
enemies, even to the shedding of blood if it were necessary; yea, and

they were also taught never to give an offense, yea, and never to raise the sword except it were against an enemy, except it were to preserve their lives." Thus, defense of rights was the only moral justification for war and the aggressive use of force was against the will of God. As followers of the "Prince of Peace," we are still bound by these principles today.

This being said, should America continue the war in Iraq, attack Iran before they supposedly develop a nuclear weapon, and continue the ill-defined war on Terrorism? I submit to you that the answer is emphatically "NO."

First of all, the war against Iraq is not defensive. For those who believe that the September 11th atrocities were an unprovoked attack by Muslim extremists, there is no proof that the prior Iraqi regime had anything to do with these attacks. Furthermore, the Iraqi government never directly attacked the United States of America. This is a preemptive war, which is the shedding of blood of those who have not given an offense, and is not justifiable before the Lord.

However, even if we suppose that the war in Iraq was defensive, the Iraqi government that "attacked" us no longer rules the country. Since the so-called offender has been eliminated, it follows that we are no longer defending ourselves against an enemy who gave the initial offense. The most benign reason for our continued waging of war in Iraq is to build a democratic government and bring stability to this region. This is not a moral basis for our continued bloodshed of the people in this region. If the French government had kept a military presence in the American states after the Revolutionary War, the patriots would have attacked them too.

The *Book of Mormon* provides us with the example of Captain Moroni, who was the great military leader of the Nephites during much of their warfare. After he had defeated a Lamanite army and the attacking king had been killed (effectively destroying the Lamanite government and bringing "instability" to the Lamanite people), Moroni did not lead an army down to the Lamanite lands to ensure the establishment of a democratic government, which would be friendly to the Nephites. We are specifically told that immediately afterward he put his efforts toward preparing the Nephite lands against any future attacks (Alma 62:42). Allowing the defeated aggressors to sort out their own governmental affairs was clearly his policy. After Captain Moroni had repelled a prior attack, we read "And the armies of the Nephites, or of Moroni, returned and came to their houses and their lands" (Alma 44:22). We have no moral basis for remaining in Iraq to assist in the creation and stabilization of the new Iraqi government. We need to immediately cease the American slaughter of Iraqis and all others who have not attacked our own families, lands, rights, and religion.

The *Book of Mormon* also provides us with another clear admonition not to be the aggressors of war in 3 Nephi chapter 3. Just prior to this time, the Nephites very own government leaders had conspired together to violate the God-given rights of the individuals in the land (sounds familiar). The people eventually rose up and threw the oppressors, or Gadianton robbers as they were called, out of their land. The Gadianton robbers then proceeded to attack them from the outside "and did slay so many people, and did lay waste so many cities, and did spread so much death and carnage throughout the land" that the people decided to join together "to take up arms against them" (3 Nephi 2:11).

Initially, the Nephites were able to ward off the attacks of the Gadianton robbers. However, after the Gadiantons had gained more strength, they sent a letter to the leader of the Nephites demanding surrender or the robbers would "let fall the sword upon you even until ye shall become extinct" (3 Nephi 3:8). At this point, the Nephites demanded of their leader, who we are told had the spirit of revelation, "Pray unto the Lord, and let us go up upon the mountains and into the wilderness, that we may fall upon the robbers and destroy them in their own lands" (3 Nephi 3:20). In today's language, they wanted "to fight the terrorists over there so they would not come over here." What was his answer? "The Lord forbid; for if we should go up against them the Lord would deliver us into their hands; therefore we will prepare ourselves in the center of our lands, and we will gather all our armies together, and we will not go against them, but we will wait till they shall come against us; therefore as the Lord liveth, if we do this he will deliver them into our hands" (3 Nephi 3:21).

The Nephites, who were repeatedly attacked by the Gadiantons in the past and were directly and credibly threatened with aggression once again, were not justified by the Lord in going into the terrorists' lands to attack. With this being understood, on what principled basis are we justified in preemptively attacking Iran or any other country that has not attacked us in the past nor threatened to make us extinct if we did not completely submit to them?

Modern-day church leaders have warned us, in the *Book of Mormon* as well, that the destruction of our society will be due to the corruption of our own government from within and not from a foreign enemy. James Madison gave us this same warning – "If tyranny and oppression come to this land, it will be in the guise of fighting a foreign enemy."

Fortunately during this election we have a good and honest man who would strictly follow the Constitution as President. As a congressman, Ron Paul has used the Constitution as his iron rod for 10 terms. As a presidential candidate, he has repeatedly stood by the Constitution in its entirety, even when those in the "great and spacious building" have continually mocked him for doing so. He is also the only candidate from both major parties who "renounce(s) war and proclaim(s) peace" (D&C 98:16). It is my hope that the LDS people will put their full support behind Ron Paul and valiantly defend their agency.

Section 2b

Rock Waterman, "What is the Age of Accountability for a Latter-day Saint Servicemember?"

Rock Waterman is the creator of puremormonism.blogspot.com and this is an excerpt from an article he posted on November 25, 2009. The reader will find it both moving and provocative.

Although we don't know the particulars, my personal feeling is that accountability is reached by not only confronting one's self, but also by confronting those we have sinned against.

By way of illustration, I've spun a little tale about a soldier brought to the reality of his actions. It's a bit derivative of Mitch Albom's *The Five People You Meet In Heaven*, but it expresses my feelings and presents our theology in a way that I might have failed to convey previously. Here it is:

The time is some sixty years in the future.

After a long and happy life, an old man, a former sergeant in the Marine Corps, finally died and went to heaven.

To his surprise and delight, he found his body completely restored to the way it had been when he was in his twenties, fit and strong. And he was wearing, of all things, his dress blue uniform, the one from his days in the corps. It was sharply creased and starched with a perfection he had never seen before. He had never before given those shoes a spit-shine that glistened the way they did now. As he looked down at the hard-earned bars and medals pinned to his chest, he felt again that glow he once knew when he proudly wore that uniform those many years ago.

To the soldier's further surprise, he wasn't immediately met by the Lord or even greeted by any long lost relatives as he had expected.

In fact, the first person he came across was a girl with straight black hair and pure brown eyes sitting alone in a large, palatial room. She was on the floor on what looked to be a large round pillow or cushion of some kind. It appeared to the soldier that she sat with her legs tucked under her, as they weren't visible beneath the long white robe that settled around her and draped over the sides of the cushion.

When the soldier came near, the girl smiled a friendly greeting. The soldier sensed there was something familiar about her, and suddenly it came to him.

"Hey, I know you! I remember you from the pre-existence!"

"That's right," she replied., "You and I were friends back then. We fought together during the war in heaven."

"Yeah, now I remember! How's it going?"

The girl smiled, just a little. "Did you have a nice life?" she asked.

"Amazing life. 87 years! Wonderful wife, five kids, so many grandkids and great-grandkids I couldn't remember who belonged to who. Take it all around, I'd have to say it was a great time."

He looked at the girl, this old friend of his. "How about you?"

"Me?" She shook her head. "I never married. I do kind of wish I could have known what it was like, though; waking up in the morning next to a loving husband, stuff like that. I don't mind admitting I would have liked to know what it felt like to make love. Wish I knew what it was like to have a baby, too." She shrugged. "But I missed all that."

"Gee, that's too bad. What happened?"

"I died."

"You died? How?"

"Iraq."

"You were in Iraq? I was in Iraq! When were you deployed?"

"I wasn't deployed. I lived there with my family. They all died too."

"Oh, I get it. You were an Iraqi! I helped liberate you guys!"

She smiled sweetly. "Can't tell you how much we appreciated that."

"No sweat. Just glad I could be a part of the mission. So, how old are you, anyway?"

"I was fifteen when I died."

"Gee, that's tough. Anything I can do?"

"Well, you could apologize."

"Apologize? For what?"

"You killed me."

She said it so simply and in such a matter-of-fact way that it took him aback.

"Get outta here! I never killed any girl! I can promise you I'd remember that."

"Well, you did. You killed my whole family. You and your friends opened fire on our car."

"I would remember that," he shook his head. "Wait a minute, were you in that car at the checkpoint in Baghdad that tried to plow past us?"

"We weren't trying to plow past you," she explained quietly. "It was noisy and chaotic at that checkpoint. My father couldn't understand what you people wanted. He got flustered and thought he was putting his foot on the brake when he accidentally hit the accelerator instead. The car lurched forward for an instant. Just an instant, but that was all it took. You guys panicked and tore the car apart with your automatic gunfire."

"Yeah, I remember. A guy, his wife, and a couple of kids in the backseat. A real mess. I felt terrible about that."

"Me too."

"Well anyway, it was an accident. Those things happen in war. Your family was just in the wrong place at the wrong time."

"My family was in the right place. Baghdad was where we lived. We drove down that street all the time before you came and put your roadblocks up. You were the ones who didn't belong there. You were the one in the wrong place at the wrong time." She spoke calmly, without any anger in her voice. Still, something about her words made the soldier feel uneasy.

"Geez, back off a little, will ya? Sometimes stuff like that can't be helped. It's called collateral damage."

"I never heard God saying he justifies collateral damage."

"Look, I'm sorry you got in the way, okay?"

The girl smiled politely and changed the subject. "I see they let you bring your medals. What's that, a Purple Heart?"

"Yeah, weird, huh? I guess some things you can take with you."

"A Purple Heart . . . That's what they give soldiers when they've been injured in the line of duty, isn't it?"

"Yeah, I lost a foot when an I.E.D. went off while I was on patrol."

"I feel for you. That was a long life you lived with only one foot."

"Well, I got by. They gave me a Prosthetic."

"I lost both my legs in that accident you caused," the girl said simply. "You and your friends just kept shooting through the car door until my legs were sheared off at the hips"

"I said I was sorry."

"You said you were sorry I got in the way," she reminded him gently, "I see you have your missing foot back now, though."

"Yeah. I feel great!" He was hoping to change the subject. "Everything's completely restored and back the way it was. Like they say, 'every hair of the head', and all that."

The girl reached down and pulled her gown up part way, to show him her own resurrected legs, he thought. But he was surprised. Where her legs should have been there was . . . well, there was nothing.

"I still haven't got my own legs back," she said a bit wistfully, "I'll get them eventually, but I had to wait until you got here first."

"What are you talking about? That makes no sense. Why would you have to wait for me?"

"Because you deserve the chance to account for your actions during the war. I'm here to assist you so that you can be at peace."

The soldier was beginning to feel annoyed. "I am at peace!" he insisted, almost angrily. "Whatever it was that happened to you, also happened to a lot of other people. That's just war. It shouldn't matter now. What about the atonement? The blood of Christ? What about forgiveness?"

"Those who take innocent life are held accountable by the Lord. You have a chance to receive the Peace and Eternal Rest of the Lord only after you are held accountable, and part of that accountability is admitting guilt and seeking forgiveness from those you wronged. You are being given the chance to be accountable and to obtain forgiveness from me personally."

He shifted his weight awkwardly. "Okay, fine. What do I need to do?"

"Well, during your time on earth you didn't fully accept accountability for your part in the war. I'm here to help you take responsibility."

"What are you talking about? I hated that war! I got out of the Marine Corps just as soon as I could. And I hated being in Iraq; that place was a garbage dump and a hell hole."

"That 'hell hole' was my home. And it wasn't a garbage dump until your people bombed our water and sewage systems and turned it into one."

"Geez, why do you keep going on about something I can't do anything about? That was a lifetime ago."

"Not for me."

"What do you want from me?"

"I want you to understand. You've read Dickens' *A Christmas Carol*, haven't you?"

"I've seen the movies."

"Those ghosts didn't appear to Scrooge just to torment him, they were there to teach him. Do you believe in eternal progression?"

"Yes."

"So tell me, how do we progress?"

"Through learning, right?"

"Then let me help you learn about consequences. Do you want to see *my* purple heart?"

The girl pulled down the center of her robe a little, exposing a huge hole in the middle of her chest. The soldier could see right through her body and out her back. The sight of it caught him up short.

"There's no heart there!"

"That's right. You shot my heart clean out of me. I still don't know where it went, but wherever it is, I'm sure it's purple like yours," she smiled.

"I don't know why you're doing this."

"Then pay attention, please. You deserve to face something that you avoided facing during your life on earth. This hole in my chest was put there by you. You did this to me. It was caused by a fifty caliber bullet that you fired from your gun from atop your armored vehicle."

Her words were making him uncomfortable, but she didn't appear to be angry at all. There was absolutely no malice in her words; she was simply and calmly relating the truth. "Because of something you did to me, I experienced none of the sweetness of a full life as you did."

She may not have been angry, but she was getting him upset. "I don't have to take this from you!" he found himself shouting, "Where's Jesus? Where's Jesus Christ? I should have been met here by my Lord and Savior!"

"You will meet him shortly, and it will be the most sweet embrace. He loves you more than you have ever loved yourself."

"Then what's the hold up?" He tried to calm himself down.

"You first get to admit what you were afraid to admit to during your entire time on earth—something many people told you that you didn't have to worry about. You get to acknowledge that right or wrong, you took innocent people off the earth before their time. No matter how it was rationalized—your fault, my fault, nobody's fault—your actions resulted in the taking of human life. That is the truth, and it can't be forgotten, dismissed, or wished away."

"What are you getting at? That I did it on purpose? I didn't start that stinking war. I was only in Iraq because it was my duty."

"Your duty?"

"Yes, duty. I made sacrifices. I was a soldier in the service of my country."

"Sacrifice," she mused, "Wouldn't it be more accurate to say that you forced me to make a sacrifice? But never mind that. Tell me, did they pay you to be a Marine?"

"Of course."

"Then what did you sacrifice?"

"My time. Six years of my life."

"But you got paid for all that time, didn't you?"

"I said I did."

"And you also got paid for your service? And you had a lifetime of benefits, didn't you?"

"Why are you even asking me this?"

"So essentially you had a job."

"It's not that simple. The job I had was dangerous."

"It certainly was dangerous to me."

"What I did was not just any stupid little job! I wore the uniform of a United States Marine!"

"So you had a job and you got to wear a costume. Good for you."

"Gee whiz, are you ever going to let up?"

"Just trying to help you see reality. This is heaven. We don't deal in illusion here. I'll tell you what you were. You were an unwitting pawn of a governmental entity that had lost sight of its true mission."

"Then why blame me? Doesn't the fault lie with those who sent me to war?"

"They are being held to answer, don't worry about that. Believe me, you wouldn't want to be in their shoes. Now, do you remember the Marine Corps Code of Conduct?"

"I know it by heart."

"Then recite article six for me, please."

"Easy. 'I will never forget that I am an American, fighting for freedom, responsible for my actions, and dedicated to the principles which made my country free. I will trust in my God and in the United States of America.'"

"'Responsible for my actions,'" the girl repeated, "Do you really feel that you were responsible for your actions?"

"To the extent I could be, yes. I had no choice about where I was ordered to fight."

"But you didn't object to the fighting. You swore dedication to the principles which made your country free, did you not?"

"That's what it says."

"Where would you say those principles are embodied?"

"In the Constitution, I suppose."

"And in fact, didn't you also swear an oath to protect and defend the Constitution? Did you not take that oath seriously?"

"I took it very seriously."

"What does the Constitution say about war?"

"I'm not sure."

"Not sure? Why not?"

"Look, I didn't memorize the Constitution, okay?"

"Have you ever even read it?"

"I might have once or twice."

"Remember, you're in heaven now. No fudging."

"Okay, so I never read the entire Constitution."

"Did you ever read any of it?"

"So I never read any of it. So sue me."

"I don't wish to sue you, but I would like to understand how you can defend a document when you don't even know what's in it."

"I'm sure the president read it and knew what he was doing when he ordered America into war."

"Well that's just it. Under your Constitution, the president does not have authority to order America into war. He can only direct the war after the people have made known to congress their desire for war, and the congress has officially declared war. The decision is not the president's to make.

"Well, none of that really matters. The reality is, somebody else sent me to Iraq and I had to go to war whether I agreed with it or not."

"That's why I've met you here today. Throughout your long life you never held yourself accountable for being where you were that day."

"What day?"

"The day you took my life."

"I had no say in the matter!"

"Did you not swear to protect and defend the Constitution of the United States against all enemies, foreign and domestic?"

"I did."

"Do you agree that the founders of your country placed that limitation on the president because they didn't want any one person in government acting like a king, deciding to send the nation to war at whim?"

"I guess so."

"And wouldn't you say that when the president defies the Constitution and behaves like a king, that he has become a domestic enemy?"

"That's putting it pretty harshly."

Well, let me put it this way: did you not have an obligation, under your oath of office and under the Marine Corps Code, to defend the Constitution from usurpation?"

"I guess you could look at it that way."

"Then why didn't you?"

"Because I didn't know that was in the Constitution."

"Why didn't you?"

"I told you, I hadn't read it."

"Then why did you swear to defend it?"

"All right! I should have read it, and I should have objected to unconstitutional orders. Is that what you want me to say?"

"See? Now you're beginning to take accountability."

"Good. Are we done here?"

"Not quite. You've admitted you were lax in your duty to your country, now let's see how accountable you were to God. You were what, on earth, they called a "Mormon," am I right?"

"That's right."

"A member of the Church of Jesus Christ of Latter-day Saints?"

"All my life"

"The true church."

""The only true church on the face of the earth.'"

"And what makes that church unique is its claim to latter-day revelation, am I right?"

"Yes it does. I can bear you my testimony right now if you want."

"I have no doubt as to your sincerity. What I want to know is why, during your time on earth, did you take so lightly those revelations?"

"I didn't take anything lightly! I was active in the church all my life; I was a temple goer, Gospel Doctrine teacher, Elder's Quorum President -I was even in the bishopric and stake presidencies. I'm sure you'll find my name in the Book of Life, so why don't you just look it up and let's get this over with. I was completely obedient to my priesthood leaders."

"I'm not interested in your obedience to your leaders. I'm concerned with your fealty to God."

"Okay, test me. I followed all of the commandments."

"Did you take seriously the Lord's charge in Doctrine and Covenants chapter 98?"

"Jog my memory."

"I'll just quote a portion of verse 33: 'This is the law that I gave unto mine ancients, that they should not go out unto battle against any nation, kindred, tongue, or people, save I, the Lord, commanded them.' A few verses down the Lord makes clear that this law applies to your day, and particularly to America."

"Well, how do you know God didn't command the president to send us to war against Iraq?"

"Well, first of all, God doesn't reveal his will to rulers. He reveals it to prophets. And second, do you think the same God who, in verse 7, declared that anything more or less than the Constitution is evil, would then command the president to violate his oath and usurp the war-making powers from Congress?"

"I guess it depends on the urgency of the situation."

"Then, let's suppose God actually had commanded your country to go to war against mine. Wouldn't you have heard about this new commandment?"

"Not if the command was classified."

"So you were willing to violate your oath of office and your duty to God without even knowing whether or not the Lord had ordered war in accordance with D&C 98:33?"

"Look, I didn't know about that scripture, okay?"

"I thought you said you followed all of God's commandments."

"That one must have gotten past me."

"Let's move on. You lived 87 years on the earth. You must have read the *Book of Mormon* many times during your lifetime."

"Many times. I love the *Book of Mormon*."

"How many times did you actually read it all the way through?"

"Many times."

"How many?

"I don't know, maybe two or three times."

"This is heaven, remember."

"Okay, okay! I'm sure we read it in seminary. I know we studied it every four years in Sunday school."

"You studied parts of it in Sunday school. Those Sunday school lessons were abridged. They skipped entire sections that would have been important for you as a soldier to know about. Some of those tedious war chapters, for instance.”

“There were a lot of wars in the *Book of Mormon*, that’s for sure.”

“What do you think was the reason the prophet Mormon saw fit to include all those chapters on war?”

“I don’t know. Filler?”

“Have you ever heard the statement that the *Book of Mormon* is both a witness and a warning?”

“Sure I have.”

“So what is the witness?”

“It witnesses of Jesus Christ.”

“And what do you think is the warning?”

“I get the feeling you’re going to tell me it’s something about war.”

“War and deception in the last days… yes…Mormon wanted you to understand that there are sometimes legitimate reasons for going to war, and at those times the people have a sacred duty to take up arms and defend their lands and freedoms even unto the shedding of blood.”

“That’s what I’m saying! That’s why we were in Iraq and Afghanistan; we were defending America from the terrorists!”

“The *Book of Mormon* also demonstrates that people can be deceived into believing they are under threat when they really are not. They can even be tricked into retaliating against the wrong enemy. God used the *Book of Mormon* to warn you that corrupt leaders would come among your people willing to exploit their fears, and to convince you that you were engaged in a great battle for righteousness. In reality, the opposite was true.”

“Well, I didn’t know about any of that.”

“I know you didn’t. And that’s a shame because Mormon’s son Moroni was adamant in his warnings that the record his father passed to him was of the utmost importance to the people in your day, and to your country in particular. He foresaw the danger Americans would put themselves in by making war in defiance of God’s commandments. Saddest of all, he prophesied that many members of your church, those same people who would receive the record, would reject the warnings. Your own actions have assisted in bringing some of those prophecies to pass."

"You're killing me here. Okay, maybe I wasn't being fully accountable. Listen, I'll admit something. In the beginning I did have some doubts about what we were doing in Iraq. But then everybody back home just kept telling us that our sacrifices were noble and necessary. We got care packages from school children and letters from strangers thanking us for being their heroes. They had us believing the whole country depended upon us for its very survival."

"Flattery is one of the most effective tools of the Evil One, isn't it?"

"Well, I sure I bought into all of it. I tried to think of myself as a simple soldier just doing my duty, but all that encouragement was pretty heady stuff. It got me believing I was engaged in some great battle between good and evil."

"Those citizens who allowed the Evil One to use them in cheering you on will be held individually accountable for their part, but you yourself are accountable for not seeing through it.

"You know, I have to admit that I think I may be almost ready to accept that accountability."

"That makes me very happy. Do you remember what the war in heaven was about?"

"Of course, that's where you and I met. I always figured that the war I was fighting on earth was a continuation of the war in heaven; you know, fighting for freedom and all. We just couldn't get over the fact that you people didn't appreciate that we were there to help you get your freedom back. I lost a foot from a bomb set by some of the very people I was there to liberate."

"And still you didn't take the hint. Did you not learn anything from our victory in the war in heaven? The issue was self-determination. Nations as well as individuals deserve to be left to themselves to sort out their problems. We did not ask for your help. You imposed your will on us, just as Lucifer tried to impose his will on all the denizens of heaven."

"You're wrong about that. We liberated you from a dictator."

"And who asked you to do so? Your leaders were successful in convincing you that first we were an imminent threat to you. Then you were told that we needed rescuing from our own government. Then you were told we couldn't manage without your help. Then you were told that you were needed against the terrorists. It was always some new excuse so you wouldn't leave. Your government always had a reason to deny us our free agency. You helped me fight a war of liberty in heaven, then went to earth and became my oppressor."

He didn't know how to respond to that. "But our intentions were noble."

"What's that proverb about the road to hell? Why didn't you turn your noble intentions on yourselves? Your country had its own problems. When America was hit with floods and fires, your people learned to their dismay that most of your National Guard were stuck in my country and unavailable. God commands all nations to respect the sovereignty of each-other. You should have been home where you were needed."

"Well, some of us in the church hoped that by fighting to free the Middle East, we could open up the area some day for the spreading of the gospel."

"And who would listen to you then?"

"Everybody. We'd flood the area with missionaries."

"Did you ever know anyone who served a mission in Germany?" She asked.

"Yeah, I heard that lots of guys would spend their whole two years there and never get one baptism."

"And that was half a century after the United States defeated those people for a second time. How is the missionary work going in Vietnam and Cambodia? How about Thailand? Laos? You can't spread the gospel of the Prince of Peace using a flamethrower. If you wanted to convert us, why did you think sending your armies in first was the way to do it? We weren't infidels, you know. Before the Americans came to Iraq there were two million Christians openly living there unmolested by

Saddam Hussein's government, and free of persecution. There was mutual respect between the Christians and their Muslim neighbors. Within four years of your occupation we were all displaced or dead. It was a most unproductive method of proselyting."

"Well, the war might have been wrong, but I know God was with me while I was in Iraq."

"God did not abandon you, but that didn't mean he approved what you were doing. All that praying you did, and not once did you ask the right questions or listen for answers. God wanted you to simply live your religion. He stood at the door and knocked, but his knocking was drowned out by the sound of your machine gun fire."

The soldier could not think of anything more to say to the girl. He was suddenly overcome by sadness and regret. He had been standing the entire time; now his newfound strength went out of him and he simply sank to his knees before her.

"I'm sorry," he cried, "I really am! I'm sorry I deprived you of a full life. I should not have been in your home, and I'm sorry. You tell me I have the Lord's forgiveness, but I'm asking you now for yours. Please. I take accountability for what I did to you and your family. I am accountable for it. Can you ever forgive me?"

The girl grasped her robe near the neck and folded it closed as she slowly raised herself up. The soldier looked up in astonishment to see that she was now standing on two perfect, beautiful legs where a moment before there had been nothing.

A look of peace crossed her face. She closed her eyes in a moment of sweet contentment as she brought her right hand up and held it against her breast. It was as if she hadn't felt the sensation of a heartbeat in a long, long time, and now it was there again. The girl looked down at the now sobbing soldier and smiled tenderly. She gently touched her hand to his head. Finally she spoke.

"I forgave you before you got here."

Section 3b

Ron Madson, "Speaking Truth to Power: 9/11—My Reflections Ten Years Later"

This was a guest post on Rock Waterman's blog puremormonism.blogspot.com on September 11, 2011

In early 1943, hundreds of German women did the unthinkable—they confronted machine gun wielding Gestapo agents and demanded the release of their Jewish husbands who were part of Hitler's final roundup of Jews that were to be transported to Auschwitz. Even more remarkable, their Jewish husbands (approximately 1,700 in number) were released. This incident, now known as The Rosenstrasse Protest, was appropriately dubbed "The Day Hitler Blinked." Germans have until recently, largely ignored this story because the consensus has been and remains that the average German was powerless against their government and its anti-Semitic policies. Such thinking appears to be confirmed, as a practical matter, when focusing on individual martyrs such as the German latter-day Saint Helmuth Hubener and the occasional principled monk, priest or clergyman who defied his government's policies of war, torture and genocide. However, what set these acts of civil disobedience apart from the Rosenstrasse protest is that these latter individuals were abandoned by their own faith community, and in particular, their church leaders. Then again, the

Helmuth Hubeners of this world were responding to a higher authority and an audience unseen in this world.

Christian Nazis

My father told me that he observed that the German soldiers wore a Christian cross on their belt buckles during WWII. Their faith to the church and their country had converged into one. But consider what would have happened if every single Bishop, Priest, Pastor, and spiritual leader in Germany had denounced Hitler's invasion of Poland? What if every single Sunday the German chapels and cathedrals rang with strident denunciations of even the earliest persecution of the Jews under Nazism? If the united voices of a few hundred women could cause a hardened Gestapo to back down, then what effect could tens of thousands of German spiritual leaders condemning Germany's wars of aggression have on Germany's general population—especially if their local clergy were supported by an edict from the Pope and the leaders of all other major Protestant faiths in Germany? I submit that Hitler and Nazism would have been rendered powerless. The masses emboldened by their spiritual leaders would have isolated and paralyzed the few sociopaths that were at the core of this great evil. After reading some of my anti-war papers, a good friend asked what I consider a highly relevant question: "What is the point of all your anti-war writings and lectures?" "Or in other words, at the end of the day, what do you or anyone protesting our nation's wars expect to accomplish or change as a practical matter—within our nation, our church, or even personally?" "And how does this help build the kingdom? How does it make you or any of us better members of the church?" I will attempt to answer that by considering our nation's war policies during the last decade in light of what I believe could have been, what is, and what I believe will be if we do not repent of our current rejection of Christ's words to us in our generation as it pertains to the use of violence; and how that will play out for each of us individually as well as collectively.

What Could Have Been

Imagine it is now Sunday, September 16th, 2001. It's been five days since the devastating attacks of what will come to be known as 9/11, and our nation is still in deep shock and in the early stages of mourning over that horrific tragedy. Holy men who lead our respective Christian faiths search their souls to find the words of Jesus to teach us how to respond to our enemies. While giving comfort, they exhort us to not become the very evil we deplore. Demonstrating a mature faith, they teach us that we must begin to pray for our enemies and even search deep within ourselves for ways to do good to those that hate us. Week after week, they seek to teach us to not give into our fear and anger, which leads inevitably to a desire for vengeance. They exhort us that the price of discipleship is great at such times, but the promises are sure that if we will trust our God enough to follow the example of Christ, He will consecrate such faith and pour out a blessing to us, and even soften the hearts of those who we might believe worthy of our vengeance. Having laid such a foundation, then when those in our nation insist that we seek vengeance by first invading one nation and its citizens, and then engage in a pre-emptive attack on another nation in order to send a message, how would those tutored on a gospel of non-vengeance respond? Among faiths that take literally the words of Christ such as the Amish, Jehovah's Witnesses, Anabaptist sects, and Seventh Day Adventists, there is a top-to-bottom collective belief that they must conscientiously object (ex: how the Amish responded to the massacre of their children recently with charity toward the family of the killer). But what if all leaders of all the Christian faiths in our nation had renounced any wars of aggression and vengeance as antithetical to one's claim of a faith in Christ? Could those political leaders -the Neocons and warmongers in high places who insisted on pre-emptive invasions of Afghanistan and then Iraq- have succeeded in marshaling enough public support for such wars? Not if every pastor and bishop had denounced such attacks, confirmed by an edict from their highest leaders informing that position. Our nation's "Decider in Chief," who had told us during the Presidential debates that Jesus was his greatest hero, would have had to weigh the collective teachings of those entrusted to share the gospel each week against whether there was any popular support for commencing the works of death and destruction among the citizens of two nations who had done us no harm. Then let's suppose we, as a nation, get carried away even further with a Christ-inspired model when it comes to our perceived enemies and we spend just a tenth of what we have squandered in these two wars on direct humanitarian relief to these benighted countries we attacked. How would the narrative have changed? How many schools and hospitals might we have built and how many fewer Madrassahs would have sprung up teaching anti-American hatred for the next generation?

> "When moral contempt for a form of violence inspires so explicit a replication of it, there is only one conclusion to be drawn: The moral revulsion the initial violence awakened proved weaker than the mimetic fascination it inspired."—Gil Bailie

> "Therefore, renounce war and proclaim peace..." Doctrine and Covenants 98:16

> "And again, this is the law I gave unto mine ancients [which is still in effect today], that they should not go out unto battle against any nation ... save I, the Lord, commanded them ... And if any nation...should proclaim war against them, they should first raise a standard of peace unto that people..."
> Doctrine and Covenants 98:33-34.

So let's narrow this script and rewrite history as to our Mormon faith community. Suppose that after 9/11, our priesthood leaders instinctively turned to D&C Section 98 and raised the standard of peace and renounced commencing any wars. By "renounce" I do not mean they simply say that war is not nice and we prefer peace to war. Or worse, proclaim that we are peace loving, and like Jesus we believe in peace, while openly responding to an invitation to march to war. No! To *renounce* means to declare an emphatic NO! It means one *unequivocally rejects* a war policy that involves retribution—and especially when it involves pre-emptive acts of aggression. If the President of the Church and the Apostles had stridently and without reservation *renounced* our invasions of Afghanistan and Iraq, then what would have happened in our faith community? The main body of our faith community would have heard the clarity of the denunciation and added to the chorus rejecting the call to endorse these wars. Believing parents would have discouraged children from enlisting. Section 98 would come alive to the believing saints and they would recognize the voice of the Lord in that immutable covenant. What difference would this make? As far as immediate effect, how many of the more than one hundred LDS soldiers who have perished in Iraq and Afghanistan would not have enlisted, or in the alternative claimed status as conscientious objectors? We will never know for sure, but at many of their funerals, friends and family testified that their desire to enlist and "serve their country" had been rooted in their religious faith. What about those injured physically and mentally? What about the lives of those "enemies?" Do they even count in the equation? But I believe there is something at risk that goes beyond this sphere of existence. I believe that if we embrace the words of Christ in His revelations, then the heavens are opened for the ministering angels to pour out an even greater blessing as promised not only in Section 98 but in all our revelations. What is that blessing? Beyond peace and prosperity, there is the promise of further light and knowledge. There is the unsealing of the heavens as we receive even greater revelations and blessings, which I believe are sealed up until we actually live those revelations which we have been given.

So what would happen if, as a people, whether speaking from the Chief Seats down to the smallest primary class, we were to teach the words of Christ with *conviction*, utterly renouncing all forms of retributive violence? I believe we would find our voice. And I further believe the throngs of heavenly beings would join us. And who knows but that we, like the few hundred women at Rosenstrasse, could cause miracles to occur? And would our united voices renouncing these wars not give courage to other faith communities and like-minded people? Then, like the women at Rosenstrasse would there be enough collective refrains that those who sought moral support for their war plans would have not only "blinked" but also frozen long enough to arrest what has proven to be so evil on so many levels? We will never know.

What Happened?

There is no need to rehearse our unfortunate ten-year odyssey in Iraq and Afghanistan at length in this submission. We engaged in wars of aggression against two nations, both of which had never come against us, and both of which raised the standard of peace *and we rejected it.* We have murdered hundreds of thousands of their civilians over these past ten years, causing an irreparable cost in lives, treasure and the spirituality of our nation. In our Mormon faith community we have praised, encouraged, and elevated military service in these wars by framing it as a conflict between good and evil when in fact, as the prophet Mormon astutely observed, "It is by the wicked that the wicked are punished." We have excused and ignored our own wickedness by conflating these wars of aggression into the slogan that by invading and occupying other people's homelands, we are somehow "fighting for our freedoms." Following 9/11, many young LDS men and women enthusiastically enlisted in the military, knowing they had the full endorsement of our church leaders and their faith community. So what difference did that make? What about those whose lives we placed on our altar of war? Alyssa Peterson returned from her mission and felt it an extension of her spiritual sacrifice to then enlist in the military, only months later to find herself forced to participate in our government's own program of torture. Then there is Sergeant Cawley, one of the first LDS casualties in the Iraq war, who served a mission in Japan, married, and fathered two children. We know of his death because President Hinckley made sure we knew that when Brother Cawley was called to serve his nation he did so "without hesitation." Of course, how could there have been any hesitation when we as a people had once again rejected Section 98 in both word and deed? How could there have even been a pause to ponder among those of our faith enlisting to serve in these wars, when our authorities invited Dick Cheney and Condaleeza Rice, co-

conspirators in fabricating the evidence promoting both wars (as well as endorsing a program of torture), to speak at "The Lord's University" while rejecting the Dalai Lama's request to speak at the same forum? What has happened -and continues to happen- in regard to these wars, and our institutional silence in not renouncing these wars are reprehensible; yet it is historically predictable once a church has placed its allegiance to empire above the commandments of God. Once that wall is breached, the practice of people sacrificing their own children on the altar of war inexorably follows.

So, what are the consequences beyond a few of our children being delivered to the fires of Moloch? No big deal. Let's move along and stay focused on building the Kingdom of Jesus on earth.

What Follows?

Again, what good does it do to create bad feelings by being critical of our faith community? Of, as some call it, "attacking" Church leadership? What's the point of spending so much energy diverting us from our "real" mission to share the Gospel's good news, which is that you too can overcome your addiction to coffee, tea, and tobacco? You too can become a holy, chaste, commandment keeper, personally worthy and feeling really, really good about yourself as a member of The All Is Well For You & Me Club. Yes, you too can know those warm feelings that come from reading the scriptures, praying three times a day, attending church, wearing white shirts, excellent hygiene, home teaching, taking cookies to the new neighbor—all wrapped up in the warm blanket of personal spiritual health. All these things are nice, but if in the end one's spiritual development never matures beyond the pharisaical narcissism of "personal" self-righteousness, then what do we have? What we have are members of a Church, but nothing remotely resembling The Kingdom of God. One graduates spiritually when one takes off his or her church training wheels and becomes a contributing member of Jesus' Kingdom *by doing as Jesus did* -standing in the breach for the least among us, denouncing the evil done to others, giving voice to His words on behalf of the Samaritan, the sinners, the outcasts and yes, even one's enemies. That is the price of admission to his Kingdom and the beginning of genuine discipleship, even if it means unpopularity within one's religious community or national tribe. And what is the price if we reject His teachings and support the latest "Christian" crusade? Does it really make any difference to us individually or collectively? It made all the difference in the lives of those individuals who have suffered grievously in these wars—even if we only count those of our own faith such as Alyssa Peterson, Brother Cawley and last week's obituary. That is enough reason to renounce these wars, is it not? But there is, in my opinion, something more spiritually cosmic at work here. Latter-day Saints believe that the original church of Christ began to drift into apostasy when they deeded their allegiance to the Roman Empire and engaged in what is referred to as "The Constantine Shift." Bishops, priests, and then Popes all began to consistently set aside the words of Christ and endorse nearly every state sponsored war—and in fact taught that it was one's Christian duty to enlist. Is it any surprise that the heavens became brass, and revelations ceased despite the Catholic Church's claim to legal priesthood pedigree? Why would the Heavens commune with such a church and its leaders lest such manifestations of charismatic gifts be considered lending its imprimatur of approval on such behavior?

Of course the medieval Catholic Church continued preserving the truths from its origins but preservation is not the same as "true and living." Do we really believe that we latter-day Saints are exempt from the sealing up of the heavens if we engage in our own Constantine Shift? Can we pay lip service to the words of Christ found in our sacred texts, but in actual church policy blatantly reject His "immutable" covenant and expect further endorsement from the same God? When we trust in the "horses" and "chariots" of Egypt (Isaiah 31:1) do we not "err in vision" and "stumble in judgment?" (Isaiah 27:7). If we reject His words found in our "doctrines" and "covenants," can we then expect the same blessings as a church found in the same body of revelations that includes specifically "receiving angels," "opening up the mysteries of heaven," "communion with the Church of the First Born," and "being in the presence of God?" How can we expect to lift the condemnation that is upon us if we continue to "treat light the things (we) have received" and do not "do according to that which I have written?" (D & C 84: 54- 57).

More to the point, if we do not repent by renouncing our State sponsored wars, how can we expect the Lord to bless us? If the Lord were to send through our church leadership ministering angels as well as His direct presence, would we not interpret that as approval of our current actions? If the gifts of the spirit were again to pour out upon this church as they had in the early years of its founding, would we not assume from observing these gifts that we were on the right path? Wouldn't such marvelous gifts and healings as were abundantly experienced by the church in the Missouri-Nauvoo period serve to communicate His approbation on our church and its current leadership? What does it then tell us when we look around us and notice the near complete absence of these spiritual manifestations in the Church today? Does this plunge toward failure we seem to be heading as a nation (not to mention as a faith community) not stand as a witness of God's disapproval of our new policy of pledging allegiance to empire over His words and teachings as found not only in D&C 98, but throughout the New Testament and *Book of Mormon*? I believe so. Like the children of Israel at Mount Sinai, we have rejected the continued presence of God and his ministering angels and have chosen mortal icons to lead us as we seek to conquer Canaan—a conquest that had the audacity to teach that there is spiritual immunity when we kill every man, woman and child who stands in the way of our "freedom"—and that when we commit these abominations, it is God's will.

Where are we now as a people?

This past year I was with a group of protestors outside the Marriot Center, protesting Condeleezza Rice's appearance to speak at BYU (essentially the same group that protested Dick Cheney's speech at the same forum three years earlier). While we were gathered outside, she was in the Marriot Center telling the full-capacity stadium how our nation "had" to engage in pre-emptive wars. To speak plainly, I interpret such doctrine as "let's get them before they get us"—which includes, if necessary, dubious "evidence" obtained through torture. Her words were received by what the press called "vigorous clapping"—while our small group of no more than thirty dissidents stood outside in the cold denouncing her message justifying our nations' unprecedented pre-emptive wars. I believe that the ratio of those applauding her comments to those who protested her remarks no longer reflects the same ratio of those of our faith who endorse our nation's current pre-emptive war doctrine. In fact, I believe that increasing thousands in our faith community privately believe that it was a great sin to endorse in any way our current State sponsored wars. I believe that we first need to decide individually where each of us stands as to these State sponsored wars. Then if we believe we must renounce these wars, decide whether we are willing to do so publicly— no matter how few join with us in the renouncement. For some of us, that personal decision was made a long time ago and it is, in the end, irrelevant as to whether others join in or whether it appears we "made a difference." We are witnessing to an audience that is beyond this veil—whose approbation means everything in the final spiritual equation. What is the point of protesting our faith communities' current relationship to State sponsored wars? What will happen the next time a Dick Cheney is invited to speak or the next time a church leader endorses either our present state sponsored wars or the next wars which will surely come? What if, as the wives in Rosenstrasse, there are hundreds -no, thousands- of outraged mothers in Zion defiantly protesting? What if they, in moral outrage, say "NO MORE of our sons, our daughters, our husbands will be placed on your altar of war." And they do not say it in wilting, primary voice tones typical of church meetings. No, *THEY SCREAM IT!* Could we as a faith community have an impact? Would we force our leaders (both political and spiritual) to "blink?" Would our refusal to give the Mormon stamp of approval at least cause some of our fellow citizens to pause before offering up any more of their own children to these false gods? In the words of Martin Luther King, "there comes a time when silence is betrayal." A decade of relative silence in our faith community is enough.

We must choose to obey the Lord's commandment and publicly *renounce* these wars in the most emphatic means. I believe it will make a difference.

Section 4b

Benjamin A. Thompson, "The True Meaning of Peace"

What is peace? The Merriam-Webster dictionary gives us the following definition of peace in the English language[1]:

1: a state of tranquility or quiet: as

a: freedom from civil disturbance

b: a state of security or order within a community provided for by law or custom <a breach of the *peace*>

2: freedom from disquieting or oppressive thoughts or emotions

3: harmony in personal relations

4

a: a state or period of mutual concord between governments

b: a pact or agreement to end hostilities between those who have been at war or in a state of enmity

5

—used interjectionally to ask for silence or calm or as a greeting or farewell

In short, we can say that in the Anglo-American culture, "peace" is a lack of war or hostility. Our Lord Jesus Christ said:

Peace I leave with you, my peace I give unto you: not as the world giveth, give I unto you. Let not your heart be troubled, neither let it be afraid.

    –Gospel of John 14:27 (KJV)

In this one verse, we are left to wonder why Jesus Christ separated the version of peace that he gives and that the world gives. It is safe to say that most of the world today also assumes that peace is a lack of hostility. The world, which is made up of mankind, tends to have wrong ideas and this is because men love darkness more than light:

And this is the condemnation, that light is come into the world, and men loved darkness rather than light, because their deeds were evil.

    –Gospel of John 3:19 (KJV)

If the majority of the world is in agreement on something then it is most likely to be corrupt in some way—even if it sounds right—because most men love darkness rather than light. This is no less true for the idea of peace, as Jesus Christ said.

To first understand the true meaning of peace, you need to understand the culture in which Jesus Christ lived. This culture spoke predominantly Hebrew and Aramaic, therefore to understand peace as the Lord intends for us to then we must know Hebrew and Aramaic.

The above word is Hebrew and is pronounced *shalom* and is the equivalent of the English word "peace." In Aramaic, it is basically the same. In fact, this word generally means the same in every Semitic language—it being derived from the same root word. In Hebrew, the word *shalom* means "completeness" or "soundness." It is derived from the Hebrew word *shalam*, which also has this meaning but also means "to submit." The difference between these two words is that *shalom* has a waw in it, while "shalam" does not—but they essentially mean the same thing.

With this, we can begin to understand the Lord's definition of peace. Though *shalom* certainly has the meaning of "lack of war or hostility," it goes far deeper than that. The true meaning of *shalom*—peace—is the state of completeness: soundness (which means 'to be the way it is supposed to be'), and indirectly means to submit to God. To further explain this point, consider the words of the prophet Ezekiel:

> Because, even because they have seduced my people, saying, Peace; and there was no peace;
> –Ezekiel 13:10 (KJV)

The prophet Ezekiel is warning the people that war will come upon them and destroy them if they do not repent. This passage is not translated very well at the end; it ought to read "Peace and there is no peace." This makes more sense now. The wicked are saying there is peace at that very moment but the Lord is saying that there is no peace. There is no peace because the ultimate meaning of peace is the 'state of being when the Law (*i.e.* the Torah) is kept'. The people of Israel were not keeping the Torah and therefore they were not in a real state of peace as the Lord defines it. The Apostle Paul warns us that this same state will exist in the last days:

> For yourselves know perfectly that the day of the Lord so cometh as a thief in the night. For when they shall say, Peace and safety; then suddenly destruction cometh upon them, as travail upon a woman with child; and they shall not escape.
> –First Epistle of Paul to the Thessalonians 5:2-3 (KJV)

In the last days, which are our days, we will cry peace but there is no peace for us because we do not keep the Law that the Lord has given. No matter how many times we will strive to create peace it will fail if it is not based on the Peace that the Lord has established. The Prophet Isaiah specifically mentions this in plain Hebrew. Here is the English translation:

> And the earth is polluted because the inhabitants passed over [ignored] the Law [Torah], changed the way of doing things, the eternal covenant has no effect. Because of this, an oath has devoured the earth, and the inhabitants in her are guilty! Because of this, the inhabitants of the earth are burned, and a few men are left.
> —Isaiah 24:5-6 (Bat Tsion Bible)

Notice that the Hebrew word for Law is Torah. What is the *Torah*? The *Torah* is a Hebrew word that means "the Law." In most *Bible* translations, they render *Torah* simply as the law. Though this is certainly accurate, it does not point your mind in the right direction. The Torah also refers to the first five books of the *Bible* (*Genesis-Deuteronomy*). The Law of God is written within these first five books. The *Torah* (referring to the first five books of *The Holy Bible*) is written in such a way so as to teach principles and commandments that the Lord wants us to live by. It is very important for us to learn these principles and commandments if we are to follow the God of the *Bible*. If these principles are so important why then did the Lord not simply give us a list to use? The answer: because the Lord wants us to search his words and discover it for ourselves. The slothful will not find salvation.

We think of the *Torah* as being done away with because of the fulfilling of the Law of Moses by Jesus Christ. It is true that the Law of Moses is fulfilled in Christ, but that means we are now under the Law of the Gospel, or Christ. The *Torah* is still needed for teaching the Law of the Gospel.

The other scriptures give us an added witness of the *Torah* without most of us even realizing it. We see passages that refer to the Law, which are speaking directly about the *Torah*. We also see passages that refer to the commandments and the covenant of the fathers. Both of these phrases refer to the *Torah* as well. The commandments are those listed within the *Torah*, so if you want to learn the commandments then you have to study the *Torah*.

The phrase 'covenants of the fathers' also refers to the *Torah*. This covenant is that if the Children of Israel will accept the Lord as their God and keep the *Torah* then the Lord will preserve them in the land and bless them and save them. If they will not accept the Lord as their God and do not keep the *Torah* then the Lord will scatter them and bring curses down on them.

The traditions of our fathers have lied to us. The *Torah* is still important for us, and I urge you to study it and apply its teachings to your life. The purpose of this work is to help you to see that the Lord intended for us to keep the *Torah* and taught us a better way to interpret it. The Lord even felt that the *Torah* was important enough to take time to be restored in these last days. We now have a *Restored Torah*.

What is the *Restored Torah*? The *Restored Torah* is the *Torah* with the sealed portions returned to it. Have you never heard that the *Torah* was sealed? *The Bible* itself tells us that the *Torah* was sealed:

> "Bind up the testimony, seal the law among my disciples."
> –Isaiah 8:16 (KJV)

This verse is not translated properly, so I will translate it better from the Hebrew:

> "Bind up the testimony and seal the Torah in my disciples."

The change from 'among' to 'in' is important. The word 'among' implies that the *Torah* was held among the disciples. The word 'in' implies that the *Torah* is literally in the hearts of the disciples. The word seal means to close off so that no one could read it. No one could read the *Torah* after it was sealed? The answer: yes, in part. The sealing of the *Torah* is the removal of certain passages. Those passages could no longer be read. The reason for this sealing is so that the Lord could sort out the true disciples from the false ones.

How would the Lord determine if a person is a true disciple of the Lord? The true disciple will realize that the *Torah* teaches us to recognize that Jesus is the Messiah. So, if the test is to see if an Israelite can determine that Jesus is the Messiah, what then would have been sealed up in the *Torah*? The answer: all the passages that referred to the coming of Jesus Christ.

So what is the *Restored Torah*? It is the *Torah* with the sealed portions returned to it. Who gave us the *Restored Torah*? Joseph Smith, Jr. did. Through revelation, Joseph Smith, Jr. restored the sealed passages that refer to Jesus Christ and his Gospel being preached from the beginning of the world. We also call this the *Inspired Version* or the *Joseph Smith Translation of the Bible*. Whether you believe that Joseph Smith, Jr. was a prophet as I do or not, the *Torah* is still just as valid to the world.

To fully understand the *Torah*, we must first understand the difference between the *Torah* and the Law of Moses. The most basic explanation is that the *Torah* is the entire law of God whereas the Law of Moses is the entire law of God with the words of the everlasting covenant of the holy priesthood removed. To illustrate this point, consider these words from the *Restored Torah*:

> And the Lord said unto Moses, Hew thee two other tables of stone, like unto the first, and I will write upon them also, the words of the law, according as they were written at the first on the tables which thou breakest; but it shall not be according to the first, for I will take the priesthood out of their midst; therefore my holy order, and the ordinances thereof, shall not go before them; for my presence shall not go up in their midst, lest I destroy them. But I will give unto them the law as at the first, but it shall be after the law of a carnal commandment;
>
> –Exodus 34:1-2 (Joseph Smith Translation)

The Lord himself says that the Law of Moses that he gave the Israelites is the same one that he originally gave to them at the first, which is the same law that was given to Adam, Enoch, Noah, and Abraham. The only difference between this new law and the law that was in the beginning is that it has the ordinances of the priesthood removed and is based on commandments concerning carnality.

We already understand what these ordinances of the priesthood are, so we need to ask ourselves what is meant by "the law of a carnal commandment." The word carnal refers to something that is of the flesh or body. This describes the situation perfectly: the Israelites were not able to keep the law in their thoughts so the Lord altered the law so that it was no longer a sin to think incorrectly but only to act incorrectly. Christ himself gave us an example of this concept:

> Ye have heard that it hath been said by them of old that, Thou shalt not kill; and whosoever shall kill, shall be in danger of the judgment of God. But I say unto you that whosoever is angry with his brother, shall be in danger of his judgment;
> —Matthew 5:23-24 (Joseph Smith Translation)

The law that says 'thou shalt not kill' is a carnal commandment, or a commandment that relates only to the act of the body. The Law of Moses does not relate to thoughts, but if you physically kill someone then you are under condemnation by the law. Christ shows us that the higher law of the Gospel focuses on thoughts as well by saying "whosoever is angry with his brother, shall be in danger of the judgment of God." The law of the Gospel is a spiritual law and therefore relates to the soul, or thought, of man.

Some might argue that the law of the Gospel was never taught until Christ came. That argument is false. The Law of Moses was added to the Gospel for the sake of the Israelites because of their transgressions, thus showing us that the Israelites did originally have the Gospel of Christ. Paul writes of this fact:

> Wherefore then, the law was added because of transgressions,
> till the seed should come to whom the promise was made in the law
> given to Moses...
> —Galatians 3:19 (Joseph Smith Translation)

So the Law of Moses was added because of transgressions and it would remain until the seed, who is Christ, comes as promised by the law. Paul also says:

> And the scripture, foreseeing that God would justify the
> heathen through faith, preached the gospel unto Abraham, saying,
> In thee shall all nations be blessed.
> —Galatians 3:8 (Joseph Smith Translation)

From this, we can see that God gave the Gospel to Abraham, showing us that the Gospel existed before the Israelites. Furthermore, we know that if Abraham had it then Adam had it, since there was no change in the Law of God from Adam to Abraham except for the addition of the Law of Circumcision.

Since the Gospel was preached from the beginning, and the Law of Moses was added later for the sake of the Israelites, we must ask ourselves what then was added specifically to the Gospel? That is actually the Law of Moses. Joseph Smith, Jr. refers to the Law of Moses as the Levitical law.[2] If Joseph Smith refers to the Law of Moses as the Levitical law, then I believe that the Law of Moses is, in fact, referring to only the Levitial ordinances as contained within the *Book of Leviticus*.

Furthermore, the *Book of Mormon* would seem to confirm this idea as well:

> Behold, I am Jesus Christ the Son of God. I created the
> heavens and the earth, and all things that in them are. I was with the
> Father from the beginning. I am in the Father, and the Father in me;
> and in me hath the Father glorified his name. I came unto my own,
> and my own received me not. And the scriptures concerning my

coming are fulfilled. And as many as have received me, to them have I given to become the sons of God; and even so will I to as many as shall believe on my name, for behold, by me redemption cometh, and in me is the law of Moses fulfilled. I am the light and the life of the world. I am Alpha and Omega, the beginning and the end. And ye shall offer up unto me no more the shedding of blood; yea, your sacrifices and your burnt offerings shall be done away, for I will accept none of your sacrifices and your burnt offerings. And ye shall offer for a sacrifice unto me a broken heart and a contrite spirit.

—3 Nephi 9:15-20 (Book of Mormon)

Jesus Christ speaks to the Nephites before appearing to them and he declares that the Law of Moses is fulfilled. Jesus Christ then explains that this means that all forms of blood sacrifice and burnt offerings are done away with. The Lord then explains that the new sacrifice is a broken heart and contrite spirit. Notice that at no time the Lord ever said that the *Torah* itself was done away with. Instead, the Lord uses their knowledge of the *Torah* to restore to them the original form of the *Torah* before it was altered for the sake of the Israelites.

Notice this pattern: In *3 Nephi* chapter 10, the Lord laments over the destruction of the Nephites and Lamanites because of their wickedness. In *3 Nephi* chapter 11, the Lord shows Himself to the people and gives to them the ordinances of salvation, the baptism of water and the receiving of the Holy Ghost. This means that the Lord inserted the ordinances of salvation back into the *Torah*. In *3 Nephi* chapter 12, the Lord then explains to them blessings for obedience and for teaching the Gospel. Included in this chapter, the Lord Himself says:

Think not that I am come to destroy the law [Torah] or the prophets. I am not come to destroy but to fulfill; for verily I say unto you, one jot nor one tittle hath not passed away from the law [Torah], but in me it [the Law of Moses] hath all been fulfilled. And behold, I have given you the law and commandments of my Father, that ye shall believe in me, and that ye shall repent of your sins, and come unto me with a broken heart and a contrite spirit. Behold, ye have the commandments before you, and the law [of Moses] is fulfilled. Therefore come unto me and be ye saved; for verily I say unto you,

that except ye shall keep my commandments, which I have commanded you at this time, ye shall in no case enter into the kingdom of heaven.

—3 Nephi 12:17-20 (Book of Mormon, words in brackets added for clarification)

I have added the words in brackets to help us think of this passage properly. The Lord is telling us that he is not getting rid of the *Torah,* but that the Law of Moses is ending. We are to now keep the Law of the Father, which is a law of Spiritual commandments. The Lord then explains to them what this new law is like. He takes their understanding of the *Torah* and brings it to the next level where they shall not only keep the law in their body, but keep the law in their thoughts as well. Not only shall they not kill but they shall not even be angry. Not only shall they not commit adultery, but they shall not even lust after a woman who is not their wife. This explanation is given from *3 Nephi* chapter 12 to *3 Nephi* chapter 14, showing us in many examples that the Father cares as much about our mindset as our actions.

With this, we can understand that the Lord is trying to teach us how to use the *Torah* now that His sacrifice has been fulfilled. The Lord has now restored to us the ordinances of salvation and has given us the Spiritual commandments. When we see commandments written in the *Torah,* we are to think of it spiritually and not only physically: do not kill in the flesh (murder) becomes do not even kill in the heart (anger). Furthermore, the Lord teaches us that we are to not keep the Law of Moses—meaning the law of sacrifice as contained in the *Book of Leviticus.* Instead, when we see a passage like this:

And it shall be, when he shall be guilty in one of these things, that he shall confess that he hath sinned in that thing; and he shall bring his trespass offering unto the Lord for his sin which he hath sinned, a female from the flock, a lamb, or a kid of the goats, for a sin offering; and the priest shall make an atonement for him concerning his sin.

—Leviticus 5:5-6 (Joseph Smith Translation)

We are to change it in this way:

And it shall be, when he shall be guilty in one of these things, that he shall confess that he hath sinned in that thing; and he shall bring to me a broken heart and a contrite spirit.

Now we can see that the Lord fully intended for us to use the *Torah* that Moses gave us instead of giving us a new *Torah*. Rather, the Lord taught us how to interpret the old *Torah* in his complete way. The *Torah* contains the commandments of the Lord and Jesus said,

Whosoever, therefore, shall break one of these least commandments, and shall teach men so to do, he shall in no wise be saved in the kingdom of heaven;

—Matthew 5:21 (Joseph Smith Translation)

By not observing the *Torah*, and by not interpreting the Torah in the way the Lord has taught us to do so, we are under the condemnation of God. Joseph Smith, Jr. tried to teach the early saints this, though it fell on deaf ears:

Jesus said, there are many mansions in my Father's house, and I will go and prepare a place for you. House here named should have been translated kingdom; and any person who is exalted to the highest mansion has to abide a celestial law, and the whole law too. But there has been a great difficulty in getting anything into the heads of this generation. It has been like splitting hemlock knots with a corndodger for a wedge, and a pumpkin for a beetle. Even the saints are slow to understand. I have tried for a number of years to get the minds of the saints prepared to receive the things of God; but we frequently see some of them, after suffering all they have for the work of God, will fly to pieces like glass as soon as anything comes that is contrary to their traditions: they cannot stand the fire at all. How many will abide a celestial law, and go through and receive their exaltation, I am unable to say, as many are called, but few are chosen.

—Teachings of the Prophet Joseph Smith, pg. 331 (bold added)

We are slow to understand. I confess this for myself—may the Lord forgive me. We are not keeping the whole law because our tradition has taught us not to. That tradition is false. The *Torah*—as Christ gave it to us—is still valid. If we cannot even keep those laws, how are we supposed to keep the celestial laws? We will not be able to because the *Torah* is designed to teach us how to live celestial law. Joseph Smith also said:

I spoke to the people, showing them that to get salvation we must not only do some things, but everything which God has commanded. Men preach and practice everything except those things which God commands us to do, and will be damned at last. We may tithe mint and rue, and all manner of herbs, and still not obey the commandments of God. The object with me is to obey and teach-others to obey God in just what he tells us to do. It mattereth not whether the principle is popular or unpopular, I will always maintain a true principle, even if I stand alone in it.

—Teachings of the Prophet Joseph Smith, pg. 332

Are you convinced yet that the *Torah* is still applicable in our day? The *Torah* is the most important collection of scriptures because all other scriptures point toward the *Torah*. The *Old Testament* prophets warn us what will happen if we do not keep the *Torah*, the *New Testament* helps us to interpret the *Torah* through Christ, the *Book of Mormon* helps us to remember the *Torah*, the *Doctrine and Covenants* copies sections of the *Torah* and gives us their restored meaning, and the *Pearl of Great Price* also expounds on the *Torah*.

The *Book of Mormon* tells us to keep the *Torah*, though we do not realize it. The *Book of Mormon* also tells us that when Christ comes, we are to stop doing blood sacrifice. The *Book of Mormon* shows us that the *Torah* will be of great worth to the gentiles:

> The book that thou beholdest is a record of the Jews, which contains the covenants of the Lord, which he hath made unto the house of Israel; and it also containeth many of the prophecies of the holy prophets; and it is a record like unto the engravings which are upon the plates of brass, save there are not so many; nevertheless, they contain the covenants of the Lord, which he hath made unto the house of Israel; wherefore, they are of great worth unto the Gentiles.
> —1 Nephi 13:23

Notice the word 'covenants of the Lord'. If you remember, we already discussed that the covenant is that if you will have the Lord as your God and keep his commandments, which are contained within the *Torah*, then you will prosper and be blessed. This is further shown when we study the original British colonists who came here. They were blessed exceedingly because they humbled themselves before the Lord, but we do not consider how they did this. If you were to study the original charter documents you would find that their laws were based, and even direct quotations, from the *Torah*. The colonists were able to obtain this land because they strove to live by the *Torah*. They possessed this land and obtained liberty, thus fulfilling the promise made in *2 Nephi* 1:7

> Wherefore, this land is consecrated unto him whom he shall bring. And if it so be that they shall serve him and keep his commandments which he hath given, it shall be a land of liberty

unto them; wherefore they shall never be brought down into captivity; if so, it shall be because of iniquity; for if iniquity shall abound cursed shall be the land for their sakes, but unto the righteous it shall be blessed forever.

—2 Nephi 1:7

The Lord promises that if we keep His commandments then we will have a land of liberty. If we do not keep the commandments then we will lose our liberty. Remember that when referring to the commandments it is a reference to the *Torah*, which contains the commandments of the Lord. Look at America today: our Constitution is being overturned more and more, our farmland is becoming dead, our wealth is disappearing, and our strength is diminishing from war after endless war. All of this is because we are ignoring the *Torah* and not interpreting it as Christ taught us to.

The *Doctrine and Covenants* also validates the *Torah*. The *Doctrine and Covenants* give us copied portions of the *Torah*, yet they are not really copied but rather reworded by the Lord. Section forty-two is an excellent example of this. It teaches the Law of God as given in the *Torah* as well as the spiritual Law as given by Jesus Christ. Remember that when the scriptures say law, it is the same as the *Torah*. After the Lord discourses on His own law, He says:

Thou knowest my laws concerning these things are given in my scriptures; he that sinneth and repents not shall be cast out. If thou lovest me thou shalt serve me and keep all my commandments.

—Doctrine and Covenants 42:28-29

Here, the Lord is reminding us that all His laws and commandments are already written down in the scriptures. Where are the greatest bulk of His commandments written? In the *Torah*, of course! The Lord then adds:

Thou shalt take the things which thou hast received, which have been given unto thee in my scriptures for a law, to be my law to govern my church; and he that doeth according to these things shall be saved, and he that doeth them not shall be damned if he so continue.

—Doctrine and Covenants 42:59-60

If we are to truly be the Lord's people then we must seek to observe all His commandments that are given in His scriptures. Is the *Torah* alone enough? No, but it contains the bulk of His law and through the other books we are taught how to interpret the *Torah* and the *Torah* is explained in greater detail.

What about *Romans 7,* you say? The Apostle Paul is the most misunderstood Apostle in the *Bible*. The fact is that *Romans* chapter seven is highly corrupted and Joseph Smith, Jr. corrected it. The Apostle Paul is really trying to show the Hebrew Christians in Rome that the Law of Moses is dead. This is a true fact. There is no disagreement. When Christ came, the Law of Moses died and Paul is saying that even though he did not transgress the Law, he became full of sin because by Christ coming he was under commandment to believe in Christ. This is the same discussion that Christ gave to the Nephites when he came. In fact, Paul supports the Law by saying that the Law teaches us what sin is:

What shall we say then? Is the law [(Torah)] sin? God forbid. Nay, I had not known sin, but by the law [(Torah)]; for I had not known lust, except the law had said, Thou shalt not covet."

Romans 7:7 (Joseph Smith Translation) words in parenthesis added for clarification

So, Paul shows us that he learned about sin because the *Torah* taught him right from wrong. Paul also says:

What then? Shall we sin, because we are not under the law [(*Torah*)], but under grace? God forbid.

Romans 6:15 (Joseph Smith Translation) words in parenthesis added for clarification

So, though we are not under the Law of Moses, we still need to study the *Torah* in order to know what sin is and not do it. We also need to remember that we are under the Law of Christ that deals with the inner thought as well as the action of the body.

Ok, so what about the rituals like circumcision and all those other rituals? I know Paul specifically spoke on circumcision and denounced it. Yes, the points of those rituals were to keep the Israelites in memory of Christ. The Gentiles believed in Christ with no such thing. Those rituals are not required for salvation; to be saved one must believe in Christ. If you can believe in Christ without those things then you are not obligated to keep those rituals. In fact, many of those rituals have become corrupt and people tend to do them for the sake of doing them. They do not think of Christ as they do these things. Therefore, they are doing those things incorrectly and this offends God, and by doing so they fall under sin. It is more important to believe in Christ than to keep those rituals. So, the important thing is to study the *Torah* so that you can know what sin is. If you believe in Christ then you do not need to keep those rituals. If you sin and repent then through Christ you can be forgiven. Ignoring the *Torah,* we will not truly know what sin is and what we need to do to follow the Lord.

If we do not keep the *Torah* then we cannot have peace in our society because true Peace is the everlasting result of keeping the *Torah.* If we do not keep the *Torah* then we will continue to have corrupt governments, endless wars, infinite debt, social unrest, famine, drought, plague, and all the judgments warned of in the scriptures.

1. http://www.merriam-webster.com/dictionary/peace
2. Teachings of the Prophet Joseph Smith pg. 60

Section 5b

Tim Urling, "War!"

Overhead of a large crowd of people streak six blue and yellow jets in formation as they begin an aerial display of aerobatics and formation flying with precision. Blazoned on the sides of each jet are the words, "The Blue Angels." On July 4th, marching down a cordoned street and flanked by hordes of people, veterans in uniform from several previous wars are honored by men, women and children at a parade with their hands over their hearts, standing in silence and reverence. A coffin draped with the United States at a cemetery is wished goodbye from family and loved-ones. A twenty-two year old man is laid to rest and receives a twenty-one-gun salute from military piers for serving his country and paying the ultimate sacrifice. Commonly affixed to rear bumpers of cars are stickers with clever expressions reminding Americans of our military who keeps us safe and free. To wit:

- God Bless our Troops, Especially our Snipers.
- If You Can Speak English-Thank a Teacher, If You Can Speak English in America-Thank a Marine.
- The American soldier and Jesus Christ, one gives his life for your freedom, the other for your soul.
- Thank the troops for their service.
- My Soldier Protects Your Honor Student
- Heroes Don't Wear Capes, They Wear Dog Tags

- Land of the Free Thanks to the Brave
- Honor the Fallen, They Gave their Tomorrows so You Can have Today

At a busy parking lot are several spaces reserved for military veterans at a home improvement center close to the entrance. At an airport, passengers disembark from their airplane flight and spill into a busy concourse. A few are servicemen dressed in military fatigues coming home from the Middle East. Spontaneously, a group of people who notice them begin to clap. A handful at first and then nearly everyone grants them generous applause for their service and welcomes them home.

Examples like these are only a pittance of the whole scheme of honor and praise bestowed on our military and veterans. It only scratches the surface. No one really argues about how much America respects those who served. Of that we can be sure. However, there are questions that arise in the wake of all this immortalized glory that raise the ire of most. Why should we support the troops? Are they really our heroes? Do our freedoms come from soldiers with guns? Who are we to tell another country whether or not they may develop a nuclear weapon? Where is the authority in the U.S. Constitution to stop the Hitler's of the world? These questions come across as so inflammatory they seldom are ever taken seriously let alone even answered. Nevertheless, they deserve to be answered and when they are, some of the greatest abominations of deceit are revealed and expose some of the most evil men ever clothed in human flesh.

Support our troops for what?

We hear on an incessant basis to support our troops but never what are we supporting them for? Today, living in the age of the state it has perhaps never been so evident that to support the troops is to support our government and not the citizens or our freedoms. Former deputy secretary of war Paul Wolfowitz uncovered the real reason for the 9-11 attacks by saying it was in retaliation for our having U.S. troops on the Arabian Peninsula. But that only tells part of the story.

Throughout history the reason is repeated many times. One country attacks another because soldiers are positioned on their property. Though nothing new, the U.S. is the greatest offender. America occupies over 140 nations and has over 700 foreign bases around the world. This is in direct violation of the advice of the founders, the Constitution, and history. Babylonian, Greek, Roman, English and Soviet empires always came to an end and for the same reason: money and the destruction of the offender's currency.

Having bases and interfering with other nations around the world suppresses freedom and results in conflict. Great libertarian statesman Richard Cobden, the apostle of free trade, said "Peace will come to earth when the people have more to do with each-other and governments less." Enforcing peace around the world with a barrel of a gun is like trying to make a people prosperous through more taxes. So why would governments promote war that do not benefit or keep their citizens safe? The founders studied eight centuries of history and understood that it was during wartime that governments began to increase in power. It was primarily in the executive branch that the increase in power occurred and it was primarily in the executive branch that the decisions were made to go to war. War satisfies an age-old temptation of *libido dominandi-man's lust for power. Leaders in government are soon temped with this insatiable weakness and perhaps no one is immune to it. It was for this reason the founders forbade war-making powers into the hands of one or a few individuals.*

Banking and War

America largely stayed out of foreign entangling alliances during the 18th and 19th centuries and followed the advice of the Founders to not mettle in other countries' affairs. Much of this can be attributed to America's adherence to following the gold standard thus preventing her from going to war because of the costs. It was Abraham Lincoln who initiated the first income tax and fiat currency called 'green backs.' The cost of the Civil War far longer and more expensive than even he imagined and through a process of inflation and taxation were the war debts settled.

A country paying for wars by debasing the currency is nothing new. Henry VIII in 1544 incurred serious debts from his uncontrolled spending and continuous wars. By clipping the coins and diluting the precious metals with copper, he drastically lowered the fineness of the gold and silver without the public's knowledge. Henry received the sobriquet of "Old Coppernose" as the silver rubbed off the high point on the relief coin's design. But it was John Maynard Keynes who revealed and confessed to the evil nature of inflation when he said: <u>By a continuing process of inflation, government can confiscate, secretly and unobserved, an important part of the wealth of their citizens.</u> In order for a country to do this, there must be a central bank that issues and regulates the nation's money supply and its currency's value. This is precisely what happened in the United States in 1913. The Federal Reserve was created under ominous conditions and now we have 100 years of proof from the continuous wars since that time. Our Founders gave us the creation of the first classical liberal government but the 20th century was a 100 years of bloodshed culminating in more than 170 million people killed by governments. In WWI alone, 10 million were killed and 50 million in WWII, of which nearly 70 percent were civilians. The Federal Reserve funded America's war machine and continues to do so to this day.

"They hate us because we are rich and free."

For perhaps the first time after September 11th people have begun to ask why America would be attacked. We give countless billions of foreign aid to nations around the world, American military bases dot the earth and we're a part of every peacekeeping U.N. mission there is. Why on earth would any country want to do us harm? For decades, a faint, lone voice has been trumpeting the truth that few believed. Twelve-term congressman Ron Paul has been warning America of its dangerous interventionist foreign policy and consequence known as blow-back. Hardly new and backed up by the CIA, Congressman Paul has said when America intervenes, meddles or occupies other nations there is blow-back. Unpopular by a mile, he stated in debates while running for president in 2007 that America has to look at what we might think if other nations did that to us. We would be annoyed if China occupied our nation with military bases and roamed our streets with Chinese military men in military vehicles. In an unprecedented event and during a presidential debate, Dr. Paul promoted the principle of the golden rule of foreign policy and was overwhelmed by boos from the crowd. His message of stopping all foreign aid to other nations, bringing our troops home from all around the world and minding our own business was unpopular at the time of the debates but now he is taken seriously.

In 2005 Robert Pape wrote a book called *Dying to Win*. In his book he created the first comprehensive database of every suicide terrorist attack from 1980 to 2004. He provides proof that the attacks on Americans are not motivated by religious reasons but are a result of consequences of a failed U.S. foreign policy. His book smashed the myth that by transforming the Muslim societies was the only way America could be kept safe from the terrorists. The connection between suicide terrorism and Islamic fundamentalism is a false message the American mainstream media promotes and benefits largely from it. For example, MSNBC is owned by General Electric and G.E., which has several military contracts for war weapons and munitions. They have no desire for the war on terror to be won, only sustained.

My Country, Right or Wrong!

A common tactic to promote perpetual war for perpetual peace is the use of demagoguery. By appealing to the emotions of the citizens, convincing them that they are being attacked, and labeling the anti-war patriots as un-American, they can drag public opinion into almost any military action. False flag events are monumental in their ability to perpetrate a lie. The Civil War begun with the attack on Fort Sumter, the War with Spain was propagandized by the motto "Remember the Maine, to hell with Spain," in 1915 President Wilson lured the Germans into torpedoing the Lusitania with Americans on board, Roosevelt slipped the U.S. through the backdoor to WWII by provoking Japan into bombing Pearl Harbor, Vietnam started on the Gulf of Tonkin Incident, and September 11th wreaks of lies, cover-ups and deliberate deceit from day one. Once a false flag event has occurred it is only a matter of running the printing presses with demagoguery and sensationalism until a war proposal becomes popular. Consider the master of demagogues President George W. Bush, who according to Nabil Shaath, the Palestinian foreign minister at the time, said: "President Bush said to all of us: 'I am driven with a mission from God'. God would tell me, 'George go and fight these terrorists in Afghanistan'. And I did. And then God would tell me 'George, go and end the tyranny in Iraq'. And I did."

Over a decade since the U.S. invaded Iraq on false information, Iraq is littered with more terrorist attacks than before Saddam Hussein was removed from power. Almost 5,000 American lives have been lost and a million innocent Iraqis are dead with millions more are displaced and billions of dollars wasted. Is this what God wanted? America-the land of the free! Or maybe the land of torture, indiscriminate bombing, sanctions that starve citizens who have done nothing to us, and foreign aid that is used as a weapon to obey the U.S. policy makers. It is always easy to identify a nationalist because he repeats liberty and patriotism with a sneer. The media touts that killing is okay as long as it is sanctioned by the U.S. government. Voltaire- "It is forbidden to kill; therefore all murderers are punished unless they kill in large numbers and to the sound of trumpets."

Read the heart wrenching story from Iraq Army veteran Michael Goss:

> I have PTSD. I know when I got it – that night I killed an 8 year old girl. Her family was trying to cross a checkpoint. We'd just shot three guys who'd tried to cross a checkpoint. And during that mess, they were just trying to get through to get away from it all. And we ended up shooting all of them, too. It was a family of six.

The only one that survived was a 13 month old girl and her mother. And the worst part about it all was there where I shot my bullets, when I went to see what I'd shot at, there was an eight year old girl there. I tried my best to bring her back to life, but there was no use.

Oh, yes, President Bush! We can't forget your solemn words of wisdom:

The troops here and across the world are fighting a global war on terror. The war reached our shores on September 11th…our mission in Iraq is clear. We're hunting down the terrorists. We're helping build a free nation that is an ally in the war on terror. We're advancing freedom in the broader Middle East. We are removing a source of violence and instability and laying the foundation of peace for our children and grandchildren." –address to the nation, June 28, 2005.

Thank you, President Bush! The eight year old girl riddled with Michael Goss's bullets and I thank you for a foundation of peace.

Section 6b

Irven Hill, "Military Keynesianism"

To many, the term military Keynesianism may seem very foreign. What does John Maynard Keynes have to do with war and military spending? Who was John Maynard Keynes? Wasn't he just an economist? What does a British economist have to do with Nazi Germany? It is not the purpose of this essay to delve into Keynes and his political and economic influence. But some clarification must be made as to give the unfamiliar reader some insight into Keynes and thus "Keynesianism."

John Maynard Keynes was a British economist whose ideas have permeated much of modern economic thought, practices and ideas. His ideas are used by governments the world over, i.e. fiat currency, central banking, central planning and arbitrary central bank adjusted interest rates. Only governments provide jobs in the making of war machines, either directly or indirectly through subsidy to government contractors. Hence the use of the term military Keynesianism. Keynes is a major contributor to macroeconomics and has a following among most economists. Many economists who don't consider themselves Keynesian often adopt many of his ideas. There is one school of economic thought which opposes Keynes and Keynesianism not just in part, but completely. It is the Austrian school, brought to the forefront by Ludwig von Mises. There are many economists, past and present, of the

Austrian tradition. I will not go into that, but anyone interested in learning more can log onto Mises.org for a plethora of information of past and present Austrian economic theory and science. The major tenets in the difference in the Keynesian school and the Austrian school are--but not limited to--sound money, prices, interest rates, savings and governments role--if any--in the market. The Austrian school does not view intervention as an answer to economic problems. Austrians actually view intervention and central planning to damage, rather than help the market. Keep in mind while reading:

> Keynesianism = government view of economics.
> Austrian = free market view of economics

Military Keynesianism in Nazi Germany

In explaining military Keynesianism, it seems fitting to start with popular myths of war being an economic boon—as Keynesianism is built on fiat ideas, or "myths." A great starting point would be Nazi Germany. There is a great myth that lives to this very day--even with the hatred that most espouse for Hitler—crediting Hitler with rescuing Germany from the Great depression in 1933. He did this by building up military in Germany, which in turn, put people to work or so the story goes. The reality of the situation in Nazi Germany is actually one of rationing, starvation and general misery. The scholarly research of Richard J. Evans—Ironically a Keynesian, government interventionist—give us insight into the true story of the third Reich. In the words of economic historian Julian Adorney:

> Hitler's rearmament program was military Keynesianism on a vast scale. Hermann Goering, Hitler's economic administrator, poured every available resource into making planes, tanks, and guns. In 1933 German military spending was 750 million Reichsmarks. By 1938 it had risen to 17 billion with 21 percent of GDP was taken up by military spending. Government spending all told was 35 percent of Germany's GDP.

Many liberals, especially Paul Krugman, routinely argue that our stimulus programs in America aren't big enough, so when they fail it's not an indictment of Keynesianism. Fair enough. But no-one could say that Hitler's rearmament program was too small. Economists expected it to create a multiplier effect and jump-start a flagging economy. Instead, it produced military wealth while private citizens starved. Employed on the largest scale ever seen, military Keynesianism created only ruin.

The generally accepted belief is that Hitler had cured unemployment. Again from Julian Adorney:

> …..rearmament and nationalized industry put every available German to work. There were so many jobs that the Nazis complained of a labor shortage and brought women in to the workplace, even though they were ideologically opposed to it. Unemployment had been cured. And yet, the people routinely suffered shortages. Civilian wood and iron were rationed. Small businesses, from artisans to carpenters to cobblers, went under. Citizens could barely buy pork, and buying fat to make a luxury like a cake was impossible. Rationing and long lines at the central supply depots the Nazis installed became the norm.

If Nazi Germany provided a plethora of jobs, what was the problem? If "everyone" was working to the point of even a labor shortage, how can there be mass starvation and misery among the general population? The answer lies in the economic principles as taught by the French economist Frederic Bastiat, later Henry Hazlitt and most recently Walter Block of Loyola University, New Orleans. Namely that real economic thought and theory must contain the reality of not only that which is seen, but that which is not seen. In the case of Nazi Germany, we need to look deeper. If high employment isn't the answer, what is? To answer that question, one must look into the type of employment that exists. Does the existing employment exist because of market phenomena, or so often as is the case, government fiat? It is obvious in the case of Germany in 1933, it was government fiat, or in the tradition of Keynesian economic theory: Government intervention is necessary to prevent economic recessions and depressions. If we build tanks and planes, we can put "everyone to work." The reality of recessions and depressions, show no such thing. Government intervention or spending haven't staved off inevitable downturns. Close research and study reveals the actuality is that government intervention increases the probability of economic downturns and volatility. Germany is not an isolated example of this—though it is the biggest example of Keynesian economic intervention. Back to 1933 Germany and Julian Adorney:

> Nazi Germany proves that curing unemployment should not be an end in itself. No doubt, jobs are important. But they are important for what they produce, not just by virtue of existing. Real growth means production of what people demand. It means making cars, growing food, building laptops, or commercial planes. Private production grows the economic pie and helps everyone to prosper. Without production, all that a job does is change a man from starving and unemployed to starving and employed.

In other words, we need to look at what is seen: fiat production. And what is not seen—at least at the time in the 1930's: Employment created, not by productive naturally occurring market phenomena, but rather government fiat. Employment is not a means to an end, but only a possible positive economic factor, depending upon its wellspring. War, mass murder, pillaging and piracy cannot bring about economic vitality. Destruction does not build and building does not destroy. Simply put, we cannot destroy our way to prosperity. Only peace and mutual cooperation can lead to prosperity. Anything else is fiat and can only appear genuine for a short time. When the reality sets in as it always does, we see the true fruits of fiat government meddling. Economic fruits are subject to a market correction. The more malinvestment—

focus of investment into non-productive means—the harsher the correction will be. Nazi Germany is probably the best example of how big of an economic bubble can be created in a relatively short time and just how quickly it can burst. Actually in Nazi Germany's case, the Keynesian intervention was so large and encompassing, that real economic prosperity was never realized.

Military Keynesianism in Stalinist Russia.

While not reaching full employment because of militaristic ventures, Stalin's Russia is an excellent economic example of Keynesian failure. The people in Stalin's Russia suffered from starvation, cold and sickness; all the while producing vast military machines and very technical military technology, at times on the cutting edge. During Stalin's reign, Keynes—to be fair—did offer some scathing critiques on the "Russian experiment" as he called it. But he also offered much praise for that same experiment. Keynes went so far as to call the Russian experiment something "which every serious citizen will do well to look into." Using some lengthy and scholarly research done by Ralph Raico, one will find information to back the argument that Keynes offered at least as much praise upon Stalin's Russia as he did criticism. Russia, in essence, caused themselves the same problems as Nazi Germany. A problem that every super power faces to some degree or other. Basically fiat means produce fiat ends.

Military Keynesianism in the United States.

During the all the years leading up to Woodrow Wilson and FDR, the people of the US weren't inclined to enter into war and bloodshed. They didn't tend to see economic prosperity through the lens of destruction. They preferred to farm and build rather than poison and destroy. The general attitude was one of working, trading and contracting in a positive effort to make themselves and therefore the nation, the most prosperous the world had seen. Most in the US tended to believe what most of the founders believed; to quote Jefferson, "The spirit of this country is totally adverse to a large military force." Even during FDR's tenure, the country was apprehensive to enter World War II. The politicians worked and preached for war, but never really gained much traction. There had to be an event, an attack on America to stir the populace into support of war. Why? So that the Keynesian mixture of warfare and welfare could be realized. Investment, jobs, production, growth and prosperity—all by fiat. An idea that, before Pearl Harbor, few Americans accepted began to take root. An idea that few Americans question today.

Today, the US has the largest Military in the history of the world. We have bases in more than 150 countries. We have hundreds of thousands employed as contractors—directly or indirectly—to the US military. We have a cutting edge drone program where cowards can earn military badges for killing "terrorists" by remote control. We have a National Security Agency that spies on more people than any agency in history. The military kills women and children on a daily basis and calls it collateral damage. We have troops committing suicide at record rates upon returning home from war zones. The right worries that cutting one dime of military spending signals weakness to the rest of the world, while the left worries about what all of the soldiers would do if they weren't employed in the military.

All of this goes on while the national debt rapidly approaches $20 trillion. How long can it be sustained? We are in uncharted territory. No one knows. What we do know, is that with all things fiat, there will be an end. The longer and larger the fiat Keynesian model grows, the more devastating the burst will be. Military Keynesianism in the US will fail, just as it did in Nazi Germany and Soviet Russia. The problem being that our Keynesian model is the largest in history, making the fall the most epic of all falls. Hopefully, if there can be any good from this failure, it will be that the failure will be the death knell of all things Keynesian. And also that God may have mercy upon those of us who dared speak out about military atrocities and the system that provided the means to build it up.

Section 7b

Collin Theis, "How to Accomplish Truly Constitutional and Superior Homeland Security"

Collin is an honorably discharged U.S. Army disabled veteran, lifetime LDS and Oathkeeper, Constitutionalist, multimedia business owner, and the editor of . . . www.thelibertarianclarion.com

Part I of IV

What is truly Constitutional and superior homeland security? It is a vast contrast between what is now implemented around the world and what is presented within this essay. It is the difference between unethical anti-constitutional imperial aggression and truly ethical and Constitutional homeland security that is superior in every way, with benefits that extend far beyond military areas to all aspects of life.

In order to accurately understand anything Constitutional, we should first and foremost rely on the Constitution itself. The following are the things that are required to accomplish truly Constitutional and superior homeland security according to supreme U.S. law—the Constitution itself (which all States agree to and must abide by—including and especially the Bill of Rights—which laws cannot be superseded by anything other than the U.S. Constitution itself and <u>no natural right can be nullified</u>). The People have failed to honor most of these things, and when it seems that they have honored them then it usually turns out to be a deceitful mockery of what truly Constitutional and superior homeland security requires. Such failures result in dire consequences to the entire world. *According to the U.S. Constitution:*

Article I, section 8

* The Congress shall have Power To lay and collect Taxes, Duties, Imposts and Excises, to pay the Debts and provide for the common Defense and general Welfare of the United States; but *all* Duties, Imposts and Excises **shall be uniform** throughout the United States; [emphasis added]

* To coin Money, regulate the Value thereof, and of foreign Coin, and fix the Standard of Weights and Measures [How does the 'Federal Reserve' fit into this, except as an abomination? The words 'coin' and 'money' are used together to emphasize that the government is to use money that is backed by precious metals, as explicitly required in article 1, section 10, clause 1];

* To declare War [power that does not rest with the executive or judicial branches], grant Letters of Marque and Reprisal, and make Rules concerning Captures on Land and Water;

* To raise and support Armies [meaning the military as a whole and not the 'U.S. Army', which did not even exist until much later], but no Appropriation of Money to that Use shall be for a longer Term than two Years [clearly this clause applies to all of the U.S. military.];

[Next, the Constitution talks about what kind of 'Armies' that we are to have and what functions they are to serve]

* To provide and maintain a Navy;

* To make Rules for the Government and Regulation of the land and naval Forces [the Militia of the Several States and the U.S. Navy];

* To provide for calling forth the Militia to execute the Laws of the Union, suppress Insurrections and repel Invasions;

* To provide for organizing, arming, and disciplining the Militia, and for governing such Part of them as may be employed in the Service of the United States, reserving to the States respectively the Appointment of the Officers and the Authority of training the Militia according to the discipline prescribed by Congress;

* To make all Laws which shall be necessary and proper for carrying into Execution the foregoing Powers, and all other Powers vested by this Constitution in the Government of the United States, or in any Department or Officer thereof. **Article I, Section 9**

* The Privilege of the Writ of *Habeas Corpus* shall not be suspended, unless when in Cases of Rebellion or Invasion the public Safety may require it.

* No Bill of Attainder or ex post facto Law shall be passed [no trial without Due Process of law and no laws that change the consequences of things that were done before the new law]

* No Capitation, or other direct, Tax shall be laid (the income tax 'amendment' is actually anti-Constitutional and therefore nullified because it infringes on the rights of the people by taking by force from their substance when the unpolluted Constitution specifically forbids the government from doing so, and for many good reasons.]

* No Tax or Duty shall be laid on Articles exported from any State.

* No Preference shall be given by any Regulation of Commerce or Revenue to the Ports of one State over those of another: nor shall Vessels bound to, or from, one State, be obliged to enter, clear, or pay Duties in another.

* No Money shall be drawn from the Treasury, but in Consequence of Appropriations made by Law; and a regular Statement and Account of the Receipts and Expenditures of all public Money shall be published from time to time [How does the 'Federal Reserve' fit into this, except as an abomination?].

* No Title of Nobility shall be granted by the United States: And no Person holding any Office of Profit or Trust under them, shall, without the Consent of the Congress, accept of any present, Emolument, Office, or Title, of any kind whatever, from any King, Prince, or foreign State.

Article I, section 10

* No State shall enter into any Treaty, Alliance, or Confederation; grant Letters of Marque and Reprisal; coin Money; emit Bills of Credit; make any Thing but gold and silver Coin a Tender in Payment of Debts; pass any Bill of Attainder, ex post facto Law [these things are so important that they included them at least 3 times in the U.S. Constitution, yet modern executive branch administrations flagrantly violate them through things such as the NDAA, the assassination of American citizens without due process of law—including children—and more], or Law impairing the Obligation of Contracts, or grant any Title of Nobility.

* No State shall, without the Consent of the Congress, lay any Imposts or Duties on Imports or Exports, except what may be absolutely necessary for executing its inspection Laws: and the net Produce of all Duties and Imposts, laid by any State on Imports or Exports, shall be for the Use of the Treasury of the United States; and all such Laws shall be subject to the Revision and Control of the Congress.

* No State shall, without the Consent of Congress, lay any Duty of Tonnage, keep Troops, or Ships of War in time of Peace, enter into any Agreement or Compact with another State, or with a foreign Power, or engage in War, unless actually invaded, or in such imminent Danger as will not admit of delay.

Article II, section 2

* The President shall be Commander in Chief of the Army and Navy of the United States [the "Army and Navy" being the same entity, with the Marines being the 'Army' element of the Navy, which always had personnel that were trained to fight on land as well], and of the Militia of the several States, when called into the actual Service of the United States; he may require the Opinion, in writing, of the principal Officer in each of the executive Departments, upon any Subject relating to the Duties of their respective Offices, and he shall have Power to grant Reprieves and Pardons for Offences against the United States, except in Cases of Impeachment.

Article II, section 3

* He shall from time to time give to the Congress Information of the State of the Union, and recommend to their Consideration such Measures as he shall judge necessary and expedient; he may, on extraordinary Occasions, convene both Houses, or either of them, and in Case of Disagreement between them, with Respect to the Time of Adjournment, he may adjourn them to such Time as he shall think proper; he shall receive Ambassadors and other public Ministers; **he shall take Care that the Laws be faithfully executed** [especially supreme U.S. law—the Constitution], and shall Commission all the Officers of the United States.

Article II, section 4

* The President, Vice President and all civil Officers of the United States, shall be removed from Office on Impeachment for, and Conviction of, Treason, Bribery, or other high Crimes and Misdemeanors.

Article III, section 2

The Trial of all Crimes, except in Cases of Impeachment, shall be by Jury; and such Trial shall be held in the State where the said Crimes shall have been committed; but when not committed within any State, the Trial shall be at such Place or Places as the Congress may by Law have directed.

Article III, section 3

* Treason against the United States, shall consist only in levying War against them, or in adhering to their Enemies, giving them Aid and Comfort. No Person shall be convicted of Treason unless on the Testimony of two Witnesses to the same overt Act, or on Confession in open Court.

* The Congress shall have Power to declare the Punishment of Treason, but no Attainder of Treason shall work Corruption of Blood, or Forfeiture except during the Life of the Person attainted.

Article IV, section 1
* Full Faith and Credit shall be given in each State to the public Acts, Records, and judicial Proceedings of every other State. And the Congress may by general Laws prescribe the Manner in which such Acts, Records and Proceedings shall be proved, and the Effect thereof.

Article IV, section 2
* The Citizens of each State shall be entitled to all Privileges and Immunities of Citizens in the several States.

* A Person charged in any State with Treason, Felony, or other Crime, who shall flee from Justice, and be found in another State, shall on Demand of the executive Authority of the State from which he fled, be delivered up, to be removed to the State having Jurisdiction of the Crime.

Article IV, section 4
* The United States shall guarantee to every State in this Union a Republican Form of Government, and shall protect each of them against Invasion [which duty the U.S. Constitution only expressly assigns to the well-regulated and localized Militia of the Several States rather than the much more centralized imposters that exist today]; and on Application of the Legislature, or of the Executive (when the Legislature cannot be convened), against domestic Violence.

Article VI
* This Constitution, and the Laws of the United States which shall be made in Pursuance thereof; and all Treaties made, or which shall be made, under the Authority of the United States, shall be the supreme Law of the Land; and the Judges in every State shall be bound thereby, any Thing in the Constitution or Laws of any State to the Contrary

notwithstanding [meaning that anything that stands against the U.S. Constitution is nullified].

* The Senators and Representatives before mentioned, and the Members of the several State Legislatures, and all executive and judicial Officers, both of the United States and of the several States, shall be bound by Oath or Affirmation, to support this Constitution; but no religious Test shall ever be required as a Qualification to any Office or public Trust under the United States.

"A **well-regulated Militia**, **being necessary** to the **security** of a *FREE* **State**, the right of the people to keep and bear Arms shall **NOT** be infringed."

—U.S. Constitution, 2nd amendment (emphasis added)

The above are only some of Congress' ongoing Constitutional obligations, long betrayed and continually neglected concerning true and superior homeland security. The most dangerous failure is that the Constitutional and local Militia of the Several States have been supplanted by centralized and non-local imposters like the U.S. Army and the National/State Guard that are under the direct control of the federal government and are unable to operate as true Militia that are Constitutionally obligated to 'execute the Laws of the Union, suppress Insurrections and repel Invasions' from enemies both foreign *and* domestic. How did things get this way and how should we respond? To answer that, we will start at the beginning of the history of what became the U.S. Militia.

In the 1770's, the British Empire had the greatest military ever known on the face of this Earth, having dominated for centuries. During the North American Revolutionary War against them, these vaunted armies, navies, spies, and commanders were beaten by a mere 3% of the colonists—primarily Militia members with excellent Native American support and French assistance. Following the colonial victory, U.S. Founders were faced with a critical choice concerning how to defend and preserve their new nation. On one hand, they now had the opportunity to establish a centralized standing army as most of the world had, and the argument was made by some from the beginning to do so. On the other, it had just been historically proven, yet again, that defensive local Militia can succeed where the best centralized standing armies ever known cannot, so the benefits of allowing the defensive Militia to continue accomplishing national security were clearly known and promoted by the Founders rather than centralized standing armies that are inferior and demonstrably dangerous to world-wide peace and prosperity.

Still, many continue holding the belief that Militia as military organizations are inferior to centralized standing armies and that only the latter can handle modern dangers. However, the opposite is actually true. Explosive, chemical, and biological 'terrorism'/warfare existed at the time of the Militia's official adoption by U.S. government, yet the Founders still chose defensive Militia over aggressive standing armies, especially when it comes to the duty of responding to government corruption—which centralized standing armies are more prone to contribute to than defend against, unlike local Militia composed of local people whose chain of command begins with local authority. Even in modern times we see the superiority of smaller, often more primitive decentralized forces against more imposing centralized militaries that are *considered* to be the greatest armed forces on earth. Consider the Soviet losses to comparatively feeble and primitive Middle-Eastern Militia, or the defeat of centralized U.S. forces in Vietnam, who were then baited to repeat the Soviet mistake in the Middle-East—causing the U.S. to continue suffering attrition and blow-back from the fundamental treason against the Constitution that centralized standing armies and aggressive warfare are.

Consider why nations like Israel and Switzerland continue to utilize Militia rather than extensive standing armies, and why the Militia is even immortalized in supreme U.S. law as the only military entity authorized and obligated to 'execute the laws of the Union, suppress Insurrections, and repel Invasions'. Consider why Congress is constitutionally bound to appropriate resources for the Militia of the Several States and ensure that they are ready and able to be called forth into service. This is an obligation that Congress has long failed, corrupt politicians having supplanted the localized U.S. Militia with centralized military forces now exclusively under federal control, rather than the military chain of command being buffered between the States, their localities, and the federal government—as intended and required by the Constitution of the United States.

What's the difference between the Army/Reserve/National Guard/FEMA/DHS/TSA/*etc.* and the true Militia of the Several States and why is it such a big deal that the U.S. Militia was and still is supplanted by such imposters?

1. Chain of Command

The Militia is meant to have an external chain of command that goes from County Sheriff, to State Governor, to Commander-in-Chief (the President), to Congress, to WE THE PEOPLE. This chain is rooted at the most local levels possible upward and is more likely to successfully nullify attempted unlawful or unjust actions and is not exclusively under federal control, so not nearly as subject to the dangers of centralized corruption as is currently the case with most modern armed forces.

2. Locality

For homeland security, local people know their territory best, how to defend it, and have the most motivation for doing so successfully—more so than centralized forces who are continually deployed as pawns to foreign places to serve those with harmful political and economic agendas rather than truly defending their Homeland, the constitution, Freedom, or any other military recruitment pick-up line.

3. Upkeep

Not only are well-regulated and localized Militia militarily superior to more centralized standing armies, they are also much more economically superior! It costs much less to achieve and maintain national security through a well-regulated and defensive Militia rather than through aggressive and ever-expanding centralized federal forces that are wasted in ways such as the endless and deceitful global 'War on Terror', costing less even if Militia members were to be paid more than current federal forces. A defensive Militia based at home can significantly stimulate industry, agriculture, and many other aspects of local and national economy.

Unfortunately, the economy of the U.S. is now in dire straits due to the people's ongoing failures to heed the warnings of Founders such as Thomas Jefferson about how dangerous both standing armies and central banking are to Freedom, Liberty, and Justice. Consequently, we now live under the economic slavery and conspiratorial tyranny of every force that we were warned against and we do so without our only truly effective and authorized last resort against these threats to the people of the U.S.—the true Militia of the Several States.

If you still think that the Militia is unimportant, then please consider that in 1786, the U.S. was already dealing with a sinister collusion between corrupt politicians and corrupt bankers that allowed those in debt to be imprisoned and otherwise cruelly persecuted. The crushing economic and legal environment of government and financial corruption was enabled by the unworkable form of government that was first authorized by the Articles of Confederation. That same year, several veterans who had fought in the North American Revolutionary War against England began a rebellion because domestic enemies threatened the Freedom, Liberty, and Justice of all.

Daniel Shays and his followers were brave, yet misguided people without which we may still be laboring under a system where bankers can imprison people for debt and subject them to the horrors of incarcerated abuse. They intended to capture the Springfield Armory and use the supplies to overthrow the corrupt government and intended to live thereafter without any government in anarchy. Shays' rebellion was quelled by the well-regulated Militia, which allowed the Founders to respond to the concerns of the brave yet misguided rebels by replacing the failed Articles of Confederation with the U.S. Constitution and its Bill of Rights (again choosing the well-regulated Militia to accomplish national security when they could have instead created centralized standing armies such as are still ignorantly and pridefully maintained). If the well-regulated Militia did not intervene and the U.S. had dissolved into anarchy then it would have left the People subject to other nations—especially the recently repelled British Empire. There are also many other instances where the well-regulated and localized Militia were required to do what centralized forces either cannot or cannot do nearly as well—such as executing the laws of the union, protecting people's voting rights and other natural rights against government corruption, or against complete anarchy and the bloodbaths that would have resulted.

These are only some of Congress' ongoing Constitutional obligations, long betrayed and continually neglected concerning the Militia of the Several States:

1. "To provide for organizing, arming, and disciplining the Militia, and for governing such Part of them as may be employed in the Service of the United States, reserving to the States respectively the Appointment of the Officers and the Authority of training the Militia according to the discipline prescribed by Congress;"

2. "To provide for calling forth the Militia to execute the Laws of the Union, suppress Insurrections and repel Invasions;"(U.S. Constitution, Article 1, Section 8)

Consequences of failing to truly live the Constitution and its Second Amendment through the Militia of the Several States:

Twice the United States was born and preserved primarily thanks to its well-regulated Militia and it will soon die with terrible and widespread destruction if true Homeland Security through the Militia of the Several States as prescribed by supreme U.S. law—the Constitution—is not immediately restored and the ever-expanding unconstitutional Nazi/Soviet-type police state that promises security yet is eternally incapable of delivering and has treacherously supplanted it is done away with and never allowed to return.

In order to operate, the truly Constitutional Militia of the Several States must first be revitalized, and before the question of how to accomplish that is addressed, it's important to understand their absence and how to avoid a harmful repeat of it.

In 1812, the United States proto-Militia—while ferocious—also still lacked discipline, equipment, and uniform training and regulation across all units. When the British regrouped and violently returned to America in the War of 1812, it was clear that the U.S. was woefully deficient in Naval warfare against the British and the poorly trained and still poorly-equipped U.S. Militia only proved to be reliably effective fighting units within their own States, not in other States or when working with unfamiliar units who may have been trained in completely different ways, with differing commands, formations, tactics, and standards of achievement in contrast to the superior cohesion, discipline, and resources of the British military. General George Washington, among others, called attention to these long-standing deficiencies and their remedies. It was determined that Congress appropriate enough resources for the Militia to be provisioned and called forth into the actual service of any of the several States. All Militia units also needed to receive uniform training, and to that end the West Point military academy was established for the training of officers who were appointed by the States, who would then return to their States to train their Militia personnel accordingly. None of the above was successfully implemented in time to benefit the Militia of the Several States by the War of 1812.

Unfortunately, the partial defeat of U.S. proto-Militia by British forces was enough to allow certain corrupt politicians to rekindle arguments for a federalized standing army under their direct control rather than retaining and improving the localized Militia. The local and decentralized Constitutional Militia were (and remain) primarily undesirable to corrupt politicians because although the Militia now had uniform training as prescribed by Congress, it also comes with local authorities who have the potential to interfere with unethical schemes involving domestic force.

These anti-Constitutional politicians persisted with their anti-Militia philosophy despite the historical fact that beyond just the North American Revolutionary War, it is only thanks to the Militia that the United States was able to exist and survive at all (a fact enshrined for posterity within the 2nd Amendment), slowly chipping away over time at the Constitutional local Militia of the Several States to be replaced by the federal forces that they wanted so badly.

This hypocritical anti-constitutionality on the part of the United States is a primary cause of the ravaged state of the world today as a result of aggressive rather than actually defensive warfare, which has been waged by corrupt federal politicians, indoctrinated federal military forces, and corrupt corporations. This unethical, hypocritical, and oath breaking anti-constitutionality has brought famine, plague, war, and death and will continue to do so until the Constitution is fully restored through the localized Militia of the Several States and the political corruption that destroyed the Militia is subdued by the implementation of the Public Servant's Uniform Code of Justice (PSUCJ).

Public Servant's Uniform Code of Justice (PSUCJ) proposal:

Problem: In order to prevent the might of the military from getting out of control through stealing, enslaving, murdering, and all manner of other dishonorable acts, we implemented a Uniform Code of Military Justice to specifically and clearly define the code of conduct for military personnel and the severe consequences of dishonoring that code. Military personnel now not only have to obey civil laws--and foreign laws when applicable—but their conduct must also adhere to the UCMJ, which is their strongest restraint and one tailored specifically for them in order to prevent unconscionable acts that are historically observed to be committed by militaries that are completely unrestrained in such a way. We established the military safety measure of the UCMJ and then conveniently ignored the men in charge of issuing orders to the military itself—the politicians who answer to no specific code, and to civil laws that intentionally aren't equipped to address the historically observed unconscionable acts of unethical politicians.

Solution: Nullification in answer to political tyranny is a temporary remedy. The argument has been made by history itself that in order to sustain an ethical government it must be operated by those bound to a PUBLIC SERVANT'S UNIFORM CODE OF JUSTICE that ALL public servants—including and especially politicians—must abide by **in addition** to United States civil law and their public oaths of office, similarly to what is required of our military personnel. The PSUCJ would clearly define the consequences of government corruption to be enforced by the well-regulated Militia of the Several States according to Supreme U.S. law—the United States Constitution.

Implementation: 1. Form a committee of those with a proven record of honoring their oaths of public office and upholding the philosophies of non-aggressive freedom, liberty, and justice. This committee would be comprised of individuals such as Ron Paul, Justin Amash, Thomas Massie, Gary Johnson, Judge Napolitano, Sheriff Richard Mack, Judge Gray, Stewart Rhodes, Jesse Ventura, *etc.* who will construct, promote, and support a Public Servant's Uniform Code of Justice to then be submitted and passed by Congress or be ratified by the sovereign people of the United States in the form of a national referendum, or be established as a result of an Article V Constitutional convention.

2. This code will first and foremost nullify all laws not in keeping with the United States Constitution as interpreted from the firm foundation of limited government, limited taxation, and maximum personal liberty through personal responsibility and community voluntarism rather than insidiously encouraged (and/or forced) government dependence. The PSUCJ will lead to the prosecution of those who pushed through traitorous anti-liberty legislation, and will effectively nullify future efforts with strict penalties for political corruption. No more Patriot Act, NDAA, or Federal Reserve. No lobbying and therefore no subsequent special treatment for companies such as Monsanto and Goldman Sachs that are ruining our health and economy, etc.

Result: Under the PSUCJ politicians won't even be able to be taken out to lunch . . . they can have their family pack something up from the organic gardens at home that will be legal again because of the

PSUCJ's having nullified the unlawful restrictions on all such PERSONAL PROPERTY rights.

It would seed a new awareness of the philosophy of non-aggressive freedom, liberty, and justice, serving its key part in bringing about the rightful restoration of such principles.

As the corrupt politicians mark themselves with their opposition to this Code of Justice, the ethical ones will call for its tonic as though freedom itself depends on it--because they'll understand that it does. The ethical ones will be established into office and honorably bound by the PSUCJ for the duration of their term, and the rest will be utterly cast down.

Your Part:

This solution doesn't require anyone to fight upstream to achieve the Presidency or compromise themselves by wading through an infiltrated and subverted system that clearly needs its Guardians to restore it. With your support, we will soon become a wave of justice too overwhelming for those politicians that are corrupt to withstand and the PSUCJ will severely limit their ability to internally compromise these United States ever again. Those corrupt politicians still at large during the implementation will have to submit, flee, or die.

All you have to do to make this happen is to simply share and support this idea in every way you know how. Are liberty and justice worth that much to you?

You can't rollback an idea whose time has come. _____In the next part, we'll examine the many attractive benefits of truly restoring the Militia of the Several States and the questions of voluntary service, compensation, personal, local, national, and international impacts, and what life would be like if the people truly live according to our own Constitution and stop being pseudo-patriotic hypocrites at the cost of self-destruction.

Part II of IV

One of the first questions that comes to the mind of many as they consider what life would be like with truly Constitutional Homeland Security is "what would happen to the current armed forces?." There are currently millions of service members across all branches and forms of military service and none would lose employment if they chose to keep it with the new Constitutional Armed Services. There are hundreds of thousands of 'homeland security' employees who would have the same option.

There would be no more things such as the U.S. Army, National Guard, or DHS (including TSA, FEMA, DEA, etc.). The reorganized Constitutional Navy, the Militia of the Several States and the Constitutional Sheriffs and Peace Officers serve the functions of all these agencies and more and they do so better in every way. Only the military bodies expressly authorized through the Constitution will remain, those being the well-regulated Militia and the Navy. The Air Force will also cease to exist, their functions being fully served by the reorganized Constitutional Navy. Special Forces not currently part of the Navy would be integrated into it. The Marines would remain as part of the Navy and maintain the bases and other foreign positions which our formal allies have officially invited us to maintain and which invitation our allies officially reaffirm at least once every 2 years by the time of the United States Congress' military appropriations deadline, and if we are not officially asked by that legitimate allied government to remain, or if we are officially asked before that time to leave, then we return home.

Current Intelligence agencies—other than legitimate private-sector security/defense/privacy businesses and/or associations—would cease to exist with the Navy given full responsibility over military Intelligence and Militia special agents given responsibility over counter-espionage within their localities. Local Sheriffs would have authority over all investigations within their jurisdiction which previously was allowed to agencies such as the FBI, DEA, ATF, etc. There would be no more FBI, CIA, NSA, DIA, NRO, etc. or the wasteful drain on resources and threat to the Constitution that they have historically represented—often proving to be the source of danger to the U.S. through direct anti-constitutionality, treasonous conspiracy, or unintentional blow-back rather than accomplishing true National Defense (especially not in a Constitutional and often not in an ethical way), though the NCIS would continue and work with local Militia counter-espionage agents and with the Constitutional Sheriffs and Peace Officers when, where, and however appropriate.

All current service members (including current 'homeland security' employees) would be given the opportunity to be integrated into the new Constitutional Armed Services or be freed from service. Unlike proto-Militia, which are typically unpaid, modern Militia would be paid along with the Navy and Constitutional Sheriffs and Peace Officers at least 10% more than current armed forces, which is an affordable incentive for transitioning given how much less expensive and more effective Constitutional Homeland Security is to accomplish and maintain. CAS members would also be paid in gold and silver-backed tender as required by Supreme Law (according to article I, section 10 of the U.S. Constitution), which they can then voluntarily convert to any currency that they want in the new and truly Free Market, such as crypto currencies—including emerging ones that are backed by metals. Personnel who opt to stay in the CAS and do not become part of the Navy or the Constitutional Sheriffs and Peace Officers will be integrated into the Militia of the Several States, returning to their home locality to render defensive service there.

The Native American Tribes are an essential part of true Homeland Security and they would be invited to train with the well-regulated Militia. Constitutional Homeland Security would be coordinated with the Native American Nations when, where, and however appropriate.

Letters of Marque and Reprisal would be issued as required to meet all other needs of true Homeland Security.

With the Constitutional Armed Services and truly Constitutional homeland security, the command structure would go from a chaotic and centralized failure with many agencies that compete and interfere with one-another and the People, to the Constitutional order that we are meant to have and which every member of the current armed forces swore or affirmed that they would uphold—and now have the opportunity to truly to do so. There would be the Militia of the Several States with their external chain-of-command going from local Sheriff, to State Governor, to U.S. President, then there are the Constitutional local Sheriffs and Peace Officers, and then the Navy (including the Marines and Special Forces) with their commander, all parts being under the authority (so long as it is legitimate) of the Commander-in-Chief (the President of the United States), and the Commander-in-Chief answering to Congress, with all answering to the people through the re-established Militia of the Several States, that has the Constitutional obligation to 'execute the laws of the Union, suppress Insurrections, and repel Invasions'—to defend the people and our Constitution from 'enemies both foreign *and* domestic' (especially corrupt elements of government). When a certain part of the chain-of-command becomes corrupt then the people recognize the best, most legitimate, and most local authority possible and resist all unethical acts/orders/commands/*etc.* from the corrupt.

When there is a worldly government conflict, the power of the purse is among the most important factors that determine victory for those involved. If the federal government does not approve of a certain State's Militia, then they can reduce that Militia's funding only by an amount that continues to ensure a Constitutional level of security for that locality—as Constitutionally required of Congress—but cannot completely cut it off and be Constitutionally legitimate if the resources are available and that State remains part of the Union. Even if the federal government does cut defense funding to any of the States, there is still State funding and the goal is for State funding of truly Constitutional Homeland Security to exceed that of the federal government to the point that federal funding is not even needed—even with only a consumption tax that never exceeds 10%—because of how prosperous that State's economy is with truly Constitutional and superior Homeland Security that restores the Rights, Privileges,

Opportunities, and Independence of the people, businesses, and the several States.

If there is violent corruption within the Militia then there are the Sheriffs and Peace Officers assisted by the honorable members of the Militia of the Several States who would appropriately respond.

There would be no compulsory service any more. People who are forced into service make undesirable service members. Among other concerns, it is high-risk to entrust them with security clearances, important responsibilities, devastating technology, *etc.* They reduce the quality of the Armed Services and are not needed at all, especially in modern warfare where the size of the enemy means much less than superior intelligence and other military resources.

No one will be left out of the Constitutional, well-regulated Militia who does not want to be, and of course all other United States citizens remain part of the 'unorganized Militia' by default. Even conscientious objectors have the option to serve as unpaid voluntary or paid part-time or full-time Militia members in the fields of medicine, science, information technology, military agriculture, military industry, and much more without any combat involvement at all, or concern about aiding an unjustly aggressive entity that threatens world peace such as the current U.S. military-industrial complex. There will be combat-certified personnel and also non-coms who are equally or more essential to success, such as paid or voluntary non-combatant scientists, medical personnel, farmers, engineers, and more. No one who wants to be part of the Militia and contribute to true national defense will be left out, though Congress may determine the personnel limit of well-regulated Militia employment based on national revenue, limiting new well-regulated Militia employment to part-time or voluntary service as needed. Those who excel in their part-time or voluntary service and desire to advance to part or full-time service will be the first individuals selected to do so once funds are made available and personnel limits set by Congress allow. The Militia will be as self-sustaining as possible, growing the majority of its own nutritionally-superior organic food, with the excess saved as emergency storage or given to the poor and needy in order to avoid competing with local farmers. They will also produce as much of their own equipment as possible, and so will in many ways contribute more and be much less of a drain on national resources than current armed forces.

Full-time Militia members would be given healthcare at least equivalent to that received by our current armed forces. Part-time members would be covered by a lower plan, yet even volunteer, unpaid Militia members who contribute at least 20 hours per week of service would qualify for a basic level of healthcare and organic food benefits. This is a better remedy to the security issue of our rapidly deteriorating national health than forced health insurance, inferior food stamps, and other big government mandates and so-called welfare for those in need of better help.

Current 'homeland security' costs, <u>not including wars</u>: 750 billion (low estimate)

Cost of Constitutional Homeland Security as outlined above: 525 billion (high estimate)

Constitutional Homeland Security is not only possible to accomplish, it is also our <u>obligation</u>, which we have neglected with dire consequences and cannot any longer without suffering an even worse fate than the Roman, Nazi, and Soviet empires combined.

The first 5 things that must happen in order to truly accomplish Constitutional Homeland Security:

1. Constitutional Armed Services established as mentioned above, the Uniform Code of Military Justice (UCMJ) re-written to reflect the changes and a Public Servant's Uniform Code of Justice (PSUCJ) implemented and enforced by the Militia of the Several States to bind all politicians and bring the corrupt to Justice as outlined above.

2. Threats to agriculture ended, including geoengineering and GM agriculture. Chemtrails stopped and GM agriculture treated as the chemical and biological warfare against all life that it is and banned pending long-term scientific proof of safety due to the massive risk that it already poses to the health of the people, the environment, and our food-chain—therefore being another unacceptable national security risk.

3. Senseless Prohibition such as the failed 'War on Drugs' (against people) ended. Borders, travel, and other sensitive locations and material secured by the Constitutional Armed Services. Uruguay's example concerning drug prohibition followed in that non-violent drug offenders are freed and given treatment options rather than incarceration. Industrial hemp legalized, therefore our dependency on foreign resources such as oil minimized. Endocrine-disrupting, health-destroying petro-plastics that are extremely pervasive and reduce the health of global populations and threaten the ecosystem can begin to be replaced by superior, renewable, non-toxic and biodegradable alternatives such as hastic (hemp plastics and other plant resins). There is much less risk of about another national security catastrophe like the U.S. Gulf oil spill when we get most or all of our fuel from hemp and other domestic, renewable, and sustainable sources.

4. Phase-out of nuclear energy. Fukushima has taught us how dangerous this form of energy can be—not only to national security, but to the entire world, and many of our U.S. reactors are only as safe as the Fukushima reactors or significantly less so. This is a massive national security issue, especially when elderly activists have already proven (at great personal cost) that they can penetrate the security of these facilities as protected by the current, inferior and false 'national security' infrastructure. Germany and other energy pioneers have proven that nuclear energy is not needed, with alternative renewable energy abundantly meeting demands despite deceitful claims that alternative, domestic, renewable, and sustainable energy is impossible and/or impractical.

5. Outstanding national monetary security threats resolved: Constitutional gold and silver tender restored and the Federal Reserve abolished. National foreign debt eliminated, national balanced budget amendment implemented, a new and more sensible tax system adopted (fair and equal consumption tax never to exceed 10%, with businesses rather than citizens reporting taxes to the New Internal Revenue Service [NIRS]). Corporate welfare and tax evasion ended.

Social security phased out, no one who currently receives government welfare of any kind under reasonable circumstances would be cut off, but new people are automatically exempt from 'social security' or any other product or service that the government claims that you must pay for (including insurance), beyond those specifically enumerated within the Constitution—namely fair and just taxation such as proposed above. No new enrollments would be accepted into government-forced schemes like 'social security', which are unprofitable and truly hurt every citizen, robbing them and making them beg for uncertain scraps of the theft later in life like subjugated surfs. Better alternatives will be introduced than the welfare programs which currently exist, such as national healthcare through the Constitutional Armed Services rather than unconstitutional forced health insurance as the nation now struggles through. The money freed from those who opt out of 'social security' and a reasonable portion of available revenue from the new economic environment would be put toward paying back the national debt—which would do more to ensure true Social Security by helping to avoid World War.

_____ Constitutional Homeland Security is not only less expensive than current pseudo-homeland security, but actually solves the national budget deficit and allows us to pay back national debt in a reasonable amount of time while also restoring our national credit rating. The math to support this claim would be included in this essay, but government spending levels change so quickly that recording those numbers in this essay is pointless, though with very simple changes within government that only improve the people's welfare, the national deficit readily transforms into a surplus.

It can only be estimated what national revenue will be after the changes in the legal and tax system take place, with many government departments altered or closed, with senseless prohibition ended and agriculture and other domestic businesses having the opportunity to thrive again in the newly and truly Free Market, where the only legitimate regulations are for dangers such as radioactive materials or chemical weapons. Therefore, the ultimate personnel limit of the paid well-regulated Militia set by Congress (and national resources) is uncertain, though it is certain that should the need arise then a great number of people would volunteer for unpaid full-time well-regulated Militia service to receive organization, resources, and training in defense, if necessary—still qualifying themselves for healthcare, bonuses for exemplary service, and other benefits.

What will life be like when we Truly accomplish Constitutional and Superior Homeland Security?

Imagine: You are a modern full-time paid Militia member. You used to be in the U.S. Army, but you're happier now that you get paid more and aren't forced all over the world to do things that disturb your conscience. You happen to live in Northern Virginia and your area of operations is the District of Columbia. You notice—especially here—that the implementation of the Public Servant's Uniform Code of Justice has greatly changed the behavior of politicians. They may still use their 1st amendment right to say whatever they like, but now those who submit (or succeed in 'passing') unconstitutional legislation are arrested by the Militia of the Several States to receive public trial for their crimes—as intended by the Founders and as obligated by the Constitution itself. They now must not only swear oaths of office, but live in fear of the specific consequences of breaking those oaths and the rest of the PSUCJ, which is specifically designed to address political corruption and the consequences that are constitutionally enforced by the well-regulated Militia of the Several States.

Now national borders, travel, and all other key infrastructure is protected by the Militia of the Several States much better than ever before. There have been times when unconstitutional orders have been issued, but now that the chain-of-command is as local as possible these attempts are more effectively nullified and more perpetrators prosecuted than ever before. The revitalization of the well-regulated Militia has succeeded in maintaining true Constitutional order better than the previous police state ever could.

You notice now how much more secure the U.S. is, with all defense funding now *actually* going toward domestic defense and the development of overawing new technology that can neutralize threats more effectively than ever before. Only a few foreign positions that our allies have invited us to maintain remain, such as in South Korea, while we have withdrawn from the majority—such as from Germany and Japan.

Your spouse is a volunteer non-com Militia member who contributes to Militia agriculture and the local community's free-to-all edible 'victory gardens' that the Militia encourages all citizens to maintain and which provide renewable resources and rally points for the community when needed. They also train the people in gardening methods that easily and effectively transform into defensive earthworks, such as aquapinis, walipinis, and more. Your full-time paid Militia service qualifies your immediate family for healthcare, but you're still thankful that your retired friend on limited income also volunteers by helping the Militia with IT work for 20 hours a week and gets organic food and healthcare in exchange. She started out as a volunteer to see how she likes it, and recently told you that she's considering applying for paid part-time non-com service like her physically disabled friend, Joe.

U.S. unemployment, poverty, hunger, and mortality have all been significantly reduced thanks to accomplishing truly Constitutional and superior Homeland Security. You no longer have to worry about taxes, there is simply a consumption tax on goods and services that never exceeds 10% and the 10% consumption tax limit is what funds the government while also keeping it from becoming too large. It is fair and equal, with no exemptions or adjustments for special interest groups or favored individuals.

You are now going on vacation to Colorado. Although you enjoy cannabis, you're not going for the legalization (drug prohibition has ended throughout the United States, addiction rates significantly lowering thanks to effective treatment being offered for drug use rather than imprisonment), you are on your way to see friends and go camping.

When you get to the airport, you are not molested by TSA agents. Instead, Militia members respectfully guard the people and premises.

When you land, your friend picks you up in a non-polluting hemp-composite vehicle that is affordably fueled thanks to the revitalized hemp industry. On your way to your campsite, you pass ultra-efficient turbine-less wind generators and super-efficient solar collectors and realize how pleased you are to be able to enjoy the outdoors without having to worry about phased-out nuclear energy reactors, poisonous agricultural practices, fracking sinkholes and pollution, or chemtrails.

Because of the United States adopting this Constitutionally-defensive stance and ceasing global aggression, world-wide tension has greatly decreased. The problems engineered by the U.S. military-industrial complex and former 'Intelligence' agencies have been alleviated and the U.S. is now dedicated to paying its debts and continuing to live prosperously through truly Constitutional Rule of Law.

In the next part we'll examine the training and operations of the Constitutional Armed Services.

Part III of IV

The Constitutional Armed Services (CAS) consist of the local Militia of the Several States, the Constitutional Sheriffs and Peace Officers, and the U.S. Navy. This section will primarily focus on the basic organization, training, and operations of the truly Constitutional and superior Militia of the Several States.

Posse Comitatus

Some are under the false impression that the Militia fulfilling their Constitutional duty to 'execute the Laws of the Union, suppress Insurrections and repel Invasions' through the PSUCJ is not possible due to the Posse Comitatus Act and the Insurrection Act of 1807. That belief is only true when applied to modern false 'Militia' in the form of the National Guard and similar centralized imposter 'Militia' units.

Those laws specifically limit the ability of federal military forces to enforce law, calling first and foremost on the Constitutional Sheriffs and Peace Officers and the local Militia of the Several States to execute the laws of the Union. There is no conflict between these laws and the implementation of the PSUCJ, only additional support for the true Militia of the Several States to honor their Constitutional obligations.

The Revitalization

Lawmakers have historically proven able to legislate nearly anything—provided enough resources and motivation, so rather than proposing model legislation for the Constitutional Militia, this section will instead cover what qualifies as legitimate Militia legislation or as legitimate Constitutional Militia that are actually worthy of all the patriotic support that can be mustered for them. To be acceptable they must:

1. Follow all parts of the Constitution, especially pertaining to the Militia—such as:

a. [Congress is Obligated] To provide for organizing, arming, and disciplining the Militia, and for governing such Part of them as may be employed in the Service of the United States, reserving to the States respectively the Appointment of the Officers and the Authority of training the Militia according to the discipline prescribed by Congress (historically to the standards of the federal military. This should remain the same in that general Militia members who opt for combat-certification receive training and equipment at least equal to that of general Naval personnel, with specialized units trained to the standards of the Marines and their marksmen, and the most elite Militia units which will replace current elite DHS combat teams should meet or exceed the standards of other U.S. special forces.);

b. To provide for calling forth the Militia to execute the Laws of the Union, suppress Insurrections and repel Invasions;

-U.S. Constitution, Article 1, Section 8

c. A well-regulated Militia, being necessary to the security of a Free State, the right of the people to keep and bear Arms shall not be infringed.

-U.S. Constitution, 2nd Amendment

2. Have a Chain-of-Command that begins locally, with external Militia leadership going from County Sheriff, to State Governor, to U.S. President, to U.S. Congress, to WE THE PEOPLE of the United States.

3. Be bound by a UCMJ and implement a PSUCJ without which they will be unable to accomplish and maintain truly Constitutional Homeland Security and their existence will either be temporary or otherwise subverted yet again.

Organization, Training, and Operations

The legitimate Militia will follow the pattern of the federal military in most ways except chain-of-command, combat certification, and flexibility of service. The internal chain-of-command of the Militia will reflect that of the federal military, with their external chain-of-command linked to local authorities as outlined above.

People may serve in the Militia as combat-certified personnel who receive more training and compensation (BASIC training equivalent & AIT), or as non-coms who receive general non-com Militia training (which ranges from Militia laws, regulations, survival training, emergency preparedness, first aid, *etc.*) and then advanced individual training (AIT) within their specialty.

Member benefits are linked to the member's service contribution. There are voluntary or paid service options, with 20 hrs/wk for basic benefits, 30 for part time, 40+ for full-time benefits and bonuses. Assignments are aptitude and need-based, with opportunities opening up all over the United States in localities that desire certain personnel, with no voluntary or part-time Militia member relocated—except by that member's own choice.

State authorities appoint the officers of the Militia of the Several States and ensure their personnel receive the training and discipline prescribed by Congress.

The Militia would take over all homeland security functions currently usurped by the 'DHS' and all related agencies and implement the PSUCJ within their areas of operation, encompassing the entire United States, with the responsibility to arrest for public trial those who violate the PSUCJ, all according to their Constitutional authority to exist and operate as outlined above.

The basics are truly that plain and simple. ***C.D.A. Framework***

If government fails to honor their Constitutional obligations to revitalize the true Militia of the Several States then it is the natural right and responsibility of the People to do so. Here is a framework of how anyone anywhere may begin revitalization of the truly Constitutional local Militia of the Several States through Community Defense Associations (C.D.A.'s).

What is a C.D.A.?

A Community Defense Association is like a Boy or Girl Scout troop though primarily for adults (with junior C.D.A. membership available for minors) that functions as an activist group, emergency preparation and response unit, neighborhood watch group and more all-in-one, which once established may naturally evolve into actual Militia units and be prime pools which State officials would be wise to use as their first choice for appointing paid officers and enlistees to the Militia, with prior Armed Service members (including those from C.D.A.'s) receiving paid hiring preference when funds and personnel limits set by Congress allow.

How does it work?

Community Defense Associations have three main parts: Headquarters, Field Group, and Support Group. Headquarters consists of the C.D.A. leaders, Constitutional Sheriffs and Peace Officers liaison, military liaison, local and federal government liaison, media (including social media) liaison, Neighborhood Watch coordinator, local government activism team, federal government activism team, legal team, Intel sections, and all others needed. Field Group teams ideally consist of a 12-person core cadre (6 if necessary) based on a U.S. Special Forces human force multiplication model: 1 Team Leader, 1 Assistant Team Leader (ATL), 2 communications experts, 2 medics, 2 engineers, 2 scouts and/or marksmen, and 2 heavy weapons experts. These are sub-organized as needed, such as the following organization of 3 teams of 4:

Sub-team 1

Team Leader, 1 comms, 1 medic, 1 heavy

St 2

ATL, 1 comms, 1 scout/marksmen, 1 heavy

St 3

1 medic, 2 engineers, 1 scout/marksman

The field team members should have at least basic light infantry training and should cross-train each-other to achieve maximum potential competence in each team member's specialization. Beyond the 12-person core cadre, field team composition will vary depending on available personnel and the defensive objectives within each locality. Support Group consists of the Quartermaster's department and non-field, non-headquarters personnel. Support Group—along with Headquarters—are ideal assignments for those such as disabled veterans or patriotic elderly citizens whose knowledge and other non-field contributions are priceless. Within Support Group there are:

S1—Quartermaster

S2—Medical (health, nutrition, emergency treatment, *etc.*)

S3—Technical Support

S4—Accounting

Community Defense Associations meet at least twice a week, once for conference, the other for training. During conference days, members will conduct all necessary group business, inform each-other, and plan. Planning goes beyond the association's agenda of activities to ways of effectively and constitutionally defending their community—especially politically, and militarily only as their last resort according to their natural right and responsibility to do so.

Training meetings may consist of a variety of activities such as firearms training and qualification, airsoft/paintball/*etc.* battle simulation training, first aid, emergency preparedness, survival, hand-to-hand combatives, disaster relief, and more.

C.D.A. members commit one weekend each month to field training. Personal time is set aside on the mornings of these field days before breakfast and after personal hygiene which may be used at the service member's discretion—such as for religious services—so that participation in C.D.A. field training is less restrictive to members of many religious denominations while benefiting non-religious personnel as well.

Example non-drill morning field schedule:

Wake Hygiene: 20m

Personal Time: 20m

Breakfast: 20m

Operations begin no more than 1 hour after waking.

The media team from Headquarters will promote the benefits of C.D.A's and openly share their experiences. Members should be in uniform during all meetings, with each association choosing its uniform in response to its unique circumstances. The C.D.A. membership fee should never exceed $10 per month per person, with quarterly, semi-annual, annual, and lifetime membership options also available. Honest contributions should be thankfully accepted, but the C.D.A. membership fee should never exceed $10 per month per person. Any that requires more is exposed as an imposter group that violates the principles of true Community Defense Associations that are affordable to all. All C.D.A. funds will only be allowed to be invested back into the C.D.A. in ways such as funding meeting locations, group training activities, group equipment, supplies, *etc.* Voluntary donations and efforts such as bake sales and car washes will provide all other needed resources. *How do I join or begin one?*

Search for 'CDA' or Community Defense Associations in your area both online and offline and if you are unable to find one then found one. Do not be discouraged; it only takes one person to start and grow a C.D.A. Recruit first from your family, friends, churches, and then all other inclined individuals and organizations within your community.

Then find physical locations to meet (preferably member-owned property). Once you have the minimum 6-person core cadre for the first field group team then you may begin field training members of the association.

Let the public know once your association is operative and network with other C.D.A.'s. Association locations and designations should be posted online and elsewhere (especially locally) by the C.D.A. media team members to help other people become aware of and have the opportunity to participate in their local Community Defense Association. Once established, introduce your C.D.A. to your local Sheriff and if they are a Constitutional Peace Officer then the C.D.A. is an asset to that Sheriff, who should be treated as the C.D.A.'s external commander similarly to how the local Sheriff is the immediate and external commander of the true Militia of the Several States within their jurisdiction. *In the next and final part, we'll examine how to establish, utilize, and maintain ethical and more effective national Intelligence resources through the Constitutional Armed Services, the Public Servant's Uniform Code of Justice, and the new UCMJ.*

Part IV of IV

As previously noted, the current U.S. Intelligence paradigm has been a wasteful drain on resources and a serious threat to the People and Constitution of the United States—often proving to be the actual source of danger through direct anti-constitutionality, treasonous conspiracy, and/or blow-back rather than accomplishing true national defense (especially not in a Constitutional and often not in any sort of ethical way). The costs inflicted on the People of the rest of the world and the resulting consequences for the People of the United States must end.

That doesn't mean that the U.S. would be left defenseless against espionage, or incapable of military Intelligence gathering and operations, as far superior national Intelligence would instead exist through the Constitutional Armed Services—in a way that doesn't violate Constitutional Rule of Law, Human Rights, and isn't guilty of the other crimes committed by the current U.S. military-industrial complex, which is primarily manipulated through the corrupt, anti-Constitutional Intelligence apparatus warned of by those such as Dwight D. Eisenhower, John F. Kennedy, and more.

All necessary counter-espionage assets would be consolidated into local Militia counter-espionage sections, except those within the Navy such as the NCIS. All non-Naval espionage investigations would be under the jurisdiction of the local Sheriff (who may at times also have joint or full jurisdiction over Naval counter-espionage investigations when necessary) with none to be conducted without their permanently documented authorization and supervision. Sheriffs would oversee such investigations as prescribed by the portion of the PSUCJ that will address them. Militia special agents would conduct these investigations under the local Sheriff's supervision as prescribed by the portion of the UCMJ that will address them. All necessary Intelligence assets would be consolidated into the U.S. Navy, only to be used against legitimate foreign enemies, not against U.S. citizens, allies, or neutral entities. U.S. Navy Intel will operate as outlined by the portion of the UCMJ that will address it.

While the power and authority of budgeting and other allocation remains with Congress, oversight will no longer be the sole jurisdiction of secret courts, committees, panels, *etc.* that are comprised of individual politicians with varying values, goals, and faithfulness as those who are meant to be objective checks and balances on what has proven to have become a rubber-stamped, ever-expanding Nazi/Soviet-modeled anti-constitutional Imperial police state/Intel panoply. Instead, Congress members and local authorities will oversee Intelligence operations according to the United States Constitution and the appropriate Uniform Code of Justice.

No other spy organizations will be allowed within the U.S., whether government or private. These would compete and interfere with the operations of the CAS and pose a continuing threat to the world, especially towards the People of the United States and Constitutional Rule of Law. All agents are free to apply to serve within the Constitutional Armed Services if they would like to exercise more ethical, superior, and worthwhile tradecraft as a U.S. Navy or local Militia special agent.

Results: With the military-industrial complex truly bound by the Rule of Law there will be no more of the following perpetrated by the government of the United States:

-U.S. banana republics and all related operations-Illegal assassinations

-Illegal kidnapping

-Indefinite detention

-Torture-False/black flag operations

-Heinous programs and operations such as Paperclip, Gladio, Northwoods, MK ULTRA, Mockingbird, PRISM, the manipulation of the Western political system, economy, culture (racial & religious conflicts, drug operations, diseases, etc.), citizens, and much, much more.

Summary of Benefits of accomplishing truly Constitutional and superior Homeland Security through the CAS, PSUCJ, and UCMJ:

* Rule of Law truly honored; Supreme U.S. Law in the form of the Constitution—including and especially the Bill of Rights—fully restored, upheld, and defended

* True and far superior local, national, and international security accomplished through the CAS, PSUCJ, and UCMJ

* Global and domestic tensions, conflicts, and dangers alleviated

* Federal budget deficit eliminated and prohibited

* National debt resolved

* National credit rating and international reputation greatly improved

* Superior tax system—the only taxes being a consumption tax on purchases never to exceed 10%

* Defense of the domestic and global environment through the elimination of nuclear energy, GMO's, and a move towards truly natural, organic sustainability in the fields of energy, agriculture, and much more

*   Overall   improved   national/cultural/societal/individual Freedom, Liberty, Justice, and Opportunity

* A voluntary and vastly superior national healthcare solution

Dissemination: With truly Constitutional and superior Homeland Security implemented as outlined within this essay, the forces of the entire world could combine against the United States and they would not prevail—though they would also have no more reason to attempt to do so. Revenge would be hollow, as implementation of the PSUCJ would bring as many as are responsible for crimes against humanity to Justice as possible, and any attempts of foreign powers to avenge themselves further will not prosper.

However, how can these things be accomplished if too few champion the cause? It is fact that it only takes 3% of a population to enact great and lasting change on a very large scale—especially in the Age of Information—and this is certainly a cause worth 100% of the support that can be offered not only from the People of the United States, but from everyone regardless of their nationality due to how greatly they would also benefit from the United States accomplishing truly Constitutional and superior Homeland Security. Share this information in any way that you know how as virally as possible. Be ready and able to accurately discuss these things with your family, friends, co-workers, internet acquaintances, and more. Ask politicians running for office what they think of this philosophy and use that to inform your vote—though the ideal is for those who support these things to vote each-other into office and implement them according to the People and Constitution of the Unites States, helping elections to again become more about the candidate's actual political philosophy, record, and works rather than their appearance, affiliation, and/or momentary rhetoric.